Modern Language Association

Approaches to Teaching
World Literature

Joseph Gibaldi, Series Editor

26. Robin Riley Fast and Christine Mack Gordon, eds. *Approaches to Teaching Dickinson's Poetry.* 1989.
27. Spencer Hall, ed. *Approaches to Teaching Shelley's Poetry.* 1990.
28. Sidney Gottlieb, ed. *Approaches to Teaching the Metaphysical Poets.* 1990.
29. Richard K. Emmerson, ed. *Approaches to Teaching Medieval English Drama.* 1990.
30. Kathleen Blake, ed. *Approaches to Teaching Eliot's* Middlemarch. 1990.
31. María Elena de Valdés and Mario J. Valdés, eds. *Approaches to Teaching García Márquez's* One Hundred Years of Solitude. 1990.
32. Donald D. Kummings, ed. *Approaches to Teaching Whitman's* Leaves of Grass. 1990.
33. Stephen C. Behrendt, ed. *Approaches to Teaching Shelley's* Frankenstein. 1990.
34. June Schlueter and Enoch Brater, eds. *Approaches to Teaching Beckett's* Waiting for Godot. 1991.
35. Walter H. Evert and Jack W. Rhodes, eds. *Approaches to Teaching Keats's Poetry.* 1991.
36. Frederick W. Shilstone, ed. *Approaches to Teaching Byron's Poetry.* 1991.
37. Bernth Lindfors, ed. *Approaches to Teaching Achebe's* Things Fall Apart. 1991.
38. Richard E. Matlak, ed. *Approaches to Teaching Coleridge's Poetry and Prose.* 1991.
39. Shirley Geok-lin Lim, ed. *Approaches to Teaching Kingston's* The Woman Warrior. 1991.

Approaches to Teaching Kingston's *The Woman Warrior*

Edited by

Shirley Geok-lin Lim

The Modern Language Association of America
New York   1991

© 1991 by The Modern Language Association of America

Library of Congress Cataloging-in-Publication Data

Approaches to teaching Kingston's The woman warrior / edited by
   Shirley Geok-lin Lim.
      p.   cm.—(Approaches to teaching world literature ; 39)
   Includes bibliographical references and index.
   ISBN 0-87352-703-8 (cloth) — ISBN 0-87352-704-6 (pbk.)
   1. Kingston, Maxine Hong. Woman warrior.   2. United States—
Biography—Study and teaching.   I. Lim, Shirley.   II. Series.
CT275.K5764A3   1991
973'.04951—dc20   91-27413

Cover illustration of the paperback edition: photograph of Cheet Sing Mui
portraying the Woman Warrior in a San Francisco theater in the 1920s. Courtesy
of the Wylie Wong Collection, San Francisco.

Published by The Modern Language Association of America
10 Astor Place, New York, New York 10003-6981

CONTENTS

T
75
.5764
3
991

PREFACE TO THE SERIES

In *The Art of Teaching* Gilbert Highet wrote, "Bad teaching wastes a great deal of effort, and spoils many lives which might have been full of energy and happiness." All too many teachers have failed in their work, Highet argued, simply "because they have not thought about it." We hope that the Approaches to Teaching World Literature series, sponsored by the Modern Language Association's Publications Committee, will not only improve the craft—as well as the art—of teaching but also encourage serious and continuing discussion of the aims and methods of teaching literature.

The principal objective of the series is to collect within each volume different points of view on teaching a specific literary work, a literary tradition, or a writer widely taught at the undergraduate level. The preparation of each volume begins with a wide-ranging survey of instructors, thus enabling us to include in the volume the philosophies and approaches, thoughts and methods of scores of experienced teachers. The result is a sourcebook of material, information, and ideas on teaching the subject of the volume to undergraduates.

The series is intended to serve nonspecialists as well as specialists, inexperienced as well as experienced teachers, graduate students who wish to learn effective ways of teaching as well as senior professors who wish to compare their own approaches with the approaches of colleagues in other schools. Of course, no volume in the series can ever substitute for erudition, intelligence, creativity, and sensitivity in teaching. We hope merely that each book will point readers in useful directions; at most each will offer only a first step in the long journey to successful teaching.

Joseph Gibaldi
Series Editor

PREFACE TO THE VOLUME

To identify the major concerns of teachers of *The Woman Warrior*, we asked over two hundred scholars in the areas of American literature, ethnic literature, and women's studies to complete a comprehensive questionnaire. Of the forty-nine respondents—fourteen men and thirty-five women—eleven were scholars of Asian American descent. *The Woman Warrior* is clearly not limited in its appeal to the Chinese American community whose history and place in the United States form the substrata of its text.

As the demographics of the United States shift in the late twentieth century, from a Caucasian-based majority to a heterogeneous citizenry of diverse races and ethnicities, so too do the concerns of scholars and teachers who are attentive to the cultural needs of their students. Cultural studies assume the presence of underlying ideologies in institutions and in the disciplines these institutions support; we have learned to challenge, everywhere in the United States, the canon of American literature as delineated in traditional curricula. Indicating the sensitivity of the humanities to issues of gender, race, and class, and consequent considerations of inclusion and pluralism, the forty-nine respondents represent a wide range of institutions: research universities, public four-year and two-year colleges, small private colleges, even high schools. The respondents come from the Northeast, South, Midwest, and, of course, the West, especially California, where the impact of Asian immigration to the United States is most pronounced; they also come from outside the United States, from Japan and elsewhere.

Every respondent, noting the gap between mainstream instructors' cultural knowledge and the Chinese American world of the work, wrote about the necessity for such a volume. It is not that the essays included encompass every possible approach to teaching *The Woman Warrior*, or even that *The Woman Warrior* is the definitive Asian American text in the canon of American literature, or that it is the only work needed for students and teachers to understand the Asian contribution to American civilization.

Indeed, a major intention of this volume is to introduce teachers and students to the larger body of Asian American and ethnic literature, to inform them of the immigrant and ethnic traditions that Kingston's work comes from and contributes to, and, in so familiarizing the unfamiliar, to enable them to approach other Asian American works on their own. Within the volume, readers will find references to Asian American histories, authors, and works, as well as to other ethnic and ethnic women's works. The volume is not so much an end in itself as a part of the process of empowering teachers and students to function in a diverse American society. A collection of pedagogical essays on *The Woman Warrior* is, after all, merely a beginning, a jump start for thinking about Asian ethnics, about American writers of Japanese, Korean, Filipino, South Asian, and Southeast Asian descent, about the way these rich Asian cultural elements change, interact, transform, and are themselves transformed by their presence in the new American world.

The Woman Warrior is a complex, highly inventive, historically embedded work. It is part biography, part autobiography, part history, part fantasy, part fiction, part myth, and wholly multilayered, multivocal, and organic. When respondents urged the publication of such an Approaches volume, they often cited the lack of historical and cultural background that makes teaching *The Woman Warrior* an intimidating prospect. They requested that the volume include information on traditional Chinese and immigrant Chinese societies; the history of the Chinese in California; feminist readings; genre studies; analyses of themes, myths, talk-stories, and images; and close readings of particularly complex passages.

Maxine Hong Kingston's personal statement provides a fitting introduction to the volume, with its biographical clues, its notation on the incomplete nature of *The Woman Warrior*, which she had always intended to be read as one part of a two-volume work that includes *China Men*. Readers will find bibliographical assistance in part 1 to help them gather the sociocultural information needed for a fuller appreciation of the work. The opening essays in part 2 provide focused readings that interweave historical and cultural elucidations with close analysis. The other essays cover a range of concerns in teaching *The Woman Warrior*, from discipline-oriented approaches to thematic readings that apply for writing instructors and literary theoreticians alike. These essays speak to the significance of a work that crosses boundaries—of genre, making it particularly attractive to postmodernist interpretations; of gender and ethnicity, opening it to feminist critics and scholars of ethnic studies. *The Woman Warrior*, as figured in the organizing trope, is a transgressive work because it locates itself in the intersections of sexual, racial, and genre identities. As Kingston has said in defense of the work against the criticism that it is not an authentic account of Chinese culture, *The Woman Warrior* originates in and addresses not the high culture of China but its low culture, more specifically a transplanted oral culture, of the Say Yup (Cantonese) immigrants in California. The essays are offered as opening approaches to teaching a highly culture-specific text for instructors new to the work and to the Chinese American culture to which it refers and which it is also inventing.

In completing part 1, which surveys materials useful to classroom instructors, I owe thanks to the respondents who generously shared their reading lists, bibliographies, and syllabi with me. I am grateful to Maxine Hong Kingston for her contribution to the volume. I owe special thanks to Joseph Gibaldi, whose encouragement and patience set me on this course; Adrienne

Ward, whose advice was always useful; Charles Bazerman, who ferreted articles from interlibrary loans for me; the MLA Committee on Publications; the MLA staff; the anonymous reviewers, who made this final manuscript what it is; and numerous friends and colleagues who offered suggestions and support.

SGL

Part One

MATERIALS

Editions and Anthologies

Many instructors use the original 1977 Vintage paperback edition of *The Woman Warrior*; they especially like the provocative illustration on its cover. As one respondent wrote, the illustration "embodies the painful and empowering duality of the woman warrior, in Kingston's text and in each reader who experiences the pull between silence and the assertion of self." Also provoking discussion is the combination of categories provided in the front cover's statement, "The best book of nonfiction published in 1976—The National Book Critics Circle," and in the classification on the upper left corner of the back cover: "autobiography." All page references in this volume follow the 1977 Vintage edition.

The most recent paperback edition for classroom use and, fortunately, one of the best so far is the Vintage International Edition issued by Random House in April 1989. It features the original pagination of the hardback first edition, and many teachers find it superior to the 1977 Vintage in size (of book and print), quality, and tint of paper and binding.

Some respondents prefer the edition brought out in the Harper Torchbook series because of its larger format and the ease with which teachers and students can write notes in the margins.

The Woman Warrior has been heavily anthologized, and many respondents are pleased to use these excerpts in their first-year composition classes as a way of introducing Asian American culture to their students. One respondent was asked by a discussion group of five freshmen, "What does this term *Asian American* mean?" These anthologized pieces are seen as an excellent means of including the Asian American experience into a multiethnic perspective, both in writing classes and in introduction to literature classes.

The most frequently excerpted section is from the "No Name Woman" chapter; see *Literature* (Di Yanni 1643–50); *The Riverside Reader* (Trimmer and Hairston 59–75); *The Conscious Reader* (Shrodes et al. 44–52); *Harbrace College Reader* (Schorer 87–98); *The Written World* (S. Miller 27–38); *The Contemporary Essay* (Hall 279–90); *Responding to Prose* (Fishman 85–87); *The Norton Anthology of Literature by Women* (Gilbert and Gubar 2337–47); *Forms of Literature* (Costello and Tucker 107–17); and *New Worlds of Literature* (Beaty and Hunter 299–309).

Other excerpts available include a brief narrative titled "The Misery of Silence" in *Life Studies* (Cavitch 267–72), which focuses on the relation between silence and speech; it is also in *American Voices* under the title "The Quiet Girl" (Rosenberg 29–36). The last section of "White Tigers" (54–63 in the Vintage edition) is paired with an essay by a Vietnamese American undergraduate at Yale in *Student Writers at Work* (Sommers and

McQuade 417–23); the complete chapter appears in the *Heath Anthology of American Literature* (Lauter 2094–115); and a shorter section of the chapter is in *Patterns and Themes* (Rogers and Rogers 17–19). A segment on family photographs is in *Writing with a Thesis* (Skwire 72–74) and also in *Patterns for College Writing* (Kirszner and Mandell 117–22). Other excerpts are found in *Reading American Culture* (Colombo et al. 241–45); *Essay 2: Reading with the Writer's Eye* (Guth and Shea 480–86); and *The Short Prose Reader* (G. Miller et al. 104–07).

More recently, excerpts from *China Men* have also been anthologized in *Reflections* (Barnwell and Price 250–64); *Being and Becoming* (King and Kurtinitis 847–63); *The Writer's Sourcebook* (Kirszner and Mandell 91–99); *Thinking in Writing* (McQuade and Atwan 164–66); and *Seventy-Five Readings* (29–31).

Other Works by Maxine Hong Kingston

In addition to *The Woman Warrior*, her first book, Kingston has published a companion volume on Chinese American men, *China Men*, and a novel, *Tripmaster Monkey: His Fake Book*. Students who have read all three works have a much better sense of Kingston's evolution as a prose stylist. Kingston calls the language in *The Woman Warrior* "stilted and complicated . . . because I was trying to find a language for a very complicated story" (Carabi 11). While her goal in *China Men* was "to have a very lucid language," in the novel she uses "another voice . . . very modern, very slangy, a hip 1960s language." In the same interview, Kingston describes her increasing confidence. In writing *The Woman Warrior*, "I didn't think I could write a long book, so I did five interlocking pieces and each one was like a short story or an essay." In *China Men*, "I would have a myth, and then a modern story and then a myth." She describes her novel as having "a coherent long, long structure." Kingston calls *The Woman Warrior* "an 'I' book, it is the voices that I hear inside myself; whereas in [the novel] it is the voices that I hear around me" (11).

The Woman Warrior and *China Men* are categorized as works of nonfiction, and Kingston makes it clear that both books are based on her parents' lives—that is, both are forms of biography. While *The Woman Warrior* is based on her mother and the talk-stories her mother told her, *China Men* is composed of stories of her father's life in China and in the United States, and of the lives of various male relatives and sojourners, including grandfathers, uncles, and brother. Kingston frequently emphasizes the organic unity of the two books. "At one time, *TWW* and *China Men* were supposed to be one book. I had conceived of one huge book" (Rabinowitz 179). In the interview with Paula Rabinowitz, Kingston explains that the women's stories "have a convolution and the men's stories have more of a linear passage through time." Because the Chinese American male experience was within history, "those men were making history," while the women were caught up in "old myths." Both books, however, "are much more American than Chinese"; the characters are "American people."

A chapter, "The Making of More Americans," from *China Men* appeared as a prose piece in the *New Yorker* in February 1980. Kingston acknowledges her debt to Gertrude Stein's *Making of Americans* in the title. In this chapter, she especially constructs the Chinese American claim to the United States, as in the incident where aunts and uncles return to Stockton to visit her grandfathers' farm: "The relatives kept saying, 'This is the ancestral ground,' their eyes filling with tears over a vacant lot in Stockton" (171). In the reference to Stein, Kingston grounds her work in the American tradition. Of her "artful combination of Chinese rhythms and American slang" (Brownmiller 148), she says, "I want to work more the way Gertrude Stein did in 'Melanctha,' where she doesn't fool around with spelling: she plays around with syntax and rhythm rather than weird spelling and apostrophes" (Evory 292). Referring directly to the influence of *The Making of Americans*, Kingston says, "I am trying to write an American language that has Chinese accents. . . . I was creating something new, but at the same time, it's still the American language, pushed further" (Rabinowitz 182).

China Men tells the stories of Kingston's male ancestors, with the father as the central figure. Composed of eighteen chapters of varying length, it resembles *The Woman Warrior* in its collage of family stories, Chinese and Western legends and myths, Chinese and Chinese American history, fantasy, and memoirs. The chapters range chronologically from the legendary past of "very great grandfathers" in China (47) to the brother who returns safely from Vietnam (304).

As in *The Woman Warrior*, the boundary between memory and invention, history and myth is never clear. As Linda Ching Sledge points out, "In some respects, *China Men* is so close to the 'facts' of history that it can serve as a casebook for the evolution of Chinese-American family life over the last century; in other respects, it is wildly inventive and poetic" (3). Sledge argues that *China Men* "represents the transmutation of 'oral history' into cultural literary epic" (4). Alfred S. Wang reads *China Men* more politically, as a portrayal of "Men Warriors," a "synthesis of different generations of Chinese American males, who, defiant of being outlawed, emasculated, even silenced, were claiming forthright their shares of the American dream" (19). Pointing to the unreliability of memory and Kingston's "lack of verifiable material," Carol E. Neubauer argues that Kingston's purpose in writing *China Men* is "to reveal, if not in fact to resolve, the uncertainty and ambiguity of the available information . . . to make sense of her family's history and, perhaps more importantly, to place her family within the larger historical context of Chinese immigration and settlement in the United States" (26). Neubauer analyzes Kingston's use of photographs from the family album as a heuristic device to "provide information when other sources prove to be unreliable or incomplete," as in the photographs of her brother in military uniform in Vietnam and of her father's first fifteen years as a bachelor sojourner in New York. While some American reviewers have criticized Kingston for the inauthenticity of her "pieces of distant China lore" (Wakeman 44), Qing-yun Wu, a critic from the People's Republic of China, reads *China Men* as "historical fiction," arguing that "the freedom of fictionalization enables Kingston to transcend the limits of historical events and individuals to reveal a reality truer in essence and spirit than biography and autobiography or any history book can reveal."

Kingston claims that *Tripmaster Monkey*, unlike the first two books, is completely fiction. The narrative, set in San Francisco in the 1960s, focuses on the character of a Chinese American would-be playwright, Wittman Ah Sing, and on his attempts to produce a Chinese American epic drama. Using the classical Chinese mythical trickster figure of Monkey, the novel introduces a number of finely imagined Chinese American characters, ranging from showgirls of the 1940s to eccentric elders. *Tripmaster Monkey* portrays the hip, psychedelic 1960s culture centered in Berkeley of the Free Speech Movement. Modeling itself on Joyce's *Ulysses*, the novel uses strategies of realism, following a few days in the life of its hero to offer, self-consciously, an epic body of materials on Chinese American history and culture.

Some scholars have read the novel as a roman à clef that attacks Kingston's most vocal critic, Frank Chin (Solberg). Kingston herself sees the novel as a celebration of a Chinese American man—"I sing the Chinese American from top to toe" (Blauvelt 1)—and as a successful evolution from the "I" perspective of *The Woman Warrior* and *China Men* to the omniscient narrator.

Although fiction, *Tripmaster Monkey*—like her first two books—is a reservoir of information on Chinese American history and culture, including the cultural significance of the Gwang Goong figure (god of war and literature) for the Say Yup (Cantonese) branch of the Chinese American diaspora to which Kingston belongs.

Kingston has also published a number of articles. "Duck Boy," a sketch of an emotionally disturbed teenager, illustrates her empathy as a teacher for victims and outcasts, her understanding of the terrors and attractions of the irrational. "The Coming Book" is an idiosyncratic account of her creative process, when "the visions come assailing" (181). Written at about the time she was beginning work on *Tripmaster Monkey*, the essay alludes to Joyce's *Ulysses*, "a break from the 'I' stories I have been writing," to the aural origins of the process: "The Book will be filled with voices as heard through machines. . . . [I]t will sound like the Twentieth Century" (183). "A Writer's Notebook from the Far East" is a compilation of notes she made on a tour of Japan, Australia, Indonesia, Malaysia, and Hong Kong that generally record the oppression of citizens of Chinese origin in Islamic societies and the sexism and ethnocentrism still apparent in these regions. *Hawai'i One Summer*, composed of prose sketches, many of which appeared originally in the *New York Times*, celebrates Kingston's ten years in Hawaii and is illustrated with original woodcuts by Deng Ming-Dao.

Courses and Contexts

Survey respondents indicated that *The Woman Warrior* is taught in a wide range of courses, from lower-division courses for majors and nonmajors to upper-division electives and graduate seminars. It is taught in a number of departments, chiefly those of English literature, American culture and thought, women's studies, and ethnic studies. Respondents also noted that *The Woman Warrior* is taught as part of ethnic American history courses and as a cross-cultural reading in Asian and comparative literature courses.

The work is used, among other contexts, as a rhetorical model in freshman and sophomore writing courses. Respondents indicated that they teach only a portion of the book in such courses, primarily the chapters on No Name Aunt and on Fa Mu Lan. Passages are frequently included in composition readers, as models of style and as examples of American cultural diversity.

A popular choice of text in American studies courses, *The Woman Warrior* is taught in courses on twentieth-century and contemporary literature, folklore, popular culture, cultural pluralism, and California regional literature. It also appears in courses on autobiography, both diachronically and synchronically, together with such standard autobiographies as those of Benjamin Franklin and Henry Adams and with Twain's *Life on the Mississippi*, Hemingway's *Nick Adams Stories*, Frank Conroy's *Stop-Time*, and Lillian Hellman's *Pentimento*.

Moreover, *The Woman Warrior* is frequently a text in women's studies departments, especially those that intersect with literature and ethnic studies departments in a wide range of offerings: for example, Women and Creativity, Women Artists, Women and Popular Culture, Contemporary American Women Writers, Women of Color, Women as Leaders, Gender and Values. In these courses, the book is taught alongside works by Native American, African American, and Chicano women.

More specifically, *The Woman Warrior* usually appears in Asian American studies programs, as a model for creative writing, or as a major text in courses such as the Asian American Experience and the Immigrant-Ethnic Experience. It is also included in courses offered through ethnic studies departments, where it is read in the context of other American ethnic texts, ranging from *The Autobiography of Malcolm X* to Maya Angelou's *I Know Why the Caged Bird Sings*. More concerned with theory and formal inquiry, courses in postmodern readings examine *The Woman Warrior* as a powerfully indeterminate text, paying close attention to the ways in which it oversteps or blurs the boundaries between fiction and life story. Fewer respondents pressed this point, although a number said that what they enjoyed most about teaching the book was analyzing the postmodern aspects of Kingston's art (what their students found most frustrating)—the ambiguity between "truth," or autobiographical history, and "lies," or fictional invention. Courses titled Autobiography and Biography, Modernism in Crisis, and Postcolonial Texts allow instructors to focus on the "literary" aspects of the work.

The Instructor's Library

Respondents were asked to recommend reference and background works, biographical and critical studies, and audiovisual aids, including film, that would assist in teaching *The Woman Warrior*. The following is in no way an exhaustive compilation of works recommended; it is, instead, a summary of works most frequently mentioned and works that, in my opinion, would be most useful in explaining the cultural background of *The Woman Warrior*. Although much has been written on Kingston's writing, there is no single bibliography or book on it, and a great deal of analysis is scattered among various books, journals, and newspapers. I have limited the survey to chapters or significant passages of books and to journal articles. While the survey distinguishes among background studies, cultural background, and critical studies, no such clear distinction exists in the materials themselves, and some overlap inevitably occurs, as the book itself elicits a complex response to its cross-cultural, socioethnographic, postmodernist narratives.

Reference Works

King-Kok Cheung and Stan Yogi's *Asian American Literature: An Annotated Bibliography* contains the most useful bibliography on Kingston's work. While the book covers other ethnic Asian writers, the relevant section on primary sources of Chinese American literature (27–58) offers a valuable survey of the particular tradition in which *The Woman Warrior* is to be read. Significantly, as an indication of the wealth of the literature as against the critical work carried on it so far, the section on secondary sources (178–88) is much shorter. In the primary sources, there are eight entries on Kingston, covering various essays and prose pieces published since 1975. The entries on *China Men* and *The Woman Warrior* also note where portions of the books appeared elsewhere and particular reviews; for example, twenty-four reviews of *The Woman Warrior* are cited. But Kingston's critical prose is categorized separately, under the section on secondary sources (182); two other prose pieces are subcategorized under "Interviews, Profiles, and Commentary" (186); and articles on her work, composed of thirty-nine entries, appear under the names of the various authors and can be traced only under the index of authors of secondary materials. This clumsy division is necessary because the *Bibliography* functions for the entire body of Asian American literature. The index is indispensable in tracing specific items by and on Kingston. There clearly remains a need for a comprehensive annotated bibliography on Kingston's work, perhaps in the form of a pamphlet. Also, although Cheung and Yogi's work is called an annotated bibliography, many of the entries by Kingston and on her work are not annotated.

Briefer introductions to Asian American literature are to be found in the Spring 1985 *ADE Bulletin*. Amy Ling's brief introduction and selected bibliography is more useful for undergraduates than Cheung and Yogi's more complete work. Elaine Kim compresses a wealth of information on the social context of Asian American literature, discussing almost forty writers of major ethnic Asian groups and providing thematic summaries that she places in sociohistorical context. Linda Ching Sledge offers a critical approach to some of these texts, to elucidate the major pedagogical concerns of claiming "Asian American literature's place in the American literature curriculum" (44): the communal, Old World, immigrant contexts, the emergence of ethnic-generated genres as "historical products," and the function of "the collective ethnocentric notion of selfhood" (43) in shaping the forms of fiction. Both Kim's and Sledge's essays have useful selected bibliographies.

A dated bibliography that is helpful to undergraduates because it is attached to an introductory essay is in Suzanne Juhasz's "Narrative Technique and Female Identity" (189–90). In fact, this small bibliography carries two items of poems and a pedagogical essay Kingston published in *English Journal* in 1973 that are omitted in Cheung and Yogi.

An accessible but extremely limited bibliography is carried in *Contemporary Authors* (Evory 293–94). It chiefly provides review items. But the entry essay itself is helpful for undergraduates as it summarizes the major points made in at least fifteen reviews, interviews, and articles. Indeed, the essay is the only one so far to attempt a survey of reception of *The Woman Warrior* and *China Men*. While carrying only a limited critical analysis, it begins with a brief discussion of Kingston's techniques in these two books, leading to an examination of genre. It lists the significant themes in *The Woman Warrior*, focusing on the feminist heroics in the figures of Fa Mu Lan and No Name aunt; a much longer discussion is extended to *China Men*. There is a well-balanced summary of the controversy surrounding the "nonfiction" status of her two books, as in Frederic Wakeman's contention that "precisely because the myths are usually so consciously contrived, her pieces of distant China lore often seem jejune and even inauthentic—especially to readers who know a little bit about the original high culture which Kingston claims as her birthright." The essay is particularly useful in providing Kingston's defense to these criticisms of "spurious folklore," that she is writing in the "peasant talk-story Cantonese tradition ('low' if you will), which is the heritage of Chinese Americans" (291). The bibliography is also attached to an interview conducted specifically for this publication.

Background Studies

The survey on *The Woman Warrior* went out before Kingston's novel, *Tripmaster Monkey: His Fake Book*, appeared. Thus, while many of the survey respondents recommended that *The Woman Warrior* be read together with *China Men*, no mention (obviously) was made of *Tripmaster Monkey*. However, as Kingston's introduction to this volume makes clear, and as numerous critics and the respondents themselves specify, *China Men* is an accompanying text that "completes" the experience of reading *The Woman Warrior*.

The other text that many respondents referred to as essential background study for both teachers and students is Elaine H. Kim's *Asian American Literature: An Introduction to the Writings and Their Social Context*. While the discussion on Kingston's work forms a small part of Kim's book (199–213), *Asian American Literature* (the first and so far the only volume of its kind) provides a coherent sociohistorical background for understanding *The Woman Warrior*, particularly in the gendered context of Chinese American literary tradition, a context that many teachers may be unfamiliar with. The chapter in which Kingston's books are discussed is titled, appropriately, "Chinatown Cowboys and Warrior Women: Searching for a New Self-Image." In offering analyses of early Asian immigrant literature and of portraits of Chinatown in earlier chapters, Kim's book provides the ethnocultural background needed to understand many of the sources and reference points of *The Woman Warrior*.

A number of respondents indicated that to appreciate *The Woman Warrior* fully, readers would have to understand something of cultural analysis. Some pointed to Clifford Geertz's *Interpretation of Cultures*, Edward Said's *Orientalism*, Gayatri Spivak's *In Other Worlds*, and Reed Dasenbrock's "Intelligibility and Meaningfulness in Multicultural Literature in English" as useful pedagogical departure points for thinking about the cross-cultural challenge of teaching *The Woman Warrior*. Other respondents recommended ethnic-based background materials, such as Werner Sollors's *Beyond Ethnicity* and William Boelhower's *Through a Glass Darkly*.

In the same spirit of cross-cultural inquiry, respondents selected specific texts as useful studies of Chinese and Chinese American culture and history—for example, Jack Chen's *Chinese of America*, Judy Yung's *Chinese Women of America*, Paul C. Siu's *Chinese Laundryman*, Margery Wolf and Roxane Witke's *Women in Chinese Society*, and Houston Baker and Walter J. Ong's *Three American Literatures*.

An equal number of respondents believed that *The Woman Warrior* should be read in the context of women's writing, on the one hand, and autobiography and genre studies, on the other. Frequently, the concerns of non-ethnic-oriented respondents intersected with those of women's studies respondents in the recommended background readings on women's autobiography. These covered the whole range of contemporary scholarship on autobiography, from books by William C. Spengemann, James Olney, Albert E. Stone, and Janet Gunn, which do not deal specifically with Kingston or even with women's autobiographies, to more feminist volumes, such as Estelle Jelinek's, Shari Benstock's, Sidonie Smith's, and Domna C. Stanton's books.

Yet another group of respondents placed *The Woman Warrior* in women's studies, recommending theoretical and contextual readings such as Carol Gilligan's *In a Different Voice*, Sandra M. Gilbert and Susan Gubar's *Madwoman in the Attic*, and Elaine Showalter's edited collection *New Feminist Criticism*.

The range of background studies recommended by the respondents indicates less a controversy over how to read *The Woman Warrior* than the enormous popularity and broad appeal of the book. While clearly an ethnic text, coming from and addressing a Chinese American history and community, it is not ethnic-bound. Its power as a literary artifact forms its dominant appeal to mainstream teachers; hence the number of background texts dealing with autobiography and genre studies suggested. Moreover, it is both an American cultural document and a strong feminist articulation, albeit complicated and nuanced by race and class. Because *The Woman Warrior* is a multivocal text, capable of speaking to immediate and wider audiences, the background studies recommended are multidisciplinary, diverse, even divergent and loose.

Cultural Background

Many instructors asked for readings that would help them fill in the cultural background of an unfamiliar people and history. The information in a number of histories of Chinese immigration to the United States, Chinese labor in California, and Chinese women in America can help in an appreciation of the cross-cultural materials in *The Woman Warrior*—for example, Victor Nee and Brett Nee's *Longtime Californ'*, Chen's *Chinese of America*, Rose Hum Lee's *Chinese in the United States of America*, Stanford M. Lyman's *Chinese Americans*, Ruthanne Lum McCunn's *Chinese American Portraits*, Stan Steiner's *Fusang: The Chinese Who Built America*, Betty Lee Sung's *Mountain of Gold*, and Henry Shih-shan Tsai's *Chinese Experience in America*. Of particular relevance are Him Mark Lai, Genny Lim, and Judy Yung's *Island: Poetry and History of Chinese Immigrants on Angel Island: 1910–1940*, which provides translations of pioneer Chinese immigrants' poems in response to the stresses of dislocation, detention, and immigration.

Judy Yung's *Chinese Women of America: A Pictorial History* is a vivid history that captures the experiences of Chinese women caught in the intersection of race and gender in the United States. Another source frequently mentioned is Margery Wolf and Roxane Witke's *Women in Chinese Society*. Wolf's essay "Women and Suicide in China" gives the No Name Woman episode a sociopolitical grounding, providing a fuller appreciation of the Chinese and female cultural contexts. Kay Ann Johnson's *Women, the Fam-*

ily, and Peasant Revolution in China is knowledgeable in its analysis of women's roles and images in a Chinese patriarchal system. The seemingly ambiguous position of women as both strong and weak, dangerous and victimized, in *The Woman Warrior* is illuminated by Johnson's discussion of how the pattern of sexually irresponsible women juxtaposed against cultural ideals of nurturant, submissive mother-wives is most pronounced in extended patrilineal, patriarchal societies.

Michael Omi and Howard Winant's *Racial Formation in the United States from the 1960's to the 1980's*, an analysis of the sociopolitical origins of racial ideology, helps us to view *The Woman Warrior* as a text negotiating the constitution of Chinese American identity. Teachers of *The Woman Warrior* will find Paul C. Siu's *Chinese Laundryman: A Study of Social Isolation* useful background on the lives of Chinese sojourners as portrayed in Kingston's first two books; Siu's study explains the kind of misogyny that permeated Chinese bachelor society and that *The Woman Warrior* portrays. Because immigration laws did not permit wives from China to join their husbands in the United States, Chinese American society was largely male up to the middle of the twentieth century. This enforced bachelorhood encouraged deviant and misogynistic attitudes toward women in a culture that was already strictly patriarchal.

The introduction to *Aiiieeeee! An Anthology of Asian American Writers* (Chan, Chin, Inada, and Wong) represents a male view of Asian American literary tradition that has been highly critical of Kingston's success. Amy Ling's *Between Worlds: Women Writers of Chinese Ancestry* places *The Woman Warrior* in the tradition of anglophone writing by women of the Chinese diaspora. Some respondents indicated the usefulness of reading *The Woman Warrior* together with other Chinese American women's writing, such as Jade Snow Wong's *Fifth Chinese Daughter* or Amy Tan's *Joy Luck Club*.

Biography

No single biographical essay exists on Kingston. Many biographical facts are included in Susan Currier's entry in *Dictionary of Literary Biography Yearbook 1980* and in Jean W. Ross's interview in *Contemporary Authors*. Most of Kingston's interviews skirt personal questions to focus on her writing, but biographical data relating her background to her writing process do emerge in some interviews. The interview with Arturo Islas (1983) in *Women Writers of the West Coast* gives insights into the relation between *The Woman Warrior* and Kingston's own life. These insights are elaborated and updated in the interview with Paula Rabinowitz (1987) and in the *Humanities Discourses* interview (1988). Kingston talks about her relation to her critic Frank

Chin in an interview with William Satake Blauvelt (1989) and the influence of her education on her work in the interview with Angeles Carabi (1989). A taped interview with Kay Bonetti provides interesting background information (1986), and a video interview with Bill Moyers on Public Television's *World of Ideas* is also thought-provoking (1989).

Critical Studies

Since its publication in 1976, *The Woman Warrior* has been the subject of many critical studies, as a single-text study or as part of a broader analysis of Kingston's writings and of other ethnic women's texts. Among the more illuminating single-text studies are Sidonie Smith's chapter on *The Woman Warrior* in her *Poetics of Women's Autobiography* and Sau-ling Wong's essay in *MELUS*. Smith's chapter, another instance of postmodern interpretation, reads the work as "an autobiography about women's autobiographical storytelling" (150), in which "the hermeneutics of self-representation can never be divorced from cultural representations of woman that delimit the nature of her access to the world and the articulation of her desire" (151), and weaves close readings of specific passages with thematic considerations of mother-daughter conflicts and bonds. Wong's essay, a defense of *The Woman Warrior* against continued criticism of the elements of fantasy in it, views the book as a thematic development of the tension between the Chinese immigrant acceptance of necessity and the human impulse toward extravagance.

David Leiwei Li's essay locates *The Woman Warrior* in its cross-cultural context. Focusing on the primacy of names and pronouns in the book, Li provides the Chinese cultural information necessary to balance our reading of this *Chinese* American text. Deborah Homsher, however, approaches the work as "an autobiography of a second-generation American," a dramatic form that enacts "the central problem of [Kingston's] life, that she is not completely Chinese" (95), and Homsher's essay is useful in its discussion of *The Woman Warrior*'s crossing of the boundaries of the genres of autobiography and fiction. Margaret Miller, Amy Ling, and Carol Mitchell, among others, discuss specific thematic concerns in the text.

A number of studies focus on *The Woman Warrior* and *China Men* as a paired opus. Suzanne Juhasz's "Narrative Technique and Female Identity" explores the differences between *The Woman Warrior* and *China Men* in terms of the differences in female identity evolved between the daughter's relations to the mother and her relations to the father, "a self formed at the source by gender experience" (174). Leslie Rabine's essay in *Signs* explores Kingston's double ambivalence to her parents' Chinese culture and to American culture and examines the "proliferation of gender arrangements" in *The*

Woman Warrior and *China Men* to show how gender systems change across cultures as well as how symbolic gender and social gender change between cultures (474). Roberta Rubenstein's "Bridging Two Cultures" and Elaine Kim's "Visions and Fierce Dreams" analyze both books as "reconciling the immigrant and American-born Chinese" (147). One of the few critics to incorporate a discussion of *Tripmaster Monkey*, James Aubrey reads Kingston's work as artistic displacements of actual war.

Essays that discuss *The Woman Warrior* in the tradition of Asian American literature include Pat Lin Blinde's "Icicle in the Desert," a comparison of Jade Snow Wong's *Fifth Chinese Daughter* with *The Woman Warrior*. Cheng Lok Chua examines the various versions of the American dream as portrayed by Louis Chu, Lin Yutang, and Kingston; and Shirley Geok-lin Lim interprets *The Woman Warrior* in the tradition of twelve Asian American writers whose works focus on defining identity: communal, ethnic, American, and existential.

Many essays approach *The Woman Warrior* as participating in a broader ethnic women's thematics. King-Kok Cheung's *PMLA* essay focuses on voice, narrative, and oppression in Alice Walker's *Color Purple* and *The Woman Warrior*. Elizabeth J. Ordóñez places *The Woman Warrior* among black, Chicano, and Jewish women's writing as an example of Chinese American female and ethnic sociohistorical identity that moves beyond cultural nationalism to a textuality that reshapes female history and personal and collective identity.

The Woman Warrior is increasingly read as part of a larger body of thematics drawn from a canon of literature, be it contemporary American literature, regional California literature, women's writing, or world literature. Shirley K. Rose discusses Kingston's work together with that of male ethnic autobiographers. Marilyn Yalom, for example, discusses the theme of female madness in *The Woman Warrior* in *Maternity, Mortality, and the Literature of Madness*. For his part, Michael M. J. Fischer reads *The Woman Warrior* as one of the ethnic autobiographies that explore a "pluralist, post-industrial, late-twentieth-century society" (195). Stephanie Demetrakopoulos studies the mother-daughter relations in the book, one of the four women's autobiographies she considers, while Lynn Z. Bloom discusses the work as one of many twentieth-century women's texts that treat the daughters' responses to their mothers' heritage.

Finally, *The Woman Warrior* is examined frequently as an example of postmodern narrative that blurs/pushes/breaks/collapses the traditional boundaries of autobiography-fantasy-poetry-fiction. Juhasz analyzes the form of the feminist autobiography in Kate Millett and Kingston's work. Paul J. Eakin gives a close reading of *The Woman Warrior* as an ontogenetic account of self, linking the autobiographical act to the linguistic inventions of self;

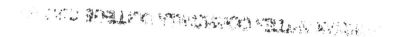

he later offers Kingston as a "new model autobiographer" whose conviction of textuality is expressed in intensely narrative structure and practice (38). Celeste Schenck interprets *The Woman Warrior*'s treatment of voice, vocation, and the vocative in the light of the relationship between the writing daughter and the mother.

MOHAWK VALLEY COMMUNITY COLLEGE LIBRARY

VALLEY COMMUNITY COLLEGE LIBRARY

Part Two

APPROACHES

INTRODUCTION

The seventeen essays in part 2 underline the volume's commitment to "critical methods that are flexible and eclectic and that avoid single-minded, myopic systems—methods that seek to combine thematic, structural, deconstructive, historical, and even biographical approaches" (Brombert 395). It is inevitable that the nineteen contributors speak with so many voices and views on the same text, as they each contextualize *The Woman Warrior* in a different tradition, canon, reading list, or course, with different student audiences in mind.

The essayists bring to their approaches the skills and expertise of a range of disciplines. The first section, on cultural and historical contexts, will prove especially useful for instructors who are unfamiliar with Asian and Chinese cultures and literary traditions. The essays by Sau-ling Cynthia Wong, Patricia Lin, and Kathyrn VanSpanckeren provide in readable form a wealth of information that ground *The Woman Warrior* in specific Asian and Chinese American allusions, offering the kind of multicultural literacy that E. D. Hirsch, Jr., had somehow omitted from his version of cultural literacy. Robert G. Lee's historiographic analysis introduces the reader to the gendered politics underlying Asian American writing and its reception and to the uses and abuses of "cross-cultural" stances (or Orientalist positions) in literary interpretation.

The second section, on pedagogical contexts, begins with Vicente Gotera's survey of student responses to *The Woman Warrior* and proceeds to discussions of how the work is taught in various environments: women's studies, military college classes, writing classes, history courses, high school and community college classes.

The last section, on critical contexts, demonstrates the flexible, eclectic methodology of the volume. *The Woman Warrior* is examined as postmodernist text, women's autobiography, a part of the tradition of women's writing of the body, mythopoeic strategies, subjectivity inseparable from language resources, and textuality that challenges the boundaries between fiction and nonfiction and that constructs an ethical domain. The two concluding essays are examples of the kinds of thematic readings that *The Woman Warrior* attracts by its very complexity and density, linguistic and narrative features that Bakhtin has inscribed on our consciousness as "heteroglossia," characteristic of hybrid cultural forms.

Space limitations made it impossible to include another ten or twenty different approaches to teaching *The Woman Warrior*. We hope the beginning instructor will find much that is useful in these essays and that the experienced teacher will find valuable insights shared by contributors from different disciplines or contexts. What all the essays agree on, however, and what I hope readers will also agree with, is that the work itself, with its sheer literary luminosity even as it transgresses and transforms traditions and canons, is what makes the teaching worthwhile.

Personal Statement

Maxine Hong Kingston

I must write in a way that makes readers care about the people I create on paper. No matter that critics question what my genre is—fiction? nonfiction?—there is a reader in every audience who will ask: "How's your mother doing?"

My mother is fine, thank you, though she has high blood pressure and ought to be taking her prescription pills rather than the latest Chinatown remedy—honey and lemons just now, because specific herbs have not been available since June 4, 1989. She worries too much, and talks-story about the drug dealers on the block and their blatant m.o.'s. I advise her to pretend she doesn't notice. Should I tell her my idea? Put the pyramids of food and fruit and the shot glasses of Seagram's V.O. outside the gate. On the other hand, you aren't supposed to feed the bears at Yosemite; you call attention to yourself, and they don't understand when you run out of largesse.

Readers also ask how she feels about my writing. Well, since she doesn't read English, she can't get the fullest impact and power of my work. She reads the translations that have been pirated in Taiwan, Hong Kong, and China. Since pirates work fast, they use ready-made literary forms. They do not take the care to experiment with language or to try new shapes—to find the new shapes that I'm working in. The easiest given form is soap opera, which fakes passion and revelation. I suppose my mother thinks I am strong on plot and very entertaining, like her favorite American book, *Gone with the Wind*. She takes the world's praise of my work at face value and assumes that she and our family come off well.

My father's reactions to my work have been more satisfying. I directly challenge him in *China Men*: "You'll just have to speak up with the real stories if I've got you wrong." The Hong Kong pirated edition of *China Men* has nice wide margins, in which my father wrote commentary in his beautiful calligraphic hand. Commentary is a poetic and religious tradition, writers answering one another in verse, furthering and finishing rhymes and ideas. Confucius wrote commentary on the *I Ching*. I donated that copy of *China Men* to the Bancroft Library. I took my father there to show him his words on display. He said in English to the people around him, "My writing."

To best appreciate *The Woman Warrior*, you do need to read *China Men*. You'll see that "I" achieve an adult narrator's voice. And you'll find out what else the people do. Brave Orchid comes to New York and takes up the role of wife. The feminist narrator journeys to the Land of Men. She finds the ancestors and sympathetically follows the brothers to Vietnam. "I" am nothing but who "I" am in relation to other people. In *The Woman Warrior* "I" begin the quest for self by understanding the archetypal mother. In *China Men*, "I" become more whole because of the ability to appreciate the other gender.

Young women on campuses carry *The Norton Anthology of Literature by Women* like a talisman, like a shield. Just so, they carry *The Woman Warrior*; they call it "the book." "We're studying the book in class." "Will you discuss the book with us?" I don't like all this overpraising of my daughter and rudeness toward my sons—especially since my writing has gotten better— wiser and more skillful—as I've gone along.

China Men was almost part of *The Woman Warrior*; I wrote much of those two books at the same time. I once meant for them to be one large book. But the women's stories and the men's stories parted into two volumes, naturally replicating history and geography: the women stayed in China and maintained communities; the men sailed off to the Gold Mountain, where they built bachelor Chinatowns. The Quality Paperback Club printed *The Woman Warrior* and *China Men* as a boxed set, the most correct presentation.

The use of myths in the two books is quite different. The myths and the lives in *The Woman Warrior* are integrated in the women's and girls' stories so that we cannot find the seams where a myth leaves off and a life and imagination begin. Fa Mu Lan is a fantasy that inspires the girls' psyches and their politics. The myths transform lives and are themselves changed.

In *China Men* the myths are separate from the men's adventures in the modern world. That book is like a six-layer club sandwich or cake. I tell six present-day stories, and between them are the myths. The men have trouble keeping Chinese ways in new lands. What good are the old stories? How can we live up to the ancestral heroes? What are myths anyway? Religious directives? Warnings? Amusing stories? Old-country baggage? Quest maps to the Gold Mountain? Why not be rid of the mythical, and be a free American?

Sinologists have criticized me for not knowing myths and for distorting them; pirates correct my myths, revising them to make them conform to some traditional Chinese version. They don't understand that myths have to change, be useful or be forgotten. Like the people who carry them across oceans, the myths become American. The myths I write are new, American. That's why they often appear as cartoons and kung fu movies. I take the power I need from whatever myth. Thus Fa Mu Lan has the words cut into her back; in traditional story, it is the man, Ngak Fei the Patriot, whose parents cut vows on his back. I mean to take his power for women.

I visited China after I'd written the mythic China that we in the West have made up. The actual China is much the way I imagined it and affirms the accuracy of talk-story. (It also brings up the philosophical problem of how to see through preconceptions.) If I could rewrite *The Woman Warrior*, though, I'd make some changes in setting: the well in "No Name Woman" is actually next to the Hong family temple. I'd write a scene of the men standing on its steps and teasing the girls; my mother was so flustered that she broke her jug. The other adjustment I'd make would be to bring living spaces closer together, house added upon house. Having always lived in the United States, I could not imagine how very close the people in China crowd together. The "lanes" are alleys; you step over the raised threshold of the "great front door" on to dirt floors. The dwellings I've seen that most resemble my family's adobe villages are the pueblos in New Mexico and Arizona. A branch of our tribe lives in each room; everyone's behavior reverberates community-wide.

There are omissions that I'm sorry I didn't think of until long after I'd finished *The Woman Warrior*. I don't know why I didn't write down such obvious, important details. One is that Fa Mu Lan was a weaver. The chant begins with the sound of her shuttle and loom: "Jik jik jik" 'Weave weave weave.' I love it that *texture* and *text* come from the same root word. The other thing I wish I could add is that when Ts'ai Yen, the woman warrior who composed eighteen songs for the barbarian reed pipe, looked up in the sky, she saw home-flying geese that made formations of words—her letters home.

CULTURAL AND HISTORICAL CONTEXTS

Kingston's Handling of Traditional Chinese Sources

Sau-ling Cynthia Wong

"*The Woman Warrior* is an American book," declares an exasperated Kingston in an essay entitled "Cultural Mis-readings by American Reviewers." "Yet many reviewers do not see the American-ness of it, nor the fact of my own American-ness" (58).

The Woman Warrior is indeed a distinctly American book (by now an American classic, some believe [M. Chin, "Writing" 17]). It is also a book that makes extensive use of traditional Chinese sources. These two facts are entirely compatible if we see Chinese Americans as active users and creators of culture. In fact, it is only by reading *The Woman Warrior* as an American book that we can make sense of its "Chinese" elements, which freely alter their sources in both spirit and letter. However, many non–Chinese American readers have been blinkered by the stereotype that Chinese Americans, even those several generations removed from their ancestral land, are unassimilable aliens with some mystical genetic hotline to China's great traditions. As a result, they tend to focus disproportionately on the "Chinese" parts of the book, in particular "White Tigers," the chapter on the young girl's fantasized adventures as a woman warrior. As Kingston notes, some critics are put off by the unfamiliar air of the "Chinese" elements and find in them a confirmation of notorious Oriental inscrutability; others are only too ready to be delighted by the exotic, taking all the fabulous details at face value ("Cultural Mis-readings" 56). Neither response does justice to Kingston's chief artistic enterprise, which is to establish the legitimacy of a unique Chinese American (as opposed to "Chinese Chinese") experience and sensibility.

To help students grasp the centrality of this self-fashioning, self-affirming project, teachers who assign *The Woman Warrior* must be prepared to tackle that inevitable question from students, Do the Chinese really do that?— which translates to the broader and more theoretical question, How "Chinese" is *The Woman Warrior*? "Doing that" could refer to committing female infanticide, or training for years in the art of sitting still, or believing in ghosts and exorcism. The question may express innocent inquisitiveness, general epistemological confusion caused by the book's narrative complexities, uneasiness at ways of life so different from one's own, or a host of other attitudes. Whatever the motive, the question is far from simple; how one answers it would shape the students' understanding of what *The Woman Warrior* is all about.

One could bypass the question altogether by dismissing it as irrelevant, by redirecting the students' attention to the "universal" aspects of the book and asking them to connect an exotic-sounding detail to their own lives (e.g., from the standpoint of a woman, a descendant of immigrants, a language user, an aspiring writer, etc.). There is certainly enough material of "universal" appeal to have made *The Woman Warrior* a fixture on reading lists in many disciplines. A responsible teacher, however, may find the danger of reductionism and cooptation too great for this approach to be satisfactory.

Yet in another, truly defensible sense, the question is indeed irrelevant, since every narrated event in *The Woman Warrior* has been mediated by the imagination and voice of the narrator-protagonist. As an American-born daughter of immigrants, the narrator has no direct access to Chinese realities. She must draw her own haphazard deductions and create a precarious coherence from the elaborate talk-story of the mother, her unexplained cultural practices, the behavior of immigrant neighbors in Stockton's small Chinatown, and, later, from bilingual dictionaries and library research (238, 104). What this specific Chinese American narrator does to validate her own life matters much more than what the "Chinese Chinese" in general really do or don't do: anthropological accuracy is not the issue. In fact, vis-à-vis the latter question, the narrator is far from privileged; she has to struggle to sort out "[w]hat is Chinese tradition and what is the movies" (6).

That said, it must be acknowledged that students might detect evasiveness in such an answer and that there are far too many vivid, curiosity-arousing details throughout the book to allow the question an early retirement. Moreover, the issue of Kingston's infidelity to her Chinese sources has been at the heart of a long-standing controversy within the Chinese American community; some critics have accused Kingston of promoting a "fake" Chinese

American culture by mutilating traditional material beyond recognition (see S. C. Wong, "Autobiography"). For these reasons, it would not do simply to tell students to stop asking whether the Chinese "really do that."

A good way to strike a balance between pedagogical effectiveness and interpretive rigor is to approach the question of "Chineseness" indirectly, by studying how a few traditional Chinese literary sources have been altered to serve as commentary on the narrator's Chinese American reality. In this essay I discuss how two such sources might be used in the classroom—the stories of Fa Mu Lan (Hua Mulan according to the pinyin system of romanization; the pinyin version of each Chinese name is given in parentheses) and Ts'ai Yen (Cai Yan). These have been chosen partly for practical reasons: for each a focused, written version is available and an English translation already exists, and the original is brief enough to be presented in full, allowing for the discussion of specific questions. (If the teacher were to concentrate on inaccessible elements of popular culture diffused through nonprint media like movies, comics, or talk-story, students would simply have to take the instructor's word for it and could not participate actively in the process of comparison and contrast.) Pragmatic considerations aside, the two sources are important because Kingston's divergences from the originals bear on central themes in the book. Once they recognize these themes, students are less likely to be distracted by questions of detail based on the erroneous assumption that traditional Chinese culture is "brought over" by immigrants much like a steamer trunk is: it can be opened or kept closed, preserved or thrown out, but never *transformed* into something different by the experience of living in America.

The Story of Fa Mu Lan

As even a cursory comparison with the traditional "Ballad of Mulan" shows, Kingston's version in "White Tigers" is a retelling only in the loosest possible sense: numerous details have been added, some from sources far removed historically from the "Ballad." The crucial questions for the reader are, Why has the Fa Mu Lan story been so altered? Do the interpolations serve any thematic function? Are they integrated with the rest of the book? Do they, rather, reflect sloppy scholarship or, even worse, crowd-pleasing exoticization, as some of Kingston's Chinese American critics have accused her of promoting (Chan, "Jeff Chan"; Tong; Fong; F. Chin)?

Before one plunges into these questions, a general reminder is in order: although the "Ballad of Mulan" is the most common and likely means by which modern Chinese children learn about the heroine, it is by no means the only extant literary work on her life. The Fa Mu Lan story has attained the status of a topos in Chinese literature, so that a number of versions exist in various genres, with authors fabricating episodes and secondary characters as they see fit. There are versions of the Mulan story in the Tang, Ming, and Qing dynasties as well as the modern period, in genres ranging from the ballad, the novel, and the opera libretto to the *baihua*, or vernacular, play; during China's war of resistance against Japanese invaders (1937–45), the Mulan story was frequently staged in patriotic propaganda plays. "Added" characters have included a sister and her love interest, and a cowardly, draft-evading cousin. (For a brief account in Chinese of the "Ballad of Mulan," see J. Zhao 77–79). Moreover, scholars throughout the ages have disagreed on many crucial details in the poem, including the heroine's name, ethnic origin, and hometown; the geographical locations of her military campaigns; the nature of the battles; as well as the historical period during which the "Ballad" was most likely composed (Yao, "Mulan congjun shidi biaowei"; Xu). If even the historical existence of Fa Mu Lan is impossible to ascertain, she should be regarded simply as a folk heroine. The debate should not be couched in terms of how Kingston's version deviates from a "definitive" one chronicling the life of a "real" Fa Mu Lan.

Two other points must also be fully appreciated before a fruitful discussion can proceed: the "White Tigers" segment on the woman warrior is meant to be read as a fantasy, not historical reconstruction, and it is meant to be read in an American context—the narrator's life as a female child in a Chinese American immigrant family. The nonnaturalistic status of the narrative can be brought out by highlighting textual clues in the first part of the chapter (e.g., the conditional subjunctive in "The call would come from a bird. . . . The bird would cross the sun" [24]) and the improbability of some of the narrated events (e.g., the woman warrior going through pregnancy and childbirth undetected by fellow soldiers). Students can be led to the second point by being asked to note the twofold structure of the "White Tigers" chapter: the woman-warrior story followed by a shorter section beginning "My American life has been such a disappointment" (54–63).

Once these two points are made clear, the teacher can begin a discussion of the "Ballad of Mulan" as a way of getting at the ambiguity inherent in the situation of a woman distinguishing herself dressed as a man. This ambiguity has made for conflicting interpretations of the "Ballad" among Chinese scholars. Some consider the story an inspiring exemplar of filial piety, about a dutiful daughter who undergoes extremities to spare her aging father from conscription (Yao, "Mulan congjun shidi bushu" 71–73). Others read it as antipatriarchal and anti-Confucian, arguing that so unconventional a heroine can only be of northern nomadic origin (Xu 81–83). The same ambiguity, greatly magnified because of elaborations, can be seen in Kingston's rendition. As is typical in wish-fulfilling fantasies, the narrator tries to eat her cake and have it too: her glorious subversion of patriarchy ends in reconciliation with it (53–54). The class can explore the narrator's simultaneous revolt against, and subscription to, sexist ideas about women and through the exploration arrive at some understanding of the artistic resolution attempted in *The Woman Warrior*.

Next, the class can examine Kingston's various additions to the skeletal Fa Mu Lan story and the psychological and cultural dynamics informing them. Because of space limitations, only a few of these changes can be reviewed here.

The original "Ballad" does not mention the heroine's childhood. Details in "White Tigers" about the young girl's training are drawn from popular *wuxia xiaoshuo*, or martial-arts novels, and their modern incarnations in the cinema (see Liu 81–137 for an introduction to the tradition of *wuxia*, or knight-errantry; Hsia 30 for an introduction to the *wuxia xiaoshuo*). The basis of this still influential genre is *wushu* (martial art), which has a long and venerable tradition in China; in its highest form it is meditation as well as self-defense and calls for lifelong dedication and discipline—a far cry from the popular American perception of kung fu as a cult of ruthless aggression and macho swagger. Taoist influences are strong (as in the notion of self-cultivation to attain immortality, exemplified by the old couple who become the narrator's teachers and surrogate parents in the fantasy). Typical plots interweave an archetypal struggle between good and evil (those who use their superhuman martial skills to uphold righteous values versus those who misuse them for self-aggrandizement); an arduous quest (for the right master, for magic elixirs or antidotes, for a secret instruction book, etc.) and attendant trials; years of endurance and tireless practice; revenge (avenging the murder of loved ones or domination by foreign invaders); and dramatic showdowns. Most of these structural elements can be seen in Kingston's version. Likewise, most of the colorful, marvelous details of "White Tigers" (for which I suspect many non-Chinese reviewers credit solely Kingston's imagination) are conventional and derivative.

With the issue of fidelity to the original placed in perspective, we might then ask, What is it about the process of martial-arts training that appeals so much to the young protagonist's imagination? In other words, in what sense is the traditional "Ballad" inadequate for the narrator? What aspects of her Chinese American female life have prompted her to compensate by grafting martial-arts images onto a sketchy poem, where fighting is described in cursory, vague, and stylized terms? Are there parallels between the martial arts and literary art? What are the conflicting demands on the protagonist as she undergoes years of training, in a protected realm away from her mundane responsibilities? How does the situation mirror her Chinese American existence?

A second major, and highly controversial, alteration to the Fa Mu Lan story is the tattooing episode. The episode is based on another well-known traditional story, that of Ngak Fei (Yue Fei), a historical hero whose mother is said to have carved four characters on his back exhorting him to serve his country with loyalty and honor (Cheung 169; Hsu 442). Furthermore, the four-character maxim has turned into an entire page of reminders of revenge (again a physical improbability). Some interesting issues to explore are these: Does Kingston's confusion betray an irresponsible attitude toward Chinese traditions? Should she not have done her "homework" better? She has defended her deviations from traditional myths as necessary: "We have to do more than record myth. . . . That's just more ancestor worship. The way I keep the old Chinese myths alive is by telling them in a new American way" (Pfaff, "Talk" 26). Is she indeed free to modify traditional material well known to the Chinese people? Why or why not? Can we assume that, like Freudian slips, Kingston's confusion is determined by some kind of hidden emotional logic and, if so, what is this logic?

Third, Kingston has incorporated elements of stories of peasant uprisings into her version of Fa Mu Lan's life. Two of the best-known works of classical Chinese fiction, *Romance of the Three Kingdoms* and *Outlaws of the Marsh* (or *Water Margin*), describe men of humble origin who have led "righteous armies" in revolt against the existing dynastic order. (Two translations of each work, one full-length and one abridged, are listed in "Works Cited" under Lo and Luo, respectively.) Episodes from these two novels, which originated as oral literature, have been retold with relish countless times over the centuries—informally, by itinerant storytellers, grandparents and parents pestered for bedtime stories, or teachers taking a break from the didactic canon; formally, in operas and, more recently, on the radio or in film. The protagonist of *The Woman Warrior* appears to have been brought up on oral material derived from these classics, judging from some of the modifications made to the Fa Mu Lan story. Whereas the heroine of the "Ballad" is depicted as a loyal retainer, the one in Kingston's version is a rebel against a wicked baron and the tyrannical emperor he represents. The traditional woman warrior reveals her gender in a final moment of glory, surprising her comrades-in-arms; Kingston's, after her triumphant return from the mountains, has more work to do. She has to assemble a peasant army, fight her way to the capital, behead the evil emperor, and inaugurate a new one—a male peasant under whom she gladly serves as a general. (Note again the ambivalence toward patriarchy: her rebellion is far from radical.)

Kingston's injection of peasant revolt motifs shifts the ideological center of gravity of the Fa Mu Lan story. Once again, contrasting the two versions, students might ask, What values are affirmed by turning Fa Mu Lan into a Robin Hood type? Why is so much made of the woman warrior's recruitment of peasant sons? or of the confrontation with the baron? What is the point of inventing a mercenary female army formed by liberated concubines? Does the narrator's preoccupation with community even in her most farfetched fantasies imply a certain attitude toward fellow Chinese Americans? How does the peasant origin of the ragtag army relate to Chinese immigration history (see, e.g., Chen 16)? What are the parallels in Chinese American life to the wicked baron or the tyrannical emperor?

Apart from investigating how the "Ballad" has been fleshed out by the young protagonist, it would also be useful to think of the "White Tigers" fantasy as resonating with the lives of other women portrayed in *The Woman Warrior*. In this connection, it should be noted that Brave Orchid and Moon Orchid are named as if they were sisters of Fa Mu Lan, whose given name, Mu Lan, if translated literally character by character, would be Sylvan Orchid (Li 501). In what sense can one call the narrator's mother and aunt modern-day sisters of the woman warrior? What affinities or contrasts among the three can be discovered? The teacher may wish to address these questions and consider the concept of a symbolic sisterhood as a structuring mechanism for the entire book.

The Ts'ai Yen Story

Kingston ends *The Woman Warrior* with a version of the story of Ts'ai Yen, author of "Eighteen Stanzas for a Barbarian Reed Pipe," the long poem from which the title of the final chapter ("A Song for a Barbarian Reed Pipe") is derived.

Unlike Fa Mu Lan, Ts'ai Yen was definitely a historical figure. The standard source on her life is *Hou Han Shu* (History of the Latter Han Dynasty), compiled in the mid-fifth century; Guo provides a review of research on the biographical details (96–137). Ts'ai Yen was born about AD 177, daughter of a scholar-statesman, Ts'ai Yung (Cai Yong), who had a rough career in officialdom and died in prison. (Kingston's description of "princess" is not to be taken literally.) Ts'ai Yen was known for being a superb scholar, speaker, and musician. Widowed at a young age, she was captured from her parents' home by raiding Southern Hsiung-nu (Xiongnu) horsemen (identical to the Huns who later invaded Europe) in the year 195. During her twelve years' sojourn in barbarian lands, she was made the wife of a commander and had two children by him. In the meantime, in Han (ethnic Chinese) land, the Han dynasty fell. The new emperor of Wei (one of the "Three Kingdoms"), Ts'ao Ts'ao (Cao Cao), was a good friend of Ts'ai Yen's father; troubled that the unfortunate man would have no heir, Ts'ao Ts'ao sent envoys with ransom gifts to the southern Hsiung-nu and secured Ts'ai Yen's return. She was married a third time. Three poems have been attributed to her: two entitled "Lamentation" (in different verse form; see Liu and Lo 36–39) and "Eighteen Stanzas."

Kingston's few "factual" references to Ts'ai Yen's life, as we can see, are based on research. Because "Eighteen Stanzas" is much longer than the "Ballad of Mulan," was written in a far from vernacular style, and has been less popular as well, Kingston almost certainly did not learn of the poem as part of an oral tradition. Like Fa Mu Lan's story, however, Ts'ai Yen's has been retold; a recent version was a 1959 play (Guo 1–86). Both the authenticity and literary merit of "Eighteen Stanzas" have been questioned (Guo 96–137). For the anglophone reader interested in getting a sense of the tenor and typical images of Ts'ai Yen's poem, the matter is further complicated by the lack of a full-length translation in English. The closest approximation available is a translation of a later "imitation" of "Eighteen Stanzas" by Liu Shang (c. AD 773), given in Rorex and Fong's handsomely produced *Eighteen Songs of a Nomad Flute: The Story of Lady Wen-Chi*. Because of this textual limitation, one would be ill-advised to contrast it with Kingston's version in any detailed fashion. Besides, we are not sure which version Kingston had access to when she wrote *The Woman Warrior*. But broad differences in thematic emphasis can still be discerned.

The liberty that Kingston has taken with the Ts'ai Yen story is a matter of selective focus rather than sustained embellishment on a scant narrative frame. She has added some details; at the same time, she has left out a great deal that seems important in the Chinese versions. She has also taken advantage of the symbolist's license to concentrate in the person of Ts'ai Yen two different predicaments: that of the immigrant generation and that of the American-born.

In insisting on regarding China as "home" even after twelve years with the Southern Hsiung-nu, in feeling alienated from the uncivilized barbarians among whom she must live, the speaker in "Eighteen Stanzas" is like the narrator's parents in *The Woman Warrior*. "Whenever my parents said 'home,' they suspended America" (116). Though not abducted like Ts'ai Yen, the immigrant parents do feel a sense of involuntariness: they have had to leave their ancestral land to seek a better life among American "barbarians."

If Ts'ai Yen represents, in a sense, the immigrant generation suffering from nostalgia and alienation, it is not surprising to find the narrator in *The Woman Warrior* mentioning the poet's return almost as an afterthought (243), for to celebrate the event would be to negate the validity of her life as an American-born Chinese. It has been said that Ts'ai Yen's return to China has become associated with some cherished cultural ideas:

> . . . the superiority of Chinese civilization over the cultures beyond her borders, the irreconcilability of the different ways of life; the necessity for the individual to bear the burdens thrust upon one by fate; and above all, the Confucian concept of loyalty to one's ancestral family and state.   (Rorex and Fong)

If these "cherished ideas" are typical of the tradition-minded "Chinese Chinese," they obviously have little to offer an American-born Chinese;

indeed, they create demands that are quite impossible to fulfill. Because of their nativity and upbringing, the descendants of immigrants are destined to lose touch eventually with the Chinese civilization deemed so superior by their elders; emotionally it is difficult to summon loyalty toward an ancestral family and state one has never seen; and, if for their sanity alone, the American-born cannot believe that the different ways of life they encounter daily are irreconcilable.

Also conspicuously absent is any reference to the fact that Ts'ai Yen had to leave her two children behind, which is repeatedly alluded to in all three of the poems attributed to her, taking up as many as five stanzas in "Eighteen Stanzas" (even more than in Liu Shang's "imitation"). The class might wish to discuss why the narrator of *The Woman Warrior* chooses to suppress this detail. Does the omission have to do with her own mistaken childhood fear that the parents would go back to China and sell her as a slave girl (116)? When she imagines Ts'ai Yen's children, she sees them as half-barbarians mocking their mother's Chinese speech with "senseless singsong words" and laughter (242). This description echoes many passages on the Chinese American language situation found in *The Woman Warrior*: for example, how the Chinese language is denigrated as "chingchong ugly" (199) by white Americans and how the second-generation children have so internalized this view that they fall silent (200). The issue of language shift in the immigrant family can be raised in connection with "silence" and "voice" as a recurrent theme in American literatures by people of color.

The ability of Kingston's narrator to empathize with Ts'ai Yen indicates transcendence of personal grievances against her parents (particularly her mother), which in turn suggests an understanding that lack of communication is a mutual matter. In the last two paragraphs of the book, Ts'ai Yen becomes an alter ego of the American-born daughter, who has learned to articulate her pain through art rather than personal accusations. As with the Fa Mu Lan legend, Kingston has revised the ideological center of gravity of the Ts'ai Yen story by muting the significance of the return. In the historical tale the exile has been decentered and can be redeemed only by returning to China, the Central Kingdom, the seat of one's ancestral civilization. For the narrator of *The Woman Warrior*, though, the new moment of glory or validation occurs when one breaks out of silence into song: through song a new center is created right there in the desert, at the winter campfires "ringed by barbarians" (243). The American-born Chinese, Kingston seems to imply, must create their own art.

Kingston's affirmation of the communicative power of art appears closer in spirit to the "Eighteen Stanzas" attributed to Ts'ai Yen than to Liu Shang's "imitation." The former version ends with these lines (my translation; Samuel Cheung's assistance is gratefully acknowledged):

The barbarian reed pipe originated from barbarian lands.
When transcribed to the *qin* [a stringed Chinese musical
    instrument], however, its tunes remain the same.
Even though the eighteen stanzas have ended, sounds linger
    on, evoking endless sentiments.
Thus we know that the subtle marvels of strings and pipes are
    Nature's work.
Sorrows and joys vary from person to person, but when
    transformed they become connected.
Barbarian and Han lands are different, with different customs.
Heaven is separated from earth; mother and child are
    scattered east and west.
Alas, my woe is vaster than the sky.
Even though the universe is immense, it cannot contain my
    suffering.

(Liu Shang's concluding stanza stresses the joy of reconnecting with "good rituals and etiquettes.") Still, Kingston's angle on the Ts'ai Yen story is an idiosyncratic one compared with traditional Chinese interpretations. The artist, not the loyal exile and cultural preservationist, is her icon. The art she aspires to is not only personally healing, as with Ts'ai Yen's outpouring, but also translatable across linguistic and cultural barriers.

Has Kingston succeeded in creating a song that "translate[s] well" (243)? There is as yet no consensus on the subject. Undeniably part of *The Woman Warrior*'s popularity has been fueled by a misplaced fascination with traditional Chinese culture, which may mean that the endeavor to produce a "translatable" Chinese American literature is destined to be undermined by stereotyping and Orientalism. In this essay I raise some of the critical issues surrounding Kingston's handling of traditional Chinese sources, as well as provide one perspective on the "exoticization" controversy. Whether her alterations to traditional material constitute creative adaptation or willful exploitation, realistic reflection of second-generation cultural disorientation or irresponsible perversion of a precious heritage, is a question teachers must work through with their students.

It is also a question that affects all writers of color in the United States. When a writer belonging to the Euramerican tradition plays fast and loose with traditional sources such as Greek mythology, the charge of distortion seldom arises; "everybody" knows the "true" version and understands the writer's variations to be allusions, parodies, or some other artistic effort. Moreover, marginalized groups of readers are expected to be conversant with these traditional sources, as part of their education into the "cultural literacy" defined by the dominant group. In contrast, writers of color who draw on their ethnocultural traditions in any way are expected to explain their work to the "mainstream" audience (with glossaries, footnotes, etc.), on pain of being dismissed as inaccessible. As Kingston complains, "How dare they call their ignorance our inscrutability?" ("Cultural Mis-readings" 56). Because writers of color face the ever-present threat of gross misreadings, as well as a tacit demand from their own groups to act as custodians and representatives, such writers may feel constrained when they use material from their cultures as a point of departure. Teachers who assign *The Woman Warrior* in conjunction with other marginalized works may wish to explore this broader issue of the writer of color's audience and responsibility.

Use of Media and Other Resources to Situate *The Woman Warrior*

Patricia Lin

While every literary work inevitably stands on its own, the complex convergence of historical, social, linguistic, and cultural factors against which *The Woman Warrior* is projected requires the explanatory function of nonliterary texts as well as audiovisual materials at certain junctures of the work, particularly for readers who are entering the world of Chinese Americans for the first time. To that end, films and studies from the social sciences can be used as a means of situating *The Woman Warrior*.

A general familiarity with the history of the Chinese in America establishes a backdrop against which to read *The Woman Warrior*. As an ethnic group, Chinese Americans were seen as undesirable aliens. Chinese women, for their part, faced a condition of double alienation—alienation from mainstream American culture because of race and from their own communities because of the traditional Chinese practice of marginalizing women. It this double-edged social displacement that should be considered in reading *The Woman Warrior*.

Kingston provides a complementary rendition of the Chinese American experience in her second book, *China Men*. Her fictionalized accounts of men who came to Hawaii and the United States in the nineteenth century are historically accurate, as are her portrayals of Chinese life in the communities in northern California before and after World War II. In *China Men* Kingston also offers insights into the psychological consequences that ultimately beset a largely disenfranchised and misunderstood community in America.

Overall, there is a substantial extant corpus of historical studies on the Chinese in America dating from their arrival, in search of work, in the last century. Early histories include Mary R. Coolidge's *Chinese Immigration* (1909), R. C. Campbell's *Chinese Coolie Immigration* (1923), and Wu Ching Chao's dissertation, "Chinatowns: A Study of Symbiosis and Assimilation" (1928). Most of the histories depict socioeconomic factors that inevitably dictated the way in which the lives of Chinese Americans would be shaped for over a century.

In response both to the opening of the American West and to widespread poverty in China, the immigrants began arriving in the United States from the 1840s on in search of employment. Some of the men found jobs as railroad builders, agricultural laborers, and miners; others became odd-job workers, shopkeepers, launderers, fishers, and domestics. These first Chinese Americans contributed substantially, through both their labor and the taxes they paid, to the growth of the American West—a fact that is still generally neglected in the history of this nation.

Even though they provided valuable services, the Chinese were stigmatized from the beginning by their skin color and their seemingly alien culture. Because of economic recessions in the 1870s and 1890s, moreover, they were widely perceived as depriving bona fide Americans of their rightful employment.

The combination of discrimination and competition for jobs fueled race riots, lynchings, and the onslaught of anti-Chinese legislation whose residual effects have persisted into this century. (Racist attitudes and legislative measures against the Chinese also affected other Asian groups who emigrated later to the United States.) From the 1880s on, harsh laws against Chinese immigration seriously reduced the number of Chinese Americans. Other laws restricted the kinds of work the Chinese could perform and prohibited those of Chinese ancestry from becoming American citizens and from owning property, while antimiscegenation legislation in the American West specifically forbade marriage between Americans and the Chinese, who were mistakenly categorized as "persons of the Mongolian race." With the exception of the merchant class, the Chinese who came to America were also not permitted to bring their wives and womenfolk.

The economic, political, and social ostracism that Chinese Americans faced formed the backdrop against which Kingston's own family struggled to survive between the 1930s and the 1960s. Kingston's mother, a qualified doctor in China, for instance, was unable to practice medicine in America and had to find employment in one of the few occupations allowed the Chinese—that of a laundry worker.

Prohibited from living among Americans, Chinese Americans—like African Americans, American Indians, and Latinos—were either ghettoized in Chinatowns all over the United States or pushed into remote pockets on the outskirts of large communities such as Stockton, California, where Kingston grew up.

A number of films, books, and other works capture the injustice, degradation, and bigotry to which Chinese immigrants were subjected. The film *Chinese Gold* provides a historical overview of the Chinese American experience in California, while *Pickles Make Me Cry*, by Peter Chow, looks at life in one of America's Chinatowns. In a more satiric vein, Wayne Wang's film *Chan Is Missing* offers insights into Chinatown life as the movie turns the Hollywood Chinese detective genre on its head.

The effects of legislative acts to bar the Chinese from entering the United States are demonstrated in two films about Angel Island, off San Francisco. Prevented from immigrating legally to America, the Chinese at the turn of the century resorted to buying immigration papers of deceased Chinese Americans. Those who arrived in America by means of purchased identification papers were known as "paper sons." To curtail this practice, immigration officers detained the Chinese for interrogation at Angel Island for months, often years. Both *Paper Angels*, by Genny Lim, and *Carved in Silence*, by Felicia Lowe, in addition to depicting the suffering of the Chinese confined to the cramped, unhealthful conditions of Angel Island as they waited news of their fate, give ample evidence of the racial hatred directed at the Chinese.

The link between occupational sanctions and race, particularly where Chinese American labor is concerned, has been the focus of a number of studies in recent years. Alexander Saxton's *Indispensable Enemy*, published in 1971, is a classic treatise on the role that American organized labor played in its scapegoating of Chinese workers. In our own time, the persistence with which Asians are blamed for unemployment among "real" Americans is seen in Christine Choy's documentary film *Who Killed Vincent Chin?* Mistaken for a Japanese, and hence held "responsible" for joblessness among Americans in the 1980s, Vincent Chin, a Chinese American, was battered to death by disgruntled Detroit autoworkers. In two successive trials, the killers were acquitted.

Studies exploring the marginalized nature of Chinese employment include Peter Kwong's work on labor and politics in New York's Chinatown, as well as numerous articles such as Dean Lan's examination of Chinatown sweatshops and Paul Ong's "Chinese Labor in Early San Francisco."

Representations of Chinese American worklife are available on a number of films and videocassettes. For instance, *Eight-Pound Livelihood*, Yuet-Fung Ho's film on Chinese laundry workers, documents the historical, occupational, and political restrictions against the Chinese while providing insights into both the resourcefulness and toughness of Chinese immigrants in the face of prejudice. The film is a useful accompaniment to *The Woman Warrior*, whose third chapter, "Shaman," focuses on Kingston's mother, a former physician who never even had to "hang up [her] own clothes" in China but who is destined in America to "[work] her life away" in a laundry from 6:30 in the morning until midnight (122).

The tenacity of Chinese women workers is especially evident in *Sewing Woman*, a film by Lorraine Dong and Arthur Dong. Like thousands of immigrant women, one of the film's central figures, Zem Ping Dong, used her sewing skills to support her family. In garment districts in major American cities, immigrant Asian women like Zem Ping Dong even today labor long hours, often at minimum wages and under substandard conditions. These women are sustained through the tedium and hardships of their work only by the conviction that their sacrifices mean the difference between poverty and survival for their families.

The Chinese woman's ability to put aside her own needs and comforts on behalf of her family is rooted deeply in Confucianism. According to this system of belief, community needs (whether of the family or the state) take priority over individual desires, needs, or feelings. This ethic is clearly brought out in the film *Talking History*, by Loni Ding and Spenser Nakasako. Women from other Asian American ethnic groups are also depicted, but readers of *The Woman Warrior* will find the segment dealing with the Chinese woman particularly relevant, since her life story coincides chronologically with the period in which Chinese women like Kingston's mother were gradually being permitted to come to America to join the men who had preceded them. Until then, Chinese American society was mainly a so-called bachelor society—a community largely of males. The few women present were either the wives of merchants or prostitutes who had surreptitiously been brought to the United States by the *tongs*, or Chinese secret societies.

The arrival of Chinese wives and families signaled an important change in Chinese American society—families were either established or, in the case of those who had long been separated by the restrictive laws prohibiting Chinese immigration, reunited and stabilized. The children of these unions or reunions were the first Chinese to be born on American soil and could, unlike their China-born parents, make legal claims to American citizenship.

The experience of women who struggled with their husbands and children to establish themselves in a new and often hostile country before World War II has been collected in a number of publications. Oral histories of these women have been recorded by the Chinese Historical Society of Southern California in a book entitled *Linking Our Lives: Chinese American Women of Los Angeles*. A chapter in *A Place Called Chinese America*, by Diane Mei Lin Mark and Ginger Chih, also documents the significant changes and contributions Chinese women made to their community.

The willingness to place the well-being of family members above personal desires is perhaps best understood in the historical context of women's secondary position in Chinese society. *The Woman Warrior* is replete with reminders of the low status of girls and women among the Chinese. This heavily socialized attitude is internalized by Chinese women, who must justify their very existences through some form of service to the community as a whole. Thus, in turn, self-sacrifice and self-denigration are seen to justify the Chinese woman's secondary position in society. An autobiographical work that depicts some of the "old world" Chinese behavioral expectations for women is Jade Snow Wong's *Fifth Chinese Daughter*. The film *Small Happiness*, although set in contemporary China, provides evidence of the persistence with which girls are held in less esteem than boys. Inevitably, the lower value that Chinese societies place on females leads to social discrimination and such practices as female infanticide. The term "a small happiness," a phrase used by parents to describe the birth of a daughter (the birth of a son being the arrival of a "larger happiness"), perhaps says it all.

Two other films that examine the impact of a woman's inferior status on her social behavior are *Lotus* and *Paper Angels*. The former, directed by

Arthur Dong and set at the turn of the century, documents a mother's agonizing dilemma as to whether to subject her little girl to the painful practice of having her feet broken and bound. The mother herself is depicted as properly humble and subservient to authority. The only way she can free her daughter from this torturous practice, as well as from the future sub-jugation it represents, is to smuggle the girl out of the family house to a school in Canton. The act of freeing her daughter, however, entails the inevitable separation of mother and child. In *Paper Angels* one of the char-acters, Mei Lai, is a Chinese woman who has deeply internalized the dictates of Confucianism by recognizing her complete subservience first to her father, then to her husband, and, in old age, to her eldest son.

The consequences for women who do not know their places is a recurrent theme in *The Woman Warrior*: No Name Woman, for instance, is con-demned to eternal anonymity for violating the stringent Chinese codes of female chastity. Likewise, in both *Lotus* and *Paper Angels* two independent-minded young Chinese women meet less than desirable fates. In *Lotus* a young actress—who, unlike the traditional mother mentioned above, earns her own living and is accountable to no one—is, nevertheless, represented as being a part of the demimonde of shady characters. In *Paper Angels* Ku Ling, a character who rebels against the secondary status of Chinese women, is first raped by white sailors on her way to the United States and later finds that she has been sold by her own father into prostitution. The two films offer a fairly graphic dramatization of the psychological bind to which women characters in *The Woman Warrior* are subjected. There are either "good" women, who are obedient and self-abnegating, or "bad" ones, who are os-tracized from polite society. As Kingston's work shows, the choice to become a heroine, or woman warrior, is made by only a few, whose pathways are fraught with real and chimeral perils.

The polarity between traditional Chinese and American values is felt with particular keenness by American-born Chinese women. Unlike their moth-ers, such women face conflicting demands from two opposing cultures. While American-born daughters are familiar with the cultural nuances of Chinese life, their dilemmas frequently stem from having to vacillate between "Chinese-ness" and "American-ness." Their China-born mothers, in contrast, are less plagued by the complexities of being Chinese, American, *and* women. It is hardly surprising that the tensions they experience are most acute in mother-daughter relationships. *The Joy Luck Club*, by Amy Tan, another Chinese American writer, captures the essence of these tensions when the American-born daughter reflects that "my mother and I never really understood each other's meanings and I seemed to hear less than what was said, while my mother heard more" (27).

Two films in which mother-daughter dialogues closely parallel those be-tween Kingston and her mother in *The Woman Warrior* are Wayne Wang's

Dim Sum and Genny Lim's *Only Language She Knows*. In both movies, as in Kingston's work, the conflicts hinge on the differences with which China-born mothers and American-born daughters view every aspect of daily life. In *The Only Language She Knows* the filmmaker's mother is baffled by the fact that her daughter would rather struggle to make it as a playwright than use her typing skills to find a secretarial job. The mother's Chinese immigrant orientation is strictly a practical one. Questions of identity and self-expression are simply beyond her comprehension. The title of the film thus refers not only to her limited knowledge of English but obliquely to the idea that, unlike her daughter, the China-born mother is familiar only with the language of basic human survival.

Likewise, *Dim Sum* presents a situation in which the daughter's life choices are shaped predominantly by American values. She is a working woman in no particular hurry to marry or have a family. Her mother, however, deems it a serious problem that a daughter well past what would have been considered marriageable age in China appears nonchalant about her single status.

In both *Dim Sum* and *The Only Language She Knows* the characters speak to each other in a mixture of English and Cantonese. The "Cantoglish" in the two films, with its phonetic renditions of English words and Cantonese inflections and rhythms, would be helpful for readers of *The Woman Warrior* who are unfamiliar with the distinctive speech of Chinese Americans. Genny Lim, in particular, provides a devastatingly accurate rendering of the sort of "Cantoglish" that fills the dialogues in Kingston's book.

The linguistic and cultural gaps separating the Chinese in the United States from those in China are evident also in Peter Wang's *Great Wall*. In this film a Chinese American engineer and his family make a sentimental journey back to their homeland, only to discover that other than their appearance, they have little in common with their Chinese cousins.

The clear distinctions between Chinese Americans and "Chinese" Chinese are worth pointing out, because understanding the interplay of differences and similarities is pivotal to a reading of *The Woman Warrior*. The American public may be surprised by the differences, since the general perception is that Asians are fundamentally the same and that, especially, all Chinese are alike. Inherent in the view of their "all alikeness" are stereotypes that have been passed down into the public consciousness for over a century. Chinese American and Chinese women (like other Asian women) have consistently been either perceived or depicted by the American media in terms of a narrow repertoire of caricatured images and behavior. Perhaps because *The Woman Warrior*'s central motif involves the author's attempt to create an authentic self apart, yet simultaneously derived from, female prototypes from both the Chinese and the American cultures, a recognition of the ultimate destructiveness of American stereotypes about Asian women is highly instructive. *Slaying the Dragon*, a film by Asian Women United and Pacific Productions, documents the emergence and proliferation of such stereotypes—from the passive, long-suffering Madama Butterfly, to the evil vampirelike Madam Sin, to the sexually commoditized Suzy Wong. Popularized by the media and impressed onto the public consciousness, these images obliterate the realness and fullness of Chinese women. As a consequence, attempts by women themselves to develop an authentic sense of selfhood are frequently thwarted by distorted images as to what Chinese American women are "really" like.[1]

NOTE

[1]*Maxine Hong Kingston: Talking Story* was issued as this volume was going to press. The documentary, which features Kingston discussing *The Woman Warrior* and *China Men*, serves as a useful introduction to her work.

The Asian Literary Background of *The Woman Warrior*

Kathryn VanSpanckeren

The Woman Warrior may be taught as a recasting, if not a recent flowering, of a three-thousand-year-old literary tradition. The classic *Book of Songs*, traditionally attributed to Confucius, was completed around 600 BC, but the earliest parts probably extend back to the Chou Dynasty, 1122 BC. This ancient collection embraces love songs, folk songs of peasant women perhaps not unlike Kingston's No Name Aunt; it also offers the warrior song of Lady Mu, an avatar of Kingston's legendary swordswoman Fa Mu Lan. While *The Woman Warrior* is generally understood as a work that challenges and re-defines boundaries of culture, gender, and genre by transgressing them, it also appropriates and extends an Asian complex of traditions. Concepts that American students may feel familiar with, such as self, literacy, ideographic signs, and nature, take on new dimensions when seen in the Asian context. Kingston's sometimes contradictory talk-stories recall the multiple variants of Chinese narratives that grew in lush profusion from shifting oral tradition, continuous literary reworkings, and the characteristically Chinese density of allusion and symbolism (Ch'en 79–81).

Kingston's blend of autobiographical narrative and fiction is illuminated, for example, by classical Chinese attitudes toward genre. Classical Chinese literary tradition, unlike the Western tradition stemming from Aristotle, excludes fiction and drama. Fictional genres were thought to be too unim-portant to be included in traditional Chinese bibliography, whose classifi-cations consisted of *ching* (classics), *shih* (history), *tzu* (philosophy), and *chi* (collections of belles lettres) (Birch xiv). Kingston's presentation of her work as nonfictional "memoirs" situates it within the classical Chinese canon. Knowledge of this tradition helps explain why *The Woman Warrior* lacks the subjective self-probings one expects in Western autobiography, focusing instead on external events. Such literal-mindedness is an age-old aspect of Chinese historical writing, which is typically concise, avoiding contextual details and speculation regarding causation (Ch'en 47). By calling the book a memoir, Kingston privileges it within the historically oriented Chinese tradition, even as she risks marginalizing it in the Western canon, which generally elevates imaginative fiction over autobiography.

Just as genre and fictionality are issues to consider when relating *The Woman Warrior* to its Chinese literary antecedents, the profound distinction between the Western concept of an individual self and the Asian communal self needs to be noted. In China, self is largely a function of one's social identity (shaped by the Confucian values of duty, filial obligation, and piety). Confucianism, Taoism (China's indigenous religion), and Buddhism share the central belief that "self-cultivation involves the development of self-lessness, and therein lies the perfection of the self" (Hegel 7). The individualistic self and its desires and attachments are distortions ("ghosts") to be transcended. Kingston struggles with this ancient philosophical tradition, which includes belief in the overriding duty to family and in the inferiority of women. Robert Hegel suggests three qualities of the Chinese communal self: divisibility, simultaneity, and dream reality (14–15). Mind and spirit can separate; the spirit can travel, as in the case of Fa Mu Lan. From this follows simultaneous existence as spiritual and material being. Dream reality involves the notion that fantasies or dreams are meaningful in waking life.

A third general point concerns the extraordinary value placed on literacy in Chinese culture. The administrators who ruled China for thousands of years were selected through a difficult civil service exam requiring mastery of the literary classics. To be a writer in China was, therefore, a noble calling, worthy of a ruler and warrior. Traditionally, as *The Woman Warrior* shows, girls were not allowed in schools. For a woman to become a writer was to break the interdiction against education for women; it was to the unloosened ("cut") tongue what releasing the foot was to foot-binding. Still, the image of warrior woman and poet is ancient in China; the poem by Lady Mu in *The Book of Songs* voices her brave, warlike patriotism. It begins:

> I ride, I gallop
> Bearing words of comfort for the Lord of Wei,
> spurring my horse on and on to the City of Cao . . .
> You may oppose me
> But I cannot go back. My plan is less farfetched
> Than your worthless scheme.   (*Selections* 27–28)

Lady Mu's bold poem is the clearest articulation of self in the mostly anonymous collection (Lu Guanying 109–10). The concluding chapter in *The Woman Warrior*, "A Song for a Barbarian Reed Pipe," about Ts'ai Yen, is distinctly heroic as told by Kingston. It is important for students to know (though Kingston does not mention it) that Ts'ai Yen was the first great woman poet of China (Rexroth and Chung 134).

The conciseness of Chinese ideographs also affects Kingston's style. In Chinese tradition, evocative landscape painting is an extension of calligraphy; Kingston transforms ideographs into vivid landscapes evoking inspiration, nobility, passion, and enlightenment. In the journey to the mystical mountain in the "White Tigers" chapter, the call comes from a bird that "looks like the ideograph for 'human,' two black wings. The bird would cross the sun and lift into the mountains (which look like the ideograph 'mountain'), there parting the mist. . . . [T]he clouds would gray the world like an ink wash" (24–25).

The correspondence of reality and ideography, sign and thing, is central to the Taoist belief in nature as pattern and ultimate reality. In the magical mountain realm, Fa Mu Lan learns the harmony of nature and the oneness of inner and outer. Kingston refers to the story as braided, but the braids of the story are to be understood as natural and, as it were, Taoist. The description of the hut's floor illustrates this harmony. It looks as if "someone had carefully arranged the yellow, green, and brown pine needles according to age" (26), but the pattern is formed when the old women "opened the roof; an autumn wind would come up, and the needles fell in braids. . . . [She] waved her arms in conducting motions; she blew softly with her mouth" (27–28).

Each chapter displays the Asian inheritance at work. The first chapter, "No Name Woman," foregrounds the low status of women in China. Numerous contemporary works, such as the film on Chinese women *Small Happiness*, from Carma Hinton's series *One Village in China*, and Alice P. Lin's autobiography, *Grandmother Had No Name*, iterate this theme, as do early twentieth-century, prerevolutionary classics reflecting the international women's movement. In Ba Jin's novel *The Family*, for instance, the parallels between the No Name Aunt and the maidservant's suicide by drowning underscore the traditional powerlessness of Chinese women.

The concept of the divisible spirit self underlies a subplot that begins with "No Name Woman" and thickens near the end of the second chapter, "White Tigers," when a medium tells the narrator that a girl who died in a far country follows her wherever she goes. "This spirit can help me if I acknowledge her," the narrator is told (61). The book is on one level about the way the narrator finds the power to acknowledge the No Name Aunt by reconstructing a composite female self from the lives of other women, chapter by chapter, the end finally expressing Kingston's new identity and simultaneously redeeming her aunt.

In "White Tigers" the narrator's "divisible" Chinese self, or imaginative spirit, lives Fa Mu Lan's vivid adventures. For women in legend there were only two alternatives: to be "wives or slaves" or "heroines, swordswomen" (23). The No Name Aunt had been a wife and a slave; to avenge her, a swordswoman is needed. In Chinese opera, which is mentioned throughout Kingston's book, the pure, beautiful, invincible swordswoman is a favorite heroine, inhabiting a world of artistic language, song, dance, acrobatics, costume, and mystical, mountainous painted landscape. The traditional Chinese symbols crowding the dreamlike adventure narrative function simultaneously as heroic and ironic signs. The knowledgeable Asian reader smiles at the cartoonlike symbolic overkill; the naive Western reader is impressed with the exotic symbolism. The cranes that lead the swordswoman symbolize longevity (D. Scott 36); the white of the tigers is the color associated with death and funerals; tigers symbolize yin (D. Scott 22) and eat evil spirits who could harm the dead such as the No Name Aunt; tigers are traditionally depicted on tombs and tombstones in China (Latsch 28). The white tigers protect the No Name Aunt within the landscape of the book. The first chapter is a marked grave: entrance to it, via understanding, is effected only by passing by the white tigers as one reads the book.

The "White Tigers" chapter draws heavily on themes from popular culture and folklore (Mitchell), especially for Fa Mu Lan's mystical Taoist training (Ling, "Thematic Threads" 158) and swordswomanship (Tom). The fluid nature of Chinese folklore, with its many ancient written versions and political interpretations that changed over time, recalls Kingston's talk-stories and legends, similarly retold to reinterpret the past and build a stronger future identity. For example, in "The White Snake," a well-known folktale, a swordswoman rescues the virtuous White Lady from an evil monk; earlier versions had portrayed the White Lady (like the No Name Aunt) as evil (*Women in Chinese Folklore* 5). "The White Snake" contains the theme of the swordswoman saving another, symbolically submerged, woman from the evil of powerful men.

There are several points to stress in this context. (1) The numerous versions of talk-story in *The Woman Warrior* partly derive from the many versions of the oral histories and legends. (2) The existence of many versions, some diametrically opposed, allowed Kingston aesthetic and psychological freedom. Like the ancient Greek playwrights or storytellers from oral societies generally, she was empowered by the existence of a rich and varied legendary past. (3) Because she could rely on knowledge in at least some of her readers, her choice of versions and her presentation of them were meaningful. A Chinese or Chinese American audience brings a distinct understanding to the book and interprets it differently from Anglo audiences. One East Asian reader familiar with the Buddhist tradition has noted, for example, that the No Name Aunt is comparable to the ultimate reality of the Tao (All, Way), which is called the Nameless throughout the *Tao Te Ching* (Shishedo 56).

A sensitive Asian reader familiar with Buddhism would certainly grasp the significance of the rabbit in "White Tigers." In a famous anecdote, the Buddha is hungry in the wilderness. All the forest animals bring him food offerings except for the selfless rabbit, who leaps into a fire to sacrifice himself. From this the Buddha teaches that he who forgets himself shall reach enlightenment (Latsch 72–73). In *The Woman Warrior* a rabbit similarly leaps into the fire to provide food for Fa Mu Lan. The episode shows that she has reached the state of Buddha-hood, or enlightenment, after her many years of spiritual training. Immediately after she eats the rabbit, she sees an epiphany in which the cosmos reveals itself as two golden people "dancing the earth's dances." This image of yin and yang united as female and male dancers is pan-Asian: "high Javanese bells" merge with "Indian bells, Hindu Indian, American Indian" (32). The unity of seeming dualism is the essence of the vision that sustains Fa Mu Lan. It informs Kingston's novel, as well, which delineates differences of gender, genre, and culture but ultimately transcends them through aesthetic design (Kingston's image of the braid is a spatial analogue of this cosmic dance). Only after this vision is Fa Mu Lan ready for her final "dragon" lessons, in which she learns to make enlightenment a permanent quality of mind: "I learned to make my mind large . . . so that there is room for paradoxes" (35). Enlightenment involves widening the field to accommodate contradictory cultural and gender codes. Enacting the dragon of the Tao, Fa Mu Lan rights the imbalance of all the oppressed. Singing between battles, she leads her army straight to the capital city, led by "Kuan Kung, the god of war and literature" (46). In a sense, each chapter is one of her songs.

The third chapter, "Shaman," stresses the mother's heroism, scholarship (in the long, detailed description of the mother's diploma), and power as a role model. The scholarly mother bests "hairy beasts whether flesh or ghost because she could eat them" (108). "Big eaters win," the narrator explains, citing famous ancient ghost-eating scholars (105). The mother learned modern medicine in the ancient Chinese way, by rote-chanting memorization, and her memory is the source of much of *The Woman Warrior*. Yet this fearless woman, one of only 37 graduates out of an entering class of 112, feels inadequate because she can not remember as well as her husband, who, trained in classical literature, could recite whole poems. Memory itself was a male preserve that Kingston's warrior woman appropriates, with words from the past—names and injustices—carved on her back. The warrior woman may be seen as the immortal spirit of literature—upright, carved like a stele with words, inarguable, historic, and victorious. History is a war in which truth, the past, must always be re-created, lest it vanish into evil, shape-shifting, ghostlike fragments. Only a big eater, like the mother and the narrator, can survive in this war. To do so they must be able "to eat bitter" (a Chinese phrase meaning to be disciplined and able to withstand hardship). The scholar-midwife mother can face the "were-people, the apes" that dropped out of trees, rose "out of bridge water," or came "out of cervixes" (98). Kingston's persona must gain strength from this shaman of a mother without being harmed by her—as Moon Orchid, her aunt, is harmed.

"At the Western Palace," the fourth chapter, dramatizes the dangers the daughter faced. A cautionary sequel to "Shaman," it suggests the mental illness that might have awaited the narrator had she been weak-minded, like Moon Orchid. Culture shock and inability to assimilate were typically manifested in the emotional disturbance so prevalent among Kingston's Chinese immigrant women. The chapter poetically recalls the myth "Goddess Chang Ascends to the Moon," told during the Mid-Autumn Harvest Festival, during which moon cakes are traditionally made (Kingston uses the round moon cakes to evoke the Chinese worldview in "No Name Woman" (15). The legend of the moon goddess has inspired Chinese women writers for thousands of years (Rexroth and Chung 123); it weaves together the idea of renewal (the elixir of eternal life), the yin symbol of the moon, and the theme of a woman's eternal separation from her husband. The legend tells how Chang E lost her husband, Hou Yi, a great archer who used magical bow and arrows to save the scorched earth from drought by shooting down nine extra suns. According to one version, the Queen Mother of the West, embodying yin (D. Scott 28), rewarded him with the pill of immortality, but Chang E ignorantly swallowed the pill and instantly became able to fly. She fled to the moon, where she still lives. Her husband lives in a palace on the sun, from which he shoots arrows at her. They are said to symbolize the two cosmic forces of moon and sun, yin and yang (Latsch 74–75). The moon (foundation of calendrical time, agriculture, and human culture) was honored on the day of the festival itself with a moonrise ceremony conducted entirely by women (Latsch 75–77). The festival tied rebirth (the lunar cycle) to the separated woman, who, like the carefully named Moon Orchid, merely lives a life of reflected light, dependent on her absent husband. Kingston's work intertextually links Moon Orchid with the pregnant No Name Aunt, whose fertility causes a chaotic lantern-lit attack that parodies the traditional lantern-lit Mid-Autumn Harvest Festival.

The five chapters of Kingston's book parallel the five different fruit offerings of the Mid-Autumn Festival: each chapter embodies a different woman in the Hong family, each, as it were, brought forward to make the offering of her life story and thus to exemplify phases of yin, the female principle of the moon. The author's chapter comes last, not only because she has needed the "ancestral help" (10) of her older female relatives in order to construct her identity, but also because in the ritual offerings to the moon around which *The Woman Warrior* seems loosely structured, the rebirth of the female identity is a culmination. The submerged ceremonial narrative structure underscores the work's profound femininity, for the book itself is an offering (like a moon cake) to woman.

Though Kingston's narrative inexorably moves from Asia to the West, it inscribes the cycle of death and rebirth within acculturation. The stages of the cycle are suggested in the naming of the chapters after phases in a cosmic drama. "No Name Woman" dies unrecognized, therefore wronged and unavenged. "White Tigers" recounts the stage of preparation and spiritual training. "Shaman" depicts a ghost-fighting woman at the peak of her powers. "At the Western Palace" suggests pilgrimage to the realm of yin (feminine) spirits. "A Song for a Barbarian Reed Flute" begins a new ritual and seasonal cycle with images of rebirth and song, for Ts'ai Yen is ransomed from the barbarians. Through her gift of poetry, she creates cross-cultural songs that speak for all women and move individuals from many different cultures. Because the book ends with the figure of Ts'ai Yen, the ceremonial cycle of the feminine is completed and a new phase is begun. This is one meaning of the narrator's statement that her mother began the story that she, the narrator, is completing. The same idea is expressed in the second chapter, when, after avenging her family and liberating the oppressed with her army, which wears the red of the New Year celebration (44), Fa Mu Lan initiates the new order with a calendrical reference by announcing, "This is a New Year . . . the year one" (53). While Fa Mu Lan overthrows the corrupt emperor as the popularly acclaimed leader of a peasant uprising (43), Kingston's book overthrows patriarchy, installing a discourse that merges women's lives into an enlightened, inclusive text, residing in the timeless moment of the cosmic dance.

Kingston's works as a whole do justice to male and female principles. The three major festivals of the year were also used for the literal settling of accounts. These were the Spring, or Brightness, Festival (associated with the legend of the victimized White Lady), the Dragon Boat Festival of Mid-Summer (evoked in *China Men* and associated with Ch'u Yuan), and the Mid-Autumn Harvest Festival, sacred to the Moon Goddess Chang E. The ceremonial substructure of *The Woman Warrior* parallels the theme of settling accounts, in order to begin anew. Ch'u Yuan (340–278 BC), China's Homer, is the subject of the last legend in *China Men*; syntagmatically he is equivalent to Ts'ai Yen. Together they are the cosmic male and female dancers, the first man and woman of poetry, both Han patriots, victims and—through their immortal writings—avengers, progenitors of rebirth.

Still, *The Woman Warrior* shares a profound affinity with the earliest autobiographical literature by Asian women, including *The Tale of Genji*, possibly the greatest Japanese novel. This classic of world literature is indebted to the diary keeping of aristocratic ladies of the Heian era (AD 795–1185), including Murasaki Shikibu (978?–1031?), to whom the novel is attributed. The diary form exercised a powerful appeal to Asian women, like Lady Murasaki, who were confined to private lives. Literacy and writing provided a precious link with the outside world and a means of articulating private experience. Diaries, like letters, allow Asian and Western women to express "unladylike" emotions such as aggression and to locate an authentic voice lacking in many women's public narratives, as Carolyn Heilbrun has shown in her excellent *Writing a Woman's Life* (24–25).

One mark of a work's distinction is its thematic density: *The Woman Warrior* not only dramatizes the finding of a woman's voice, it touches on virtually every important issue in recent Asian or Asian American women's writing. Desire for education and freedom conflicts with abiding loyalty to family in the letters of Raden Adjeng Kartini (1879–1904) of Indonesia. Kartini's account of the first wife's hidden anguish when her husband takes new wives (114) provides a context for Moon Orchid's mental illness. The struggle for identity against a dominant mother, the power of tradition, and "ghosts" appear in Eileen Chang's *Golden Cangue*, while the Moon Lady, multiple realities, and magic dominate Amy Tan's *Joy Luck Club*. *The Woman Warrior* is an archetypal expression of the Asian response to the contemporary United States as well. Mystical, pure mountains and a remote, all-powerful father are associated with an Asian childhood and an Asian source of strength, while loss, separation, culture shock, mental illness, and suicide in America characterize (Burmese American) Wendy Law-Yone's harrowing autobiographical *Coffin Tree* and *The Woman Warrior* alike. Kingston's work is the best known of a significant and growing body of writing by emerging Asian and Asian American women authors. To read Kingston deeply is to acknowledge this new voice in the context of Asian and Western traditions.[1]

NOTE

[1] I thank Mary Ellen Giunta and the University of Tampa Honors Program for research assistance.

The Woman Warrior as an Intervention in Asian American Historiography

Robert G. Lee

When *The Woman Warrior* was first published, it was much praised in the mainstream press as a representative and authoritative artifact—that is, as an ethnography. In contrast, a number of Asian American critics, most prominent among them the playwright and essayist Frank Chin, have taken *The Woman Warrior* to task on the grounds that it is insufficiently rooted in the historical experience of the Chinese in America; that it distorts the traditional myths and legends on which it relies; and that, as a result, it exoticizes the Chinese aspect of the Chinese American experience, thereby catering to the Orientalist prejudices of its white audience. Chin has written that *The Woman Warrior* is a "fake" book, an autobiography of Christian conversion that serves the totalitarian art of a racist state (110, 121–23). Indeed, it is safe to say that the argument over *The Woman Warrior* is the most heated debate in Asian American studies circles. At the heart of the matter is a struggle over Asian American history: To whom does our experience belong? Who gets to speak for us? What gets to be said?

Frank Chin was among the editors of *Aiiieeeee! An Anthology of Asian American Writers*, which in the early 1970s was instrumental in the recuperation of an Asian American literary tradition. Chin and his colleagues have had as their project the restoration of an "authentic" Chinese American identity through a confrontation with America's emasculating, racist stereotypes and the restoration of the voice of a heroic tradition of Chinese immigrants in America. Kingston's *Woman Warrior*, with its claim to autobiographical and thus historical status, at once demanded that new terrains of Chinese American history be explored and subverted the conventions of authenticity by which that history was to be framed. The battle for subjectivity, how Asian American history is to be reconstructed and by whom, was thus joined.

The point of departure shared by Chin and Kingston is the silence of Chinese American history. This silence has been imposed by an Orientalist ideology that has constructed Asians in American culture, men and women alike, as alien, ahistorical, and without voice. All relationships between Asia and the West, Edward Said has argued, are based on the unequal power between them, and those inequalities are reproduced in the realm of culture by the West's presentation of self as itself and representation of Asia as the Oriental other. This construction of the Asian as Oriental takes the form of a sexual domination in which the Orient is portrayed as a feminine and silent object of conquest, simultaneously devalued and denied subjectivity. Key to the Orientalist's appropriation and control of discourse (and language itself) is a denial to the Asian of sanity, rationality, and maturity, all defined as male attributes. Portraying the Orient as not merely gendered female but as infused with female sexuality is a patriarchal strategy for reestablishing the difference between the West, now defined as rational, intellectual, and historical, and the East, now defined as irrational, sensual, and mute. Silence and passivity are crucial to the Orientalist domination because the Orientalized female allows Orientalists to think what they please; she does not battle for subjectivity.

This imperialist hegemony extends to the cultural construction of the Orientalized male. In order to continue this domination over Asia, the Orientalist must maintain objectivity over and distance from the sexuality and physicality that the feminized Orient represents. While the Orientalized female is represented as sexual pleasure incarnate, the Orientalized male is condemned to a perpetual infantile search for sensual pleasure. Represented as unable to ascend to the objectivity and distance needed for "mature" control over art, language, science, and history, the Oriental male is also denied subjectivity and voice.

The silence imposed on Asian Americans by Orientalism is not confined to the age of high imperialism. American social scientists since the turn of the century have subsumed Chinese American subjectivity to the discourse of the Social Problem. On the rare occasions that they have appeared in American history or social science, the Chinese in America have been represented as being without historical agency. From the turn of the century to the late 1920s, American social scientists presented the Chinese as either servile coolies or innocent pawns in the struggle between white labor and white capital. Beginning in the late 1920s, in the debates over assimilation and acculturation, sociologists represented the Chinese in America as sojourning social isolates. Since the crisis over racial civil rights and affirmative desegregation that emerged in the mid-1960s, Chinese Americans have been portrayed as the "model minority" for taking advantage of opportunities without demanding "special considerations." Represented in American culture by social scientists, the Chinese Americans have been simply the passive object of other, "larger" American social forces. The language of ethnicity and assimilation thus becomes, in practice, a refinement of the Orientalist tradition, adding yet another blanket of silence over the Asian American voice.

In an effort to confront and correct the stereotypes that are products of the Orientalist hegemony, Frank Chin has attempted to recover an authentic Asian American tradition that can restore a sense of lost manhood. Chin asserts an Asian American voice in the individual author's claim to subjectivity. In an imagined conversation with Guan Goong, the patron deity of the overseas Chinese, Chin attempts to define an authentic "Chinaman's" sensibility free of white Christian ideology. Tired of being objectified under the white people's "I," Chin appropriates the deity's voice and writes:

> I speak in the Chinaman "I" and write a Chinaman act. . . . Mine is
> the Chinaman "I." Whatever language a Chinaman speaks, it is always
> Chinaman and the first person pronoun "I," in any language, means
> "I am the law." (110)

Chin stakes his claim to subjectivity through the act of controlling a written
language in order to manipulate the forms that authenticate the experience
he defines as "Chinaman's" history. For Chin, access to language is critical
to reassertion not only of a Chinese American sensibility but also of manhood.
The two projects become one as he writes:

> Language is the medium of culture and the people's sensibility, in-
> cluding the style of manhood. Language coheres the people into a
> community by organizing and codifying the symbols of the people's
> common experience. . . . Without a language of his own, he is not a
> man. (Chan, Chin, Inada, and Wong xvii)

Chin's quest for an ethnic authenticity with which to fight racism is thus
itself deeply bound in the Orientalist construction of gender and leads to a
reassertion of patriarchy. The Orientalist's value system is nowhere challenged by the editors of *Aiiieeeee!* when they write:

> The white stereotype of the acceptable Asian is utterly without man-
> hood. Good or bad, the stereotypical Asian is nothing as a man. At
> worst, the Asian American is contemptible because he is womanly
> effeminate, devoid of all the traditionally masculine qualities of orig-
> inality, daring, physical courage and creativity. (xxxi)

Chin's valorization of a proto-Confucian "authentic Chinaman" as a reassertion of manhood is at once heroic and authoritarian. Chin dismisses all
Chinese American autobiography as a genre of Christian confession "celebrating the process of conversion from an object of contempt to an object
of acceptance" (122). The basis on which subjectivity, voice, and manhood
can be established is on the "real" and "universal" heroic tradition of Chinese
culture. Chin locates this timeless culture in popular folktales and classical
Chinese literature. In this reconstruction of an epic tradition, however,
contradiction, dislocation, and discontinuity are covered over. Experience
is sealed off and the stability and centrality of the authorial "I" is maintained
by reducing history to an ever-smaller idealized essence. Thus while Chin
rebels against the position assigned to him by Orientalist and assimilationist
discourses, he is ultimately unable to challenge the contradictions of the
problem itself.

The attempt to reconstruct "authenticity" and authority in the mirror image of Orientalism leads us into an ambush that the text, read strategically, might help us subvert. Orientalism is a practice not only of cultural production but of cultural consumption as well. It is a reading sufficiently strong to draw even the most oppositional texts into its discourse. The damage wrought by racist stereotyping and the urgent need to rediscover lost texts and buried history notwithstanding, we should not let ourselves be pushed into a blind empiricism in which the distance between Asian American literature and Asian American history is foreshortened by a demand for literal correspondence. This position is ultimately a reductionist one that leads us to an ethnographic reading of literature in which we follow the paths set by colonial administrators and anthropologists and end up simply extracting data on subject peoples. The reduction of literature to its data not only strips the text of its subjectivity but prevents us from seeing its complexity as a locus of social contradictions. As a result, we may fail to recognize that history itself is a terrain on which struggles for meaning are continuous. The oppositional, or subversive, value of a text can be realized only by a strategic reading—that is, one that both situates the text within the social contradictions of its production and locates within the text the social contradictions of its own project (Volosinov 18). Only if we take into account the artistic complexity of the text can we appropriate literature as a weapon in the struggle for a historical voice.

The Woman Warrior begins with a historiographical problem in the secret history of the No Name Aunt. Kingston's mother is driven to bring her daughter into the realm of history by the necessity not only to warn her that "what happened to her could happen to you" but also to test "our strength to establish realities." The task of the second generation of Chinese in America is to write their own history:

> Those in the emigrant generations who could not reassert brute survival died young and far from home. Those of us in the first American generations have had to figure out how the invisible world the emigrants built around our childhoods fits in solid America.   (5–6)

It is precisely the discontinuities, dislocations, and erasures in the history of Chinese women in the United States that *The Woman Warrior* interrogates, thereby challenging both the silence imposed by Orientalism and the authoritarianism of a reasserted patriarchy that threatens to seal Chinese American women's experiences off in its masculinized revision of history. This interrogation, an intervention in Chinese American history, must break the silence imposed on Chinese women not only by racism but by the material conditions of their existence both in Chinese and in American society. This intervention requires a strategy that emphasizes uncertainty and multivocality in the reconstruction of a historical experience from the terrains of history, memory, and myth.

The silence that *The Woman Warrior* confronts is a product not only of Orientalism but of the historical evolution of patriarchal capitalism in Chinese society. From the twelfth century onward, China developed a two-tier political economy in which the tension between the traditional tributary economy of the Confucian state and the emergence of a new petty capitalist mode of production based on the extended family was contained by neo-Confucian ideology. The anthropologist Hill Gates has argued persuasively that this ideology successfully preserved the two-tier system well into the nineteenth century by recapitulating patriarchal family relations at all levels of the Chinese polity. It thus served the purposes of both the tributary central state and the patriarchal households that were at the forefront of an expanding market economy. It was a political economy in which women were increasingly treated like commodities not only in the expanding labor markets but within the kinship system as well. Capital, in the form of property, labor, and women themselves as objects of exchange, was transferred from women to their male relatives. As the conflict between competing demands of the traditional tributary economy and the petty capitalist economy grew, women were admonished both by state ideology and obliged by the demands of their families to consume only what was necessary for subsistence and reproduction and to occupy as little social space as possible (Gates 799).

The penetration of European and American capitalism in nineteenth-century south China exacerbated the pattern of exploitation and erasure. The opium trade and the introduction of cheap manufactures, war taxes, and reparations brought about severe inflation and economic dislocation (see R. G. Lee). For poor families, who bore the heaviest burden of taxation, usury, and crushing land rents, surplus value extracted from the labor of women and their sons was often the margin for survival, while the presence of more women than required for labor and reproduction threatened the survival of such families. Many families facing ruin turned to female infanticide and the sale of young women into indenture or slavery (see Jashok). These economic conditions also gave rise to banditry, ethnic and class violence, rebellion, and widespread emigration out of south China.

Chinese women in the United States became pawns in the struggle between the white labor movement and capitalists over the issue of Chinese immigration. As Lucie Cheng has observed, the scarcity of women in California before the 1870s made the importation of Chinese women as willing or unwilling prostitutes a highly profitable enterprise (Cheng and Bonacich). In 1870, the California legislature, after hearings on the "problem of Chinese prostitution," passed the Act to Prevent the Kidnapping and Importation of Mongolian, Chinese, and Japanese Females for Criminal and Demoralizing Purposes. The first law to restrict immigration on the basis of race (and gender), the act preceded the federal prohibition against the immigration of Chinese workers (both male and female) by twelve years. Over fifty laws and ordinances aimed at Chinese and other Asian immigrants sharply limited the number of Chinese women in America until the 1960s. At the turn of the century there were only 8,217 Chinese women in the United States, compared with a population of 89,863 Chinese men (Cheng 420). In 1940, only 12 percent of Chinese males in the United States had wives in this country. On the other side of the Pacific, these restrictions resulted in the development of emigrant communities, in which a high proportion of male family members of working age were absent for extended periods of time (see Chen Ta). Increasingly dependent on remittances from abroad, these emigrant communities in south China, like their "bachelor" counterparts in America, were demographically distorted and highly vulnerable to stress. In a hostile racial environment the fear of violence, kidnapping and enslavement, or deportation dictated a culture of secrecy on the part of Chinese immigrant communities in California, reinforcing traditional Confucian attitudes that favored patriarchy and kept women silent.

Kingston at first resents the burden of history that immigrant parents stuff into the heads of their children like "the suitcases which they jam-pack with homemade underwear" (102) but nevertheless recognizes its necessity to her own search for subjectivity. Frustrated by the secrecy and suppleness of the immigrant culture, she realizes that recovering a Chinese tradition untransformed by the American experience is an impossible task. It is, in fact, camouflage, subterfuge, and surprise that enable the immigrant traditions to survive and imbue them with power for resistance. In the end, Kingston writes ironically, "I don't see how they kept up a continuous culture for five thousand years. Maybe they didn't; maybe everyone makes it up as they go along" (216).

In order to establish realities to ground her own story, Kingston must question the silences about Chinese women in both Chinese and in American histories. *The Woman Warrior* thus takes the form of a collective autobiography, with Kingston at once the listener and the reporter of the stories of her female relatives, actual and legendary. Kingston's authorial "I" is necessarily decentered and unstable. Instead of establishing authority over a history in which she is not the visible subject, the narrator holds open a space for heretofore unheard voices. Kingston's narrator simultaneously interrogates, resists, and appropriates the stories of her real and mythical kinfolk. The decentered "I" of *The Woman Warrior* is a child who asks, "What is Chinese tradition and what is the movies?" (6). This question reminds us that a naive narrator is fundamentally a radical, whose real or professed ignorance forces a confrontation with established authority and requires us to revise our understanding not only of the historical event but of the way it is framed (Bakhtin 403). In opening itself to many voices and by subverting its own claim to authority, the autobiography relinquishes its power to paper over the contradictions of Chinese American history and instead enters into an open-ended, interrogative, or dialogic relationship to them.

Kingston begins by breaking the historical silence imposed on her father's sister. The story of her aunt's suicide and subsequent erasure from her family's public history is part of the secret history that "[y]ou must not tell anyone" (1) but must be passed on by mother to daughter as a cautionary tale. Secret histories and unofficial histories played an important role in traditional Chinese historiography because, unlike the official dynastic histories, they revealed the actual intrigues of the court and provided the moral and political lessons for the next rulers. The Hong family's secret history is such "a story to grow up on" (5). It is told in bare bones, with no questions entertained: "My mother has told me once and for all the useful parts. She will add nothing unless powered by Necessity, a riverbank that guides her life" (6).

The story of No Name Aunt also confronts a fundamental problem of Chinese American history. Is Chinese life in America, as the mother's attitude insists, driven by necessity, or are there opportunities for resistance in the practice of everyday life? Is No Name Aunt simply a passive victim of rape and revenge, or is an alternative reading of the story possible? Kingston reverses the cautionary purpose of the tale to explore the possibilities of resistance. In the mid-nineteenth century, tens of thousands of women from all over south China joined the Taiping rebellion, with its militarized gender egalitarianism; in the later part of the century, thousands of women in the Canton delta resisted marriage by delaying for years taking up residence in their husbands' households, by buying substitutes for marriage, or by joining sworn spinsterhoods and convents (Ono; Stockard). Perhaps her aunt resisted her marriage in this smaller, personal way.

"Adultery is extravagance," Kingston writes (7), but it is an exceedingly dangerous one in an emigrant community, with its fragile demographic and moral balances, where there is no distance between public and private realms. Kingston observes, "Poverty hurt, and that was their first reason for leaving. But another, final reason for leaving the crowded house was the never-said" (12). The failure of everyday resistance carries a heavy cost for the poor and the weak. The neighbors are peasants who recognize resistance and its limits. Coldly calculating the price of upsetting the fragile human ecology, the "villagers were speeding up the circling of events because she was too shortsighted to see that her infidelity had already harmed the village, that waves of consequences would return unpredictably, sometimes in disguise, as now, to hurt her." The neighbors were people "who refused fatalism because they could invent small resources [and] insisted on culpability" (15).

Like her No Name Aunt, the legendary Fa Mu Lan is called on by Kingston for ancestral help. "My American life has been such a disappointment," the narrator says, because everyday success at assimilation seems not to be enough to please her parents. When Kingston reports straight A's on a report card, her mother, knowing that to "reassert brute survival" in America will take more than good grades in school, replies, "Let me tell you a true story about a girl who saved her village" (5–6, 54).

Fa Mu Lan is a legendary relative; her given name, Mu Lan, may be translated as Magnolia, or more literally Wood Orchid. With Kingston's mother, Brave Orchid, and her aunt, Moon Orchid, she shares the generational name of the women of the narrator's family. However, before Fa Mu Lan can be a source of ancestral help, Kingston must radically revise her story. The written version of the original folk poem celebrates the filial daughter who marches off to war in her father's stead (Liu and Lo 77). In her own woman warrior legend, Kingston's swordswoman borrows elements from a number of popular heroic characters including Li Nojia, the boy warrior armed with Taoist magical bangles, and Ts'ai Yen (Cai Yan in pinyin), whose story of exile ends in her return to a desolated home village.

Kingston's woman warrior is not in service to the emperor for her father's sake. Her mission is her own. She takes revenge against an evil baron for having drafted her brother into his army and for having stolen her childhood. In the final confrontation with the baron, Kingston's swordswoman loses her Taoist amulets but instead is armed with stories of the injustices done to her family carved on her back. She achieves victory over the baron only in that moment in which he is startled to discover that she is both a woman and the bearer of history:

> "You've done this," I said, and ripped off my shirt to show him my back. "You are responsible for this." When I saw his startled eyes at my breasts, I slashed him across the face and on the second stroke cut off his head. (52)

For Kingston, myths, necessarily rebuilt, have a strategic value in helping to analyze contemporary events. She recognizes that the power of myth resides in its capacity to be recontextualized and inscribed with new meanings:

> From the fairy tales, I've learned exactly who the enemy are. I easily recognize them—business-suited in their modern American executive guise, each boss two feet taller than I am and impossible to meet eye to eye. (57)

The power of myth is limited, however, to helping in the sorting out of realities; it cannot substitute for practice. Even reshaped into American "gun and knife fantasies," myth is powerless when "urban renewal tore down my parents' laundry and paved over our slum for a parking lot" or when her bosses ignore her "bad, small-person's voice" or simply fire her when she objects to their most overt racism (57–58).

The legend of Fa Mu Lan, even revised, provides little support for the voice Kingston needs in her battle against racism. Because its original text is so rooted in Confucian patriarchy, in order to draw strength from it at all, Kingston must first "get out of hating range" (62) of her family before she can rework the story into her own weapon. The secret weapon of Kingston's swordswoman is not Taoist magic but personal history. Unable to dismantle the system of oppression, her revenge is confined to reporting. History itself becomes the medium of resistance; writing is an act of war and revenge:

> What we [the swordswoman and Kingston] have in common are the words at our backs. The idioms for *revenge* are "report a crime" and "report to five families." The reporting is the vengeance—not the beheading, not the gutting, but the words. And I have so many words—"chink" words and "gook" words too—that they do not fit on my skin. (62–63)

Kingston envisions her mother as a shaman whose strategy for dealing with oppressors is to turn them into ghosts. Brave Orchid derives charismatic power from her ability to tell stories, to manipulate language, legend, and history. She tells her schoolmates that ghosts are nightmares or, at the very least, "an entirely different species of creature" (77). Taking up a struggle against a ghost in medical school, where she is otherwise immersed in Western science, is an act of resistance to the hegemonic discourse of Europeanization. Her struggle with the ghost in medical school prefigures the struggle with ghosts in America.

In the United States the ghost is the commanding metaphor for white people—Japanese, Filipino, Mexican ghosts also appear but "[s]ometimes ghosts put on such mundane disguises, they aren't particularly interesting" (79). It is the White Ghost whose presence is most constantly and oppressively felt. Ghosts are reduced to their immediate function—the Mail Ghost, the Newspaper Ghosts, the Teacher Ghost, all without memory or culture. Unlike Chinese ghosts however, White Ghosts cannot be defeated by resorting to tradition or reason. "This is terrible ghost country, where a human being works her life away. . . . I didn't need muscles in China," says Brave Orchid, who can now "carry a hundred pounds of Texas rice up-and-downstairs" (122). In order to "assert brute survival" in America, you need muscles.

In America, Chinese can become ghosts too, silenced people bereft of history and culture. The story of Brave Orchid's sister, Moon Orchid, is the experience of a Gold Mountain "widow," one of the thousands of women left behind in emigrant villages in Guangdong. After three decades of separation, Moon Orchid arrives in America to claim her new life. Moon Orchid's husband, succumbing to the lure of assimilation, has adjusted to life in the United States and accommodated its racism. Indeed, he recognizes that his success as a professional depends on his ability to efface his own identity as an immigrant Chinese. Moon Orchid's arrival threatens that success. In a scene that recapitulates a thousand Angel Island interrogations, Moon Orchid's husband takes the part of the hostile immigration official (see Lai, Lim, and Yung): "He looked directly at Moon Orchid the way the savages looked, looking for lies. 'What do you want?' he asked. She shrank from his stare; it silenced her crying" (177). Moon Orchid, her voice stifled by her husband's American gaze, recognizes that the system of racial oppression is not confined within America's borders but reaches out to incorporate the emigrant communities of south China. Neither she nor her husband has been sheltered from its harm:

> Moon Orchid was so ashamed, she held her hands over her face. She wished she could also hide her dappled hands. Her husband looked like one of the ghosts passing the car windows, and she must look like a ghost from China. They had indeed entered the land of ghosts, and they had become ghosts. (178)

To understand a language, the first step in assimilation, is to become dominated by the ideology it fronts. Moon Orchid's husband understands enough English to become a successful doctor who must entertain "important American guests" (178) and who cannot afford to be embarrassed by a Toishanese-speaking wife. In his final parting with her, he recognizes the totality of the domination: "It's as if I had turned into a different person. The new life around me was so complete; it pulled me away. You became people in a book I had read a long time ago" (179).

It is the apprehension of her own history and the exclusion from a language with which to voice it that finally drives Moon Orchid to paranoia. As she explains on a return trip to Stockton:

> "I heard them talking about me. I snuck up on them and heard them."
> "But you don't understand Mexican words."
> "They were speaking English."
> "You don't understand English words."
> "This time, miraculously, I understood. I decoded their speech. I penetrated the words and understood what was happening inside."
> (181)

Without the power to control or manipulate the language, Moon Orchid can only be victimized by it. This is a position that she finds unbearable, one from which she retreats into permanent fantasy.

For Kingston, "talking and not talking made the difference between sanity and insanity. Insane people were the ones who couldn't explain themselves. There were many crazy girls and women" (216). For Brave Orchid, the mentally ill were those who had only one story left to tell and repeated it over and over. Voice is critical to asserting subjectivity, claiming history, and maintaining sanity. In American school, the principal site of acculturation and assimilation, the Chinese American girls whose voices are normally "strong and bossy" are forced to invent "an American-feminine speaking personality" to make their voices "American-feminine" (200). At American school her voice is like "a crippled animal running on broken legs. You could hear splinters in my voice, bones rubbing jagged against one another" (196). Nevertheless, she recognizes the necessity of establishing a voice. Her violence against a silent alter ego at school only results in an eighteen-month-long illness that she sees as punishment. At home, under the domination of her mother's voice, which seems still to speak in the language of patriarchy, Kingston speaks in her "pressed-duck voice," resisting perceived attempts by her mother to marry her off. It is also born of her resentment of her mother for cutting her frenum, an act she believes was meant silence her.

Only when Kingston can hear that her mother's voice speaks in a separate language from a separate historical terrain can Brave Orchid's explanation for cutting her daughter's frenum make sense: "I cut it so that you would not be tongue-tied. Your tongue would be able to move in any language" (190). Only then can a reconciliation take place. It is in the coda recalling Ts'ai Yen's exile on the Chinese frontier, a story in which the feelings conveyed through Ts'ai Yen's songs overcome the silences imposed by her exile, that the two distinct voices of mother and daughter become joined. This reconciliation makes possible the heteroglossia, the introduction of voices speaking from different terrains, that emerges to resist silences of history.

While Frank Chin may have succeeded in stripping away the liberal veneer of assimilationism to reveal its Orientalist core, it is Maxine Hong Kingston who finally stands Orientalism on its head. The reconstruction of Chinese American history premised on an "authenticity" in the form of an idealized heroic past simply recapitulates the male domination at the center of Orientalism. It reimposes silence at the heart of the inquiry. The racism that excluded Chinese women and men from immigrating to America, which created the bachelor societies of Chinatown, was a gendered construction. Race and gender are inseparably at the center of the history of Chinese America.

The interrogative voices of Kingston and her unnamed and named relatives are, in the last instance, historiographical. They insist that hegemony is never complete and that we bring the hidden stories of everyday resistance into our public history. They insist that we criticize the concept of authenticity, subverting its assumption of false consciousness with the concrete complexity of the everyday. They insist that the social—past, fixed, and articulated—be confronted by the personal—present, flexible, and felt; that history be opened up by memory. They insist not only that their stories be recorded but that their questions be asked. They insist that the critical question What does it mean to be Chinese in America? includes the question What does it mean to be a second-generation Chinese American woman growing up in Stockton, California, in the 1950s and 1960s?[1]

NOTE

[1] I wish to thank Oscar Campomanes, Anne DuCille, Todd Gernes, Matt Jacobsen, Maxine Hong Kingston, Joanne Melish, Laura Santigian, Judy Yung, and Kathleen Zane for their generous readings of various drafts of this essay. I also wish to acknowledge the anonymous reviewers of the MLA for their incisive critiques.

PEDAGOGICAL CONTEXTS

"I've Never Read Anything like It": Student Responses to *The Woman Warrior*

Vicente F. Gotera

Maxine Hong Kingston's *The Woman Warrior* is "a totally different book," one of my students told me. "I've never read anything like it." Although this comment highlights the tour de force quality of Kingston's narrative style, it also underlines the difficulties students encounter in reading *The Woman Warrior*. Another typical student remark is: "A lot of the book was written in a confusing manner [because] the author was unclear in her writing." A less negative but equally typical version of this comment is: "I had trouble determining whether a particular story line was truth or fantasy." Remarks of this sort, collected via a questionnaire on students' perceptions about their experience of reading *The Woman Warrior*, serve as the basis for this essay, and my purpose is to offer some pedagogical recommendations about how we, as teachers, might alleviate such student difficulties. Using Stanley Fish's notion of "interpretive communities that are responsible . . . for the shape of a reader's activities" (322), we can create such an integrated readers' community within the classroom by forging what Fish has called "a shared basis of agreement" (317) on how to read *The Woman Warrior*.

I conducted my survey of student responses at Indiana University's Bloomington campus, which attracts, in my opinion, among the best high school graduates in Indiana. For the purposes of my survey, this student population is significant because we may infer that these students are at least potentially well trained as readers and are fairly representative, as midwesterners, of the wider pool of American students insofar as their cultural influences and experience are Middle American, both in economic class and racial representation. I realize, of course, that I have not established these assertions as statistically valid, but my general method here is more qualitative than quantitative.

I had assigned *The Woman Warrior* in a women's studies class and an ethnic-literature class focusing particularly on Asian American writing. I polled three separate groups: two different sections of my course Women and Popular Culture—an honors class and a regular class—and one section of my course Asian American Literature. As is often the case in women's studies courses, few men had enrolled: one out of sixteen in the honors group and one out of seven in the regular group. The situation was reversed in the ethnic-literature class, which had six men and four women. It is also important to note that there were seven Asian American students out of ten in the ethnic literature class, whereas there were none in the other two groups.

Women and Popular Culture was given as an undergraduate American studies course that investigated the image of women in prose writing—especially novels—and commercial movies. Along with Kingston's *Woman Warrior*, we read F. Scott Fitzgerald's *Great Gatsby*, Sidney Sheldon's *Bloodline*, Rachel Ingalls's *Mrs. Caliban*, Alice Walker's *Color Purple*, and John Varley's *Titan*. The films were Elia Kazan's *Streetcar Named Desire*, Wayne Wang's *Dim Sum*, Adrian Lyne's *Fatal Attraction* and *Flashdance*, James Cameron's *Aliens*, and Steven Spielberg's *Color Purple*.

In the course Asian American Literature we studied Chinese American, Japanese American, and Filipino American fiction and poetry, reading such seminal works as Louis Chu's *Eat a Bowl of Tea*, John Okada's *No-No Boy*, and Carlos Bulosan's *America Is in the Heart*. The other Chinese American literature we read included short stories by Virginia Lee, Jeffery Paul Chan, and Shawn Hsu Wong; excerpts from the autobiographies of Pardee Lowe and Jade Snow Wong; and poetry by Alan Chong Lau, Wing Tek Lum, Mei-Mei Berssenbrugge, Li-Young Lee, and other poets, with particular emphasis on *Dwarf Bamboo*, Marilyn Chin's book of poems.

The Questionnaire

The survey itself was composed of a series of questions, reproduced with several lines of space between items; as a result, students usually responded in short paragraphs or even a brief sentence or two.

1. What did you find most interesting about *The Woman Warrior*? Please be specific. Why was this aspect appealing to you?

2. What did you find most difficult about *The Woman Warrior?* Again, please be specific. Why did you have this difficulty?

3. What would have helped you overcome this difficulty with *The Woman Warrior?* Before reading? After reading? During class?

4. Did you feel you needed certain information or background (historical, cultural, etc.) to understand *The Woman Warrior?* If so, what kind of information?

5. Was it helpful to have other works to compare with *The Woman Warrior?* If so, which ones, and why?

6. What did you learn from *The Woman Warrior* about women's issues? What did you learn about cultural issues? What else did you learn?

7. Do you think you would have read *The Woman Warrior* if you hadn't had to read it for a class? How would your experience with it have been different in that case?

These questions were specifically phrased to elicit responses directly addressing pedagogical concerns, particularly the design of the course and individual activities both before and after students read *The Woman Warrior.*

Student Responses

1. What did you find most interesting about The Woman Warrior? *Please be specific. Why was this aspect appealing to you?* The aspects that received the most attention in responses to this item were Kingston's narrative style and use of imagination. Out of the thirty-three respondents, seven pointed to the manner in which the story was told; one member of the honors group wrote, "The lack of chronological order . . . made me think, challenged my perspective." Similarly, seven noted Kingston's idiosyncratic creativity, using terms such as "vivid imagination," "fantasy," the "supernatural," "mythological," "legend," "folklore," "mysticism"; they especially observed the preoccupation with "ghosts."

The major subjects of *The Woman Warrior* also received attention: six students cited their introduction to Chinese culture, five noted Kingston's attention to women's issues, and four were attracted to the "stories . . . about growing up." The last two areas were viewed in combination by four students, who found the relationship between the young Kingston and Brave Orchid interesting. The chapters mentioned most were "White Tigers" and "Shaman" (two respondents apiece), while the other chapters were mentioned by one student each; clearly such a response ties in with the prevailing interest in style and imagination, since "White Tigers" and "Shaman" are, in some respects, the sections that owe the least to conventional storytelling in English. The interest in these chapters also points up the students' emphases on Chinese culture, the bildungsroman, and mother-daughter relations.

2. *What did you find most difficult about* The Woman Warrior? *Again, please be specific. Why did you have this difficulty?* The aspect that students found most interesting—Kingston's style—was also what they found most difficult. Twenty-three of the respondents found Kingston's narrative montage and pastiche devices, the juxtaposition of past and present or reality and fantasy—methods some literary critics might call postmodern or metafictive—confusing. One student complained, "The book did not have a natural flow." In fact, several expressly blamed Kingston for this problem; one even suggested that the author's difficulty may have arisen from cultural displacement: "The author didn't make it very clear what was real or imagined—this could be because of a cultural difference." Several students also felt that the perceived intractability in the narrative inhibited whatever "message" they thought Kingston might be sending: "I found it difficult to understand what Kingston was saying about women." One respondent assumed that Kingston's "childhood was very strange. She seemed like a maladjusted young girl. . . . [I]t made me a little nauseat[ed]." Perhaps the most distressing difficulty was that at least one student believed that Kingston literally was the fantasized Fa Mu Lan in "White Tigers": "I didn't enjoy reading about the 'engraving' of her back with a knife. Yuck!" Of course, this student may simply be using the pronoun "her" in a general way, not to refer to the historical narrator; however, in the final exam, this same student revealed a belief that Kingston's real back was indeed scarred with pictographs. The students' general reaction is summarized by the comment that the most difficult aspect of reading the work is to try "to figure out some cohesive meaning to the stories. . . . The novel seemed disjointed, and it didn't seem to come to a conclusion or resolution at the end."

3. *What would have helped you overcome this difficulty with* The Woman Warrior? *Before reading? After reading? During class?* Twenty-two respondents felt they would have benefited from some prereading activities. Of these, six targeted the question of distinguishing the real from the fantastic. Culture was another area that seemed to require preparation: six students would have liked some background on Chinese and Chinese American history and values; two asked specifically for information on "ghosts." Information related to Kingston was requested by six respondents: four sought background on the author herself, and two thought a preview of the characters and their relation to one another would have been helpful.

Several students—sixteen in all—felt they needed some guided activity after reading *The Woman Warrior.* Some noted what they could have done on their own to aid their understanding: one student suggested writing down, for later discussion, whatever had not seemed clear; another respondent thought that taking notes of any sort—during or after reading—was imperative; one advised that each student actively avoid any judgments based on his or her own culture; another suggested "creative playing on some of the stories" (which I interpret as role-playing); and yet another suggested "re-reading the book." Several thought that the instructor should assign some postreading activities: perhaps a study guide for the whole book or "a study sheet with questions about each chapter."

The crucial in-class activity for these students was discussion; seventeen felt that it was imperative to discuss the book, while one wanted to "be told what it meant" (i.e., a lecture). Typical remarks were "I think the legends and stories have to be analyzed. . . . This book needs a lot of discussion"; "The class discussion helped to bring out points I had missed in the book"; and "Problem [was] solved in class." Clearly the consensus is that some preview information is required—particularly on how to decode the narrative, decipher real from imaginary—and that the reader should be actively engaged with the book, through some prescribed activity such as a study guide and, more important, extensive in-class discussion.

4. *Did you feel you needed certain information or background (historical, cultural, etc.) in order to understand* The Woman Warrior? *If so, what kind of information?* Historical and cultural background was the most requested—by twenty-two respondents. The areas in which such background seemed most necessary were women's role and history in China (five students), Chinese American history (three students)—particularly the term "sojourning"—and the conception of "ghosts," both in supernatural terms and in the context of prejudice and stereotype (two students). Ten respondents, however, felt that no further background was needed, and the reason most cited was that Kingston's "identity crisis can be applied to other cultures as well" or "many of the issues pertained to people of all cultural backgrounds"—in other words, that *The Woman Warrior* is universal and potentially understandable for readers armed only with their own cultural arsenal.

5. *Was it helpful to have other works to compare with* The Woman Warrior? *If so, which ones, and why?* Of the twenty-three students in both sections of the women's studies course, sixteen felt that the movie *Dim Sum* was especially helpful in illuminating various aspects of *The Woman Warrior*, particularly because of the mother-daughter conflict found in both works. *The Color Purple* was cited by four respondents as helpful because of the focus on the "mother country"—Africa as cognate to China in *The Woman Warrior*—and because any "works which show women in degrading roles [would be useful] as a contrast." Of the ten students in the Asian American Literature class, six appreciated having comparison works: three pointed to Louis Chu's *Eat a Bowl of Tea*, because of its revelations about Chinese American life, while one respondent cited *Dwarf Bamboo*, because of Mar-

ilyn Chin's focus on women's issues. Of course, there were also dissenters; six students suggested that *The Woman Warrior* is so different, perhaps unique, that it resists comparison with other works.

6. *What did you learn from* The Woman Warrior *about women's issues? What did you learn about cultural issues? What else did you learn?* The prevalent lesson, cited by thirteen students, is that the oppression of women is neither culture-specific nor ethnocentric: "I learned that women are oppressed in many cultures and share similar problems to women in our culture," wrote one respondent; another learned that "women are victims in many societies." Several students also realized the positive corollary to this viewpoint: that "women have always been leaders . . . somewhere in the world." The dissenting opinion was held by eight respondents—that women are worse off in China than they are in the United States: "Women in Chinese culture are different from American culture—treated in some respects as slaves." One Chinese American woman noted the osmosis of this attitude into Chinese American life; the important lesson she learned was that she was "not the only one." There is, however, an antidote to machismo and oppression of women: two students observed the empowerment of females in the text through "power in talk [so that they] find themselves to be . . . like the woman warrior" and through their influence within the family: "The women are quite powerless with the husband [but] quite powerful with the children." The response I found most distressing came from a woman in the honors group who found "Chinese oppression . . . just a new viewpoint of the *same old women's issues*" (emphasis mine); this woman has clearly become jaded—at such a young age!—with feminism.

Apropos of cultural concerns, eleven respondents reported that they had learned about at least one aspect of Chinese culture, especially concerning customs, superstitions—the apparently widespread belief in "ghosts," for example—and the role of women in Chinese society. At least three students cited a vast divergence between American culture and Chinese culture, although two other students felt that Chinese and Chinese Americans were similar: "Chinese Americans still go by some of the customs from China." That the culture is ineffably important as an influence on one's thinking and potential for success in one's society was cited by four respondents as their most important cultural lesson.

The most sophisticated responses to this item concerned the merger of these two areas, specifically the practical difficulty of juggling two cultures in one's life; six students made this point. One statement cited the "difficulty of trying to balance the influences of two cultures without sacrificing one to the other." The added wrinkle of this, of course, is the inclusion of femaleness in the equation: one student admitted "how hard it is to be a minority woman. It is a double whammy." If we believe—Stanley Fish notwithstanding—

that meaning ultimately resides *within* the text, then we would probably concede that these students have received the essential, most significant message telegraphed by *The Woman Warrior.*

7. *Do you think you would have read* The Woman Warrior *if you hadn't had to read it for a class? How would your experience with it have been different in that case?* The pattern of responses to this item is startling; table 1 shows that more than three-quarters of the overall group would *not* have read *The Woman Warrior* for themselves. None of the honors students, whom we might assume to be most disposed to tackle a difficult text, responded yes. Half of the Asian American Literature students, however, said they would have read the book of their own volition; perhaps this response could have been predicted by the fact that seven of the ten students in the class were Asian American. *The Woman Warrior* is clearly an important text for these students, perhaps because they feel a close identification with the characters and situations.

Table 1. Students' Answers to Question 7

Course	Yes	No	Maybe	Abstain
Women and Popular Culture	1	6	—	—
Women and Popular Culture (Honors)	—	15	1	—
Asian American Literature	5	4	—	1
TOTALS	6	25	1	1

Okay—Now What?

The most pressing problem students have with *The Woman Warrior* is obviously to apprehend and pierce through the narrative complexities of the text. Suzanne Juhasz has argued that "*The Woman Warrior* is 'messy' insofar as its narrative patterns are several and intertwined. *Complex* is really a better word for the various kinds of narrative movements that taken together reflect the dynamics of the mother-daughter relationship" ("Kingston: Narrative Technique" 177). Clearly, then, to be baffled by the narrative is similarly to be excluded from the central character conflict in the story; at least two respondents voiced this frustration: "Since the story wasn't in chronological order and her mother was viewed in so many different lights, it was hard to figure out the author's attitude toward the mother."

In *Semiotics of Poetry*, Michael Riffaterre points out the reader's need for *competence*: first, a "linguistic competence, which . . . includes the reader's ability to identify tropes and figures" and enables the reader "to perceive ungrammaticalities"; and second, a "literary competence [which] is the reader's familiarity with the descriptive systems, with themes, with his society's mythologies, and above all with other texts" (5). That many respondents could perceive that Kingston was using both reality and fantasy indicates their linguistic competence; that they often could not distinguish one from the other within the text indicates a lack of literary competence. Whether we accept Riffaterre's premise that meaning resides finally in the text or we side with Fish's insistence that community grounds the reader's making of meaning from the text, students clearly need to be armed with specific methods or information.

A convenient way for us to do so is to confront the students with intertextual cognates before they read *The Woman Warrior*. We might, for example, use selections from Kingston's own *China Men*, in which myth and folklore are mainly segregated from biography. The shorter narratives punctuating and separating *China Men*'s longer "father" sections come twice in pairs: "On Discovery" and "On Fathers" (3–7) and "The Wild Man of the Green Swamp" and "The Adventures of Lo Bun Sun" (221–33). These excerpts can introduce students to Kingston's characteristic mode of juxtaposing folkloric, fireworksy writing and down-to-earth descriptions, while they bring up important themes: oppression of women, parent-child interaction, alienation, the hybridization of culture and artifact.

Student difficulties may spring partly from Kingston's subtitle—the word "memoirs" fueling conventional expectations about autobiography. One respondent admitted, "I think I didn't always understand what was going on because I had preconceived ideas about what was *going* to happen." One response is to acknowledge the fictional, novelizing impulses embodied in *The Woman Warrior*; such an approach would ask students to read women's fiction in which the author is experimenting with narrative to blur the boundary between real and imaginary, between mundane and surreal. Examples include Charlotte Perkins Gilman's novella *The Yellow Wallpaper*, Marge Piercy's *Woman on the Edge of Time*, and Ingalls's *Mrs. Caliban*. In each of these narratives, the protagonist—a woman beleaguered by males and masculinist society—is moved to action, to self-creation amid a welter of fantasy and reality. Although none of these authors uses myth and legend in the same way as Kingston, their narrative innovations offer the possibility of comparison with her method. Moreover, these three works highlight significant women's issues that echo important themes in *The Woman Warrior*.

The remaining aspect of *The Woman Warrior* noted most often by respondents is, of course, the Chinese and Chinese American connection. Chu's *Eat a Bowl of Tea*, the first Chinese American novel, has served me in class as an easy entry into the culture of Chinatown; fortunately a film version of this novel, directed by Wayne Wang, was released in 1989, enhancing the instructor's options in using this material. In my experience, however, the most appropriate feature film to set next to *The Woman Warrior* is Wang's *Dim Sum: A Little Bit of Heart*—the unassuming yet eloquent story of a young Chinese American woman who feels pressure to marry from her aging mother, who chooses to speak solely in Chinese. The special role of the Chinese American woman is also elegantly addressed by Marilyn Chin in *Dwarf Bamboo*; in class, Chin's technical expertise as a poet is an exciting contrast to Kingston's fictional strategies, while Chin's use of Chinese myths and history, themes of Chinese American immigration and assimilation, and themes of growing up in America gracefully complements Kingston's subject matter.

After reading *The Woman Warrior*, several respondents wanted further guidance before returning to the classroom for discussion; the most pedagogically promising of the students' suggestions is the study guide, tailored to anticipate specific difficulties. It would be counterproductive here to devise a complete set of study questions for the entire book, since the phrasing of such questions would depend on each instructor's separate agenda and emphases; instead, I will provide a brief demonstration of how such a study guide might forestall student misapprehensions. Several respondents were bewildered by Kingston's "ghosts"—are they occult apparitions? imagined ephemera? actual people? One student noted that what he found most difficult was "understanding what [Kingston] meant by ghosts. . . . I didn't know if these people were real or not." The following study questions—to be considered after reading "Shaman"—would have aided this specific student:

> "Kingston . . . mistranslates the word 'ghosts' [by using] the popular white Christian sense of the word, not Chinese-American," asserts Jeffery Paul Chan. He explains in a letter to the *New York Review of Books*, "Chinese-Americans call whites *bok gwai*, white devils, as in demons, not ghosts. Ghosts of the dead are not *gwai*, though they could be. *Gwai* are inherently unfriendly. When Chinese-Americans call a white person *bok gwai*, it is an insult. If that person is liked, the term *lo fan* is applied. A *lo fan* is a foreigner. . . . The difference between *lo fan* and *bok gwai* is as obvious to any Chinese-American as the difference between 'mister' and 'asshole.' " Do you think Chan is correct? If there *is* an error in Kingston's use of the word, could this error be strategic? Could she, for example, be dramatizing her own cultural displacement as a child? What does the term "ghost"—if it is a "white person"—imply about how Chinese Americans view mainstream Americans? What effect does Chan's translation of the word *gwai*, or *kuei*, have on the overall atmosphere of the book—is anything lost? or gained? How does reading the word *kuei* as "asshole" affect *your* interpretation of what these ghosts represent? Is the narrator also a "ghost"?

Through these questions, the student would be guided to the understanding that the term "ghosts" refers quite clearly to non-Chinese, to living persons. To translate the word *kuei* as Chan suggests limits the word's resonance to the social sphere—white people become merely villains. Kingston's usage lifts the conceit into a metaphysical plane as well: it is evident that the traditional mind-set assumes that non-Chinese are *dead*—that is, less than human—and the "Mail Ghost, Meter Reader Ghost, Garbage Ghost" and perhaps most particularly the "two Jesus Ghosts" in *The Woman Warrior* (114–15) become not mere "assholes" but figures of mortal dread to the young Kingston and her siblings, and later in the text to her aunt Moon Orchid.

It is possible to teach students how to read *The Woman Warrior*, to enable them to increase their literary competence, in Riffaterre's terminology. These students then form—as Fish has suggested—an interpretive community that empowers them to read not only this book but eventually other recalcitrant texts. The hope is that through such learning, the pool of those who would have read a book like *The Woman Warrior* for themselves and not merely because it has been assigned will increase. With such increase I trust will arise more tolerance and understanding of one another, each of us, Ghost or not Ghost.

The Woman Warrior
in the Women's Studies Classroom
Judith M. Melton

Maxine Hong Kingston's compelling autobiography, *The Woman Warrior*, is a natural choice for a text in the women's studies classroom, reflecting as it does the rigid roles of women in traditional Chinese society. In such an interdisciplinary course, in which women's concerns are explored from a variety of perspectives—historical, sociological, psychological, economic, humanistic, and others—this intensely personal work enables students to perceive how a patriarchal culture shapes the choices of the women in that society. Although the work can be read on numerous levels, in my introductory women's studies class we focus on two facets—the historical portrait of a misogynist culture, feudal China, and the struggle of a modern young woman to create a sustaining identity in the face of its lingering traditions. As the daughter of a Chinese family living in California, the narrator is imbued with the misogynist legacy of her ancestry, a legacy that reaches back to traditional China but still echoes in her Chinese American environment.

Students responding to this highly poetic work in discussions and in their journals share Kingston's fear and anger at the victimization of women in feudal China and marvel at her strength and ingenuity in eluding such victimization. They empathize with her determination to shield herself from the speech and actions of the Chinese community that demeans women. Particularly for middle-class, privileged students, her ethnic upbringing in the ghetto portrays a woman's experience that contrasts starkly with their own comfortable backgrounds. In this essay, I emphasize these two readings of *The Woman Warrior* in relation to women's studies issues.

Embedded in the intriguing account of Kingston's eccentric family and her unusual childhood is a chilling portrait of a culture viscerally different from the American society students know. Scrutinizing the customs of such a society illuminates patterns in our own culture whose contours we only dimly perceive. As the historian Richard Smith notes, "Cross-cultural analysis . . . serves as a dramatic and effective illustration of the ways in which conceptions of reality are socially constructed" (6). Traditional patterns of behavior are sometimes so ingrained that we cannot think past them and are thus imprisoned by them. Examining a radically different culture like that of China can open the doors of our conceptual and perceptual prisons. An American custom such as that of a man opening the door for a woman may seem inconsequential, but a practice such as foot-binding can jar our minds, causing us to reevaluate modes of behavior we take for granted.

If initially students empathize with Kingston as she struggles to find her place alternately in the Chinese tradition and in the Chinese American community, they subsequently perceive the stringent traditions that shaped her upbringing, particularly when materials elaborating on historical Chinese social mores supplement their reading. Having already understood the value of autobiographies as sources for women's experience, students readily understand *The Woman Warrior* both as an individual account of one woman's experience and the cultural record of many women's experience. For this reason, this work can be seen not only as Kingston's autobiography but as a biography of her mother, Brave Orchid, as at least one critic, Sidonie Smith, has noted (162). Indeed, for students in women's studies courses, the experiences of all the women in the book become important, for together they make up a kaleidoscope of the roles of women in Chinese society.

Kingston makes it clear early in the book that, growing up in the Chinese American community in California, she found her life and family background a series of mysteries. She calls out to the members of her community:

> Chinese-Americans, when you try to understand what things in you are Chinese, how do you separate what is peculiar to childhood, to poverty, insanities, one family, your mother who marked your growing with stories, from what is Chinese? What is Chinese tradition and what is the movies? (6)

As students recognize, asserting her own identity within these mysteries was confusing. Living with the legacy of "China," Kingston was terrorized by the feudal life in the family's homeland. She schemed to make herself unattractive, so that she couldn't be married off or sold if her family returned. "I did not plan ever to have a husband" (56), she writes. "I dropped dishes. . . . I picked my nose while I was cooking and serving. . . . I affected a limp" (221). The ambivalence of her mother, Brave Orchid, a pivotal figure in the work, adds to her confusion. While she tells her daughter forbidden stories about her No Name Aunt and echoes Chinese sayings that denigrate girls and women, she also glorifies the "woman warrior."

In his essay on the meaning of culture, "Thick Description: Toward an Interpretive Theory of Culture," Clifford Geertz notes that human beings are "suspended in webs of significance" that they themselves have spun (5). Kingston is caught in the mysterious webs of the Chinese cultural tradition that have structured the reality of her mother and her aunts. In creating her own identity, she questions these "webs of significance" and teases out her own meaning. In differentiating between what is Chinese, what is her own family, she comes to her own understanding of the reality of the "village" life. What her mother's generation accepts as tradition, she interprets as repulsive practices.

Empathizing with her confusion, students follow her as she tries to accommodate the contradictions of what she intuits to be real and what she is told is real. In each chapter she—and readers in turn—puzzle over traditional attitudes and behaviors, creating new meanings that support her emotionally. After hearing about the village ostracism of her No Name Aunt, she must reclaim her aunt's subjectivity, as Sidonie Smith notes (153). Her mother whispers the aunt's story as an object lesson, but Kingston mulls over the various possibilities of her aunt's behavior, finally recognizing, as do sensitive students, that her aunt was no adulterer who brought destruction onto her family; she was an ordinary woman caught in the punishing beliefs of feudal China.

In the chapter "White Tigers" Kingston reinterprets her mother's talk-story, creating a powerful fantasy that becomes the identity crux of the book. Her mother told her she would grow up to be a wife, and thus a slave, but she also taught the young girl the song of the warrior woman, Fa Mu Lan. For Kingston this meant that she "would have to grow up a warrior woman" (24). In retelling the story of Fa Mu Lan, she contrasts her fantasy of being a feared and revered warrior woman with the painful everyday reality of her girlhood, in which her mother, father, and uncles endlessly repeat the litany about girls: "Feeding girls is feeding cowbirds"; "There's no profit in raising girls"; "When you raise girls, you're raising children for strangers" (54); "When fishing for treasures in the flood, be careful not to pull in girls" (62). For readers in women's studies classes, this chapter becomes a catalyst. They begin to understand how traditions against women are enculturated.

In "Shaman" and "At the Western Palace" the narrator portrays the two distinct faces of her mother: the independent woman who became a doctor in China before coming to the United States, and the traditional Chinese wife, a strong-willed woman who bore six children in her later years and spent fifteen-hour days running the laundry. Although both figures are women of strength, the doctor stands out against the traditional patterns for women in the Chinese culture, while the matriarch continues to adhere to patriarchal traditions, at least superficially. These portrayals of Brave Orchid exemplify the contradictions of Chinese views of women.

The idea of the traditional Chinese "village," which remains alive in the minds of Kingston's mother, family, and community and is passed on to the young Kingston, offers a desolate view for women, as students quickly realize. In this superstitious and relentlessly misogynist culture, women were devalued and confined to stereotypical roles. A recent film, *Small Happiness*, which portrays the status of women in current China, can be enlightening for students reading *The Woman Warrior*. This film, produced by the Long Bow Group, records life in a small village in modern China. While this village has taken on the patina of the Communist communal ideal, the feudal way of life is still much in evidence. The film's title comes from the remarks of a man who calls the birth of his granddaughter "a small happiness," in ironic distinction to the great happiness of a boy. (Kingston asks her mother concerning the birth of her brothers, "Did you roll an egg on *my* face like that when I was born?" "Did you have a full-month party for *me*?" [55])

The film not only vividly portrays the many constraints that women face in this culture but shows how the social practices are exacerbated by China's unyielding poverty. One older woman, who speaks out in the film, tells how her father sold her as a slave when she was a young girl in order to get food for the rest of the family. She herself killed her own baby—a boy—shortly after he was born because she already had one baby who was starving.

Reading *The Woman Warrior* and viewing *Small Happiness*, students react strongly to the socially constructed traditions imposed on women in feudal China. The practice of foot-binding, originally a fashion of aristocrats, effectively kept women under house arrest. In the upper classes, women were segregated in special quarters in palaces, cared for by slaves, and allowed to travel only in closed sedan chairs. They were, of course, not expected to work. The sexual mystique of foot-binding, however—described so graphically by Andrea Dworken—caused the practice to seep into the culture at large. In Kingston's narrative we learn, for example, that while her mother's feet were not bound, her grandmother's were (241). In *Small Happiness* peasant women living in modern China talk about having their feet bound as young children. But like Kingston's grandmother, these peasant women were still expected to carry their share of household tasks.

In addition to such atrocities as foot-binding, the culture encouraged widespread practices against females such as infanticide: "The midwife or a relative would take the back of a girl baby's head in her hand and turn her face into the ashes" (101). Or abuse: "Beat me, then, beat me," a woman in an opera sings; " 'She is playing the part of a new daughter-in-law,' my mother explained" (224). As these examples show, this patriarchal culture placed women in the role of destroying or abusing other women. It was the mothers who bound the feet of their young daughters, and a stereotypical figure in the literature of nineteenth-century or early twentieth-century China is the mother-in-law who abuses her new daughter-in-law, as the story "The Child Bride" in Dorothy Shimer's anthology *Rice Bowl Women* illustrates.

Further, as Carol Pearson and Katherine Pope, in *The Female Hero in American and British Literature*, point out, women who do not follow the proscriptions of such cultures are punished: "A failure to act according to the values of conventional society may result in social ostracism, poverty, madness, or death" (17). Kingston's touching portrayal of her No Name Aunt and her account of the mad woman stoned by the villagers because they believe her to be responsible for the Japanese bombings clearly depict the devastations of outcast women.

Students recognize that even the reverberations of these practices terrify Kingston. In a culture in which women for the most part were either wives

("slaves" [23]; "dustpan-and-broom" [238]) or outcasts, and in which, like
Moon Orchid, wives could be discarded, women lacked the self-esteem for
an independent identity. Indeed, as Margaret Miller has shown in her in-
formative essay "Threads of Identity in Maxine Hong Kingston's *Woman
Warrior*," Chinese women, like Chinese men, were expected to function
in a familial role. Both were expected to continue the family hierarchy, men
as leaders who revere the past generations and look to future generations,
women as necessary, but subordinate, links in this family hierarchy. The
Western concept of the individual is foreign to cultures with such "communal
traditions" (14). In fact, Miller sees Kingston's task as a Chinese American
autobiographer problematic in trying to "turn a Chinese 'we' into a Chinese-
American 'I' " (17).

Kingston's characterization of herself throughout the book, but especially
in the last chapter, "A Song for a Barbarian Reed Pipe," hinges on her
tenacity to make herself different—that is, to see herself as an individual,
to speak in the first person. When she begins to notice that the adult women
gather "to talk about marriages," she redoubles her efforts to be unmar-
riageable (226). She clings to her way out—through American school and
college: "I may be ugly and clumsy, but one thing I'm not, I'm not retarded.
There's nothing wrong with my brain" (234). Even after she leaves her
mother's home, the traditions haunt her and she doubts her self-worth:
"When I visit the family now, I wrap my American successes around me
like a private shawl; I *am* worthy of eating the food" (62). She also cannot
let go of her sense of filial obligation. She falls sick whenever she returns,
but her duty as a daughter pulls her into the family orbit: "She [her mother]
pries open my head and my fists and crams into them responsibility for time,
responsibility for intervening oceans" (126). Someday the daughter will in-
herit a "green address book full of names" (239) and be required to send
money to relatives she has never met and who may not even be living; the
mysteries of China will continue.

Despite the ongoing messages Kingston receives telling her that as a
woman she is worthless, she pursues her independent identity. She is determined to grow up to be somebody—not a slave, a castoff, a crazy. Students
from families that nurture their self-esteem respond with incredulity at the
effacement of the individual woman's identity in the autobiography. One
student wrote in her journal, "I was really shocked at how women within
the society of the Orient were treated. . . . But the thing that surprised me
the most is their lack of identity." With anger, another wrote about the No
Name Aunt's being deserted by her family and expunged from the family
history: "How could they have done this to her! They should have been
angry with the villagers, not with her!" One stated, "I had no idea that a
synonym for marriage in Chinese is 'taking a daughter-in-law' as if she's only
a piece of property." Another pondered, "How would I feel if I was told

repeatedly that I was useless because I am a girl; how would I feel being left out of most activities, simply because boys were felt superior? Not very good about myself, I assure you."

Ultimately it is Kingston's ability to find her voice, to tell her story, that defines her identity. "I thought talking and not talking made the difference between sanity and insanity. Insane people were the ones who couldn't explain themselves. There were many crazy girls and women" (216). Although strident Chinese women's voices echo in her ears, she, like feminist critics such as Dale Spender, recognizes that women in patriarchal cultures are muted. They have no real voice. As a child, like girls of other ethnic minorities, her efforts to speak, to be heard were compounded by trying to speak aloud in a second language, English. In addition, she had to contend with the cultural clues of the American patriarchal society. "We American-Chinese girls had to whisper to make ourselves American-feminine. . . . We invented an American-feminine speaking personality" (200). Her brutal treatment of the Chinese girl who wouldn't speak (202–11) stems from her clear understanding that to be a person one must use one's voice. And she realizes that her words can make a difference. As a rebellious Chinese daughter, she speaks out to send away the mentally retarded man she secretly fears may have been selected as her husband. "The very next day after I talked out the retarded man, the huncher, he disappeared" (239). And later as an activist against discrimination, she finds the courage to speak out (57–58), even if in her "pressed-duck voice" (223). And, finally as a writer, she can create "a song for a barbarian reed pipe" (240–43).

Students empathize with Kingston as she struggles against the traditions of feudal China. Like her, they find the traditions alien and abhorrent, and most of all shocking. One young man wrote, "[*The Woman Warrior*] is just completely different to anything I've read of or experienced. . . . [It] really makes you just *sit* and think!" Reading her narrative as Kingston sorts through the mysteries of growing up and as she rejects the inexorable roles slated for women in Chinese society, students begin to realize how practices that are significant in one era or culture lose their importance in another. They commiserate with her growing up in a culture in which the word for "female I" is "slave" (56) and applaud her determination not to allow herself to be broken by her "own [tongue]" (56). Indeed, they recognize the forceful irony that it is her own tongue that empowers her. Her resolve to overcome the unrelieved negative messages of her elders' language and customs causes them to reexamine the language and customs of their own society. And finally, her veracity and candor rivet their attention. As one student remarked concerning her admiration for the book, "She tells her story with integrity." It is, perhaps, Kingston's integrity of self that strikes such a responsive chord in student readers.

Woman Warriors and Military Students

James R. Aubrey

The first time I read *The Woman Warrior*, I was teaching English at the Air Force Academy and always on the watch for literary writing on military themes. The book's title led me to expect something more in the martial spirit than what I found, so I was not surprised to learn recently that Maxine Hong Kingston has had her own misgivings about the title. In a 1986 audiotaped interview, she mentions that it was her editor who first suggested that she call her book *The Woman Warrior*. When he pointed out a year later, "You know that that's you," Kingston says that her reaction was "very negative" to the suggestion that she as writer is, like Fa Mu Lan, a warrior. "I don't feel that she's me. . . . I wish I had not had a metaphor of a warrior person who uses weapons and goes to war" (Bonetti). Despite Kingston's regrets, the title places in the foreground the question of what role women should have in military combat, and that is an issue I found worth raising for discussion when I assigned *The Woman Warrior* in two junior-level courses, one required and one elective.

I can understand Kingston's discomfort with the title of *The Woman Warrior*, for pacifism is an important theme in all her books (*China Men* 256, 278; *Hawai'i One Summer* 13–15; *Tripmaster Monkey* 306, 340; see Aubrey). Her editor's view that she as the author is a metaphorical warrior is hardly farfetched, however. Kingston concludes the "White Tigers" chapter with a paragraph whose autobiographical-sounding narrator almost insists that we regard her as a warrior and her words as a metaphorical sword:

> The swordswoman and I are not so dissimilar. . . . What we have in common are the words at our backs. The idioms for *revenge* are "report a crime" and "report to five families." The reporting is the vengeance—not the beheading, not the gutting, but the words. And I have so many words—"chink" words and "gook" words too—that they do not fit on my skin. (62–63)

Having just told the story of Fa Mu Lan, who fights as "a female avenger" (51) and whose parents have literally carved a list of grievances on her back with a knife (41–42), Kingston seems conscious that her own words in *The Woman Warrior* constitute a book report, an avenging act by a writer-warrior. The offense against women is also a matter of language, manifested in proverbs such as "Better to raise geese than girls" or, at a deeper level of grammar, in the fact that the "Chinese word for the female *I* . . . is 'slave'" (56). The juxtaposition of Fa Mu Lan's warfare and Kingston's struggle against her languages implies that she is fighting a "war" for personal identity. Like the sexist Chinese baron whom Fa Mu Lan beheads, the racist American businessman whose invitations Kingston refuses to type, later in the same chapter, is a privileged representative of the dominant culture in which she worked, and now writes (52, 57–58). As the enemy of Kingston's sword-words is tall, white, and male, it would be almost perverse *not* to view the assertive Kingston as a warrior in some metaphorical conflict.

Part of Kingston's concern seems to be a wish that her book not seem a glorification of warriors and warfare. It is not one, of course, because the warrior women in the book bring about social changes that lead to harmony, to peaceable ends that require warlike means. Violence is further justified —not glorified—because warfare in the book is a metaphor for social conflict, often between genders and cultures, and the woman warrior is a metaphorical agent for resolution of social conflict—that is to say, a peacemaker.

The idea of a woman warrior became of interest to me in the early 1970s, when the wisdom of admitting women to the service academies was being debated in public, in private, and in the essays of my predominantly tall, white, male students of freshman English at the Air Force Academy. Cadet essays on the subject were almost always hostile to the idea of admitting women (the entrance way still bears the motto "Bring Me Men"). The debates became moot in 1976 when, anticipating ratification of the equal rights amendment, Congress mandated the integration of women into all three service academies.

Such concerns about women in combat are as old in the West as Kingston indicates they are in China. Plato discussed problems but thought women should be eligible to serve as Guardians (*Republic* 235), and Joan of Arc's military prowess is legendary. Nevertheless, many Americans believe that women should not be fighting—at least not in the "front lines" (wherever those may be). The anomalousness of women already in the military can be inferred just from the existence of a long-standing Defense Advisory Committee on the Status of Women in the Services. Because the notion of women in combat is one about which males often hold strong opinions, as a topic for discussion it can bring male students, especially, to appreciate some issues at stake in *The Woman Warrior*.

By 1986, when I first read *The Woman Warrior*, the presence of female cadets at the Air Force Academy seemed widely accepted by male cadets, but I could not be sure about their deeper feelings. Although the institution encourages free discussion in the classroom, students and faculty members are subject to military regulations; so a male student cannot vigorously write or speak up in opposition to the presence of women at the academy without taking the risk that someone might interpret his remark as evidence of unwillingness to accept the official policy prohibiting discrimination against women. Despite my concern that student fear of a complaint might have a chilling effect on expression, I hoped that discussions of *The Woman Warrior* would take some interesting turns in classes that were made up, for the most part, of prospective male warriors.

I was not forgetting that female cadets also would enroll in both my classes, but the fact was—and is—that the women were not considered "prospective warriors" under the 1948 law that bars women from combat. The origin and subsequent interpretation of this law, known as the "combat exclusion," are laid out by Lori Kornblum in an article titled "Women Warriors in a Men's World." After tracing the various ways the military services have defined *combat*, and the ways in which excluding women from combat harms both men and women, in and out of the military, Kornblum shows why six arguments that have been used to justify and perpetuate the law constitute "mythology as policy" (351). She concludes with an exhortation:

> Only after structural barriers to women in combat are removed will the attitudinal barriers to women's equality in the military and in society begin to end. When these barriers dissolve, all women might become true, not imaginary, women warriors.   (445)

The resemblance of her phrase "women warriors" to Kingston's title is not accidental, for Kornblum begins her article with an excerpt from *The Woman Warrior*—the passage describing Fa Mu Lan's army, which does not rape or steal food but brings order wherever it goes (44). Kornblum notes that Fa Mu Lan achieves her military successes "in a manner different from her male counterparts" and that the possible transformative effect of women on the military has been one argument used both for and against a female presence (353). But Kornblum is most interested in the fact that Fa Mu Lan must disguise herself as a man in order to participate in war, a fact that allows Kornblum to draw a comparison between the way that Chinese society executed women who fought as soldiers and the way American society "trivializes or makes invisible women's successful combat experiences" (355) and thus perpetuates the idea that women in the military decrease military capabilities.

One particular result of the combat exclusion is to give women in the military a status similar to that of a minority group. Because they may not be assigned to combat positions as officers, women are selected for the service academies neither strictly on the basis of merit nor, as with racial minorities, in rough proportion to their numbers in the American population. The goal at the Air Force Academy since 1976 has been to admit thirteen percent women, a percentage designed to maintain the 1976 proportion of women to men in the Air Force at about 1:10 (Stiehm 117; Daniels). Thus, for better or worse, the Air Force perpetuates the status of its women as a small minority. The Air Force is, of course, justified in doing so as long as the exclusion of women from combat prevents them from flying fighters or bombers, most of whose pilots get their commissions from the Air Force Academy. And since the senior commander of any fighter or bomber unit might have to lead that unit in combat, a woman is also ineligible to hold such a command position—the kind that most consistently gets officers promoted to the rank of general. Furthermore, as feminists often argue, women will not be seriously considered eligible to hold any position of political responsibility if they are not considered capable of exercising the coercive power of the state, in combat (Weber 78; Stiehm 300; Kornblum 379).

The female minority at the Air Force Academy can usually be distinguished from male cadets by such visual markers as hair style, body shape and size, and clothing (women's uniforms are not exactly "uniform" with men's). I had imagined that my women students would identify with Kingston's narrator, whose Chinese features make her, likewise, visibly different from members of the dominant majority around her and whose gender, she is repeatedly told, makes her inferior.

As things turned out, the feminist-minority agenda made *The Woman Warrior* difficult as well as interesting to teach. I have found cadets generally quite willing to read antimilitary literature with approval. Most of them like *Catch-22* or *A Farewell to Arms*, for example, but many of my 1987 students—of both sexes—seemed to dislike *The Woman Warrior*; I believe that they were responding to the way that Kingston's book subverts deeply imbedded cultural assumptions about sex and gender, assumptions that are less susceptible to critique than assumptions about war. If negative reactions by cadets to the book were indeed responses to Kingston's feminism more than to anything else, civilian college teachers should expect similar reactions, for their students' attitudes also have been shaped within the patriarchal norms of American culture.

I was less surprised over male resistance to *The Woman Warrior* than I was to find that female students, too, thought Kingston "complained too much," as one put it. The women tended to like *The Woman Warrior* more than the men, but they were not at all eager to pick up the feminist banner. I had known better than to assume that female cadets, even though they have demonstrated career aspirations by applying to a service academy, are to be considered among the vanguard of liberated women. They typically come from conservative, middle-class families and sometimes adapt to hypermasculine military attitudes by means of "protective coloration," which can take various forms, from behaving like one of the boys to behaving like one of the girls whom the boys date. Nor were my women students, outnumbered as they may have been by males, unwilling to speak up or even to carry the discussion. It was more that they almost never would take a feminist position in a room full of male students (and a male teacher), and when one found herself close to doing so, she might begin her comment with some version of the phrase "I'm not a libber, but. . . ." I suspect that four years of living in a cadet dormitory—where military traditions tend to privilege masculinity, where the males are young and particularly susceptible to antifeminism, and where cooperation and teamwork within one's squadron and class are stressed—do not encourage women to acquire, let alone to articulate, feminist attitudes. Effacement of feminist attitudes by female cadets should not be attributed simply to what Kingston refers to as concern over "no dates," however (56). Any assertive minority threatens to interfere with ideologies like "team spirit" and to disrupt the traditional, hierarchical order especially valued in the military. Nor should nonmilitary teachers forget that the American military reflects mainstream American values, and that a similar social dynamic is probably at work in a civilian classroom with a significant number of men and women who want to succeed in business or politics, so long as those hierarchies, too, remain predominantly male.

Some students liked *The Woman Warrior*, of course, but those who did not may have learned more. A book that reads against the grain of student prejudices can be valuable in the classroom, and Kingston's book is surely not a ratification of the world most students—or teachers—know. Indeed, the book's greatest virtue as a reading assignment may be the culture shock it creates. As a white male of European ancestry, I certainly recognized that I was in a fundamentally different world the first time I read the book, and exploration of such a feeling among students can generate enlightening discussions. When I asked students to assume the role of armchair ethnologists, to consider what they could infer about Chinese or Chinese American cultural norms from what they had read in the first chapter, "No Name Woman," students were surprised by the number of insights they could discover. Attitudes toward gender and sexuality, necessity and utility, family and community—all could be discerned in tentative ways. Kingston reinforces the idea of community in that chapter, for example, by linking it with the idea of roundness (15). The word *commensal* (8), which no one seemed to know, relates to the idea of community, too. Although they saw the word *community* as positive, they were suspicious of the related word *communal* (and, of course, *communist*). And they were extremely reluctant to see that freedom of individual choice, an unquestioned value in mainstream American ideology, constitutes a fundamental threat in the tradition-based community of Kingston's No Name Aunt. Another word which is revealing but likely to be unfamiliar is *origamied*, in the last paragraph of the first chapter; if a teacher points out that Kingston has been describing the process in the preceding paragraph, students may see the wryness of her observation about writing down the story of "No Name Woman"—an observation that, incidentally, gives the chapter "roundness" in the ironic way it may refer to the opening sentence.

Other chapters, too, lend themselves to liberal-humanist readings, often as texts about the transformative power of art. As the No Name Aunt liberated herself—temporarily—by redefining the discourse of sexuality, Kingston learns in "White Tigers" to imagine a verbal discourse that transcends the conventions of gender. In the chapter titled "Shaman," Kingston learns to move among different cultural discourses. This chapter contains the most exotic material—from furry ghosts to ape men to a feast on live monkey brain—for strangeness is the stuff with which Kingston's shaman-mother works. The way Brave Orchid considers any Caucasian to be a ghost indicates that she is what anthropologists call "away" from American culture, existing across some shadow line that makes an outsider seem somehow less than real (Geertz, "Deep Play" 413). Like her mother initially, Kingston the child-narrator grows up "away" but learns to cross from Chinese "reality" to American "reality." The chapter ends with Kingston's becoming a shaman, receiving her mother's blessing to work in a world her mother considers to be filled with "Ghosts" (127). For Kingston the author, the shaman may be another self-reflexive metaphor, like the warrior, for herself as writer; for if the chapter succeeds in taking readers on a passage into its strange, intercultural world, Kingston's book has served as a magical talisman for them, her initiates.

"At the Western Palace" tells the story of a failure to cross such a threshold between cultures. When Brave Orchid's sister Moon Orchid arrives, Kingston amusingly juxtaposes her aunt's "Chinese" interpretation of events with the "American" interpretation of the nephews and nieces. When Moon Orchid seeks out her estranged husband, hoping to move in with him and to displace his "minor wife," he tells her, "You don't have the hardness for this country," (177). Gradually Moon Orchid loses what Westerners would call her sanity, which Brave Orchid defines as the ability to talk-story with variety: "Mad people have only one story that they talk over and over," she says (184). The children, including Kingston, associate Moon Orchid's "weird" qualities with her displaced Chinese outlook (183) and, overreacting, vow at the end of the chapter to stave off such insanities by Westernizing: they "made up their minds to major in science or mathematics" (186).

Kingston returns to this idea in the final chapter, "A Song for a Barbarian Reed Pipe." Her mature way of seeing, however, is no longer desperately Western but ironically detached: "Give me plastics, periodical tables, TV dinners with vegetables no more complex than peas mixed with diced carrots. Shine floodlights into dark corners: no ghosts" (237). The silence of the Chinese American girl disturbed Kingston as a child, as if having no voice and no story were also a form of madness, a "dark corner" to be illuminated. By the end of the book, talking-story, or music, or any kind of creative art has become not just an index of sanity but a means to transcend cultural difference—as Kingston does by bringing Chinese stories to American readers with this book, in her own, intercultural voice.

So the title of *The Woman Warrior* celebrates not military heroism but instead, metaphorically, the self as artist and the artist as social reformer. Classroom discussion of the literal meaning of the title, however, can help students see the book's metaphorical dimension. More important, discussion of the idea of a woman warrior can get students engaged in the ongoing social debate about women in the military and can help make other kinds of social conflict in *The Woman Warrior* seem less remote from their own lives—in short, can help them appreciate how the world of Kingston's book is, after all, their world.

Voice and Vision: *The Woman Warrior* in the Writing Class

Kathleen A. Boardman

I have found *The Woman Warrior* a particularly rich text to use in a writing class. Like Kingston in her book, many of my students are coming of age and coming to terms with themselves, even though their struggles may be less dramatic than hers. First-year college students also sense the gap between the environment they have come from and the world of academia, which seems to require new ways of looking at things and different ways of communicating. Under these circumstances, learning to see and developing a voice are critical if students are to write effectively. *The Woman Warrior* describes struggles between cultures, generations, and attitudes—conflicts with which students can identify. The book can be read as a chronicle of the process of becoming a writer: finding a voice and something to say and thus making a contribution to the community. Of course, Kingston refers to herself in the book as a storyteller rather than a writer, and she draws on many more generations of storytelling tradition than are available to most students. Still, *The Woman Warrior* lays out the difficulties and rewards of being a writer as graphically as any writing text: making inferences, learning to see, dealing with multiple versions of a single incident, locating oneself within a tradition, developing style, appealing to an audience, and dealing with misunderstanding.

Individual passages of *The Woman Warrior*, so elaborate in texture and color, are valuable not just as models for imitation but as ways of showing where an individual vision and style can lead. Kingston has also been generous with comments and interviews on her own writing process. In a helpful "Postscript on Process" for *The Bedford Reader*, Kingston invites students to learn from her experience as a writer.

For several years I have taught a second-semester freshman composition course with an emphasis on modern autobiographical writing. *The Woman Warrior* has always been on the syllabus, although the other works have varied. (I generally choose four works from a list, including the following: Margaret Mead's *Blackberry Winter*, Frank Conroy's *Stop-Time*, Mary McCarthy's *Memories of a Catholic Girlhood*, Richard Rodriguez's *Hunger of Memory*, Ivan Doig's *This House of Sky*, Maya Angelou's *I Know Why the Caged Bird Sings*, and Annie Dillard's *Pilgrim at Tinker Creek*.) Although students write critical and research papers late in the course, the emphasis during the first half of the semester is on seeing autobiography from the inside—that is, on doing autobiographical writing of their own. The books read during this early period need to be rich sources of ideas for and about writing. This is when I assign *The Woman Warrior*. Despite the sophistication it demands of readers, the book helps introduce important concepts that we build on throughout the semester.

Many of these concepts organize themselves under the general headings of *vision* and *voice*. Kingston has been discussed in terms of gaps and connections (Homsher 93)—gaps between cultures, between generations, between adolescence and adulthood, between myth and reality. With these ideas in mind, I use the well-known communication triangle (writer-audience-subject) to show students that *vision* makes the connection between subject and writer, while *voice* bridges the gap between writer and audience. Vision involves interpreting the subject, filling in gaps with new information, making sense of fragmentary or paradoxical information, and viewing subject matter from an interesting angle. Voice allows expression of this point of view to an audience. (Of course, the changing voice and vision also influence the writer herself, as we see in Kingston's book.)

Good writing, then, requires an interesting point of view and the ability to give it voice in a manner appropriate to the audience, subject, and writer. In my classes we explore these goals through discussion of Kingston's ideas and techniques in *The Woman Warrior*, and through frequent writing and revision practice, aided by journals and writing response groups. In this essay I suggest ideas related to vision and voice that might be explored in a writing class.

As they begin the book, readers often express frustration at the heavily detailed and seemingly contradictory stories. But gradually they see that their experience as readers parallels Kingston's as a young girl trying to make sense of talk-story. Kingston's first problem as she views her subject matter is to find out what is true. It is not easy to figure out how things fit or to make sense of the "baggage" left her by parents, elders, and background: "Before we can leave our parents, they stuff our heads like the suitcases which they jam-pack with homemade underwear" (102). College freshmen are often tempted to throw their own baggage out, but if they do, they sacrifice a source of color and power in their writing. Shortly after the class begins reading the first "cautionary tale" told by Brave Orchid, I invite students to explore the following topic in their journals: "What cautionary tales—'stories to grow up on'—have you been told? If and when you discovered a 'reality' that contradicted this tale, what did you think?"

Students are often troubled by the presence of so many different versions of a supposedly factual story: isn't it a writer's responsibility to point out the one true version? Kingston presents several variations on the story of the drowned aunt, two different stories of the Sitting Ghost (both told by Brave Orchid), two versions of Moon Orchid's meeting with her husband (Kingston's and her brother's). Which is real? Which is best? Students generally agree that the best version of the drowned aunt's story would be the one that gave "ancestral help": Kingston is trying to make a cautionary tale more palatable to herself. Versions of the ghost tale also vary with the needs and expectations of the two audiences (Kingston and the medical students), while the differences in the Moon Orchid story must be a matter of style: the brother is a straightforward, chronological storyteller, Kingston an "outlaw knot-maker" (190). Brave Orchid often chides her daughter for believing talk-story, taking one version for fact. Kingston says that, finally, it is not necessary to decide on a single correct version: "As a writer, after getting over the idea that I had to know only one truth, I realized that my problem is that I have too much truth to tell rather than too little" ("Postscript" 70). The idea that many different versions may point to truth frees the writer to take what she hears and make it her own, changing or adding to it as she feels necessary for her purposes.

To provide practical experience in this area, I ask students, in their journals, to rewrite the cautionary tale (or some other entry) from an entirely different point of view. Then I suggest that they use the same point of view but change the events of the story. This activity can also be done—perhaps more quickly and sociably—in response groups, with students telling the same story in various versions, changing the ending or point of view.

Of course, recognizing the usefulness of many different versions of an incident is not the same as saying that any old tale will do, or that interpretation is unnecessary. Kingston portrays her struggle to establish realities, to "infer" her mother's attitudes and her Chinese roots from bits and pieces of stories and customs. The old couple training Fa Mu Lan tell her, "You have to infer the whole dragon from the parts you can see and touch" (34); Kingston later declares, "From the configurations of food my mother set out, we kids had to infer the holidays" (215). Because we too must infer the invisible world of values, ideas, and principles from language and the world of the senses, it is helpful to deal in class with ideas of the abstract and concrete in writing, with close observation and interpretation. Brave Orchid uses rich sensory detail—from the slave girl's red ribbon to the ghost's odor—to bring the old country alive for a daughter who has never been there. Kingston does the same for her readers, selecting from a wealth of detail to show her audience what it is like to grow up between cultures. Of her writing she says, "My task, like gardening in Hawaii, is cutting and pruning and hacking back, rather than planting" ("Postscript" 70).

For practice in the use of detail and inference, I have found the following exercises helpful. I ask students to find and list a number of memorable details, trying to use as many senses as possible, from Brave Orchid's narratives and from Kingston's own stories. (If several students choose the same detail, we try to decide what makes it so memorable; often it has to do with conflict or paradox, which I will discuss below.) Throughout the semester, as students read their papers aloud to their response groups, group members also list memorable details from each student paper. After we discuss the definition of *myth* in class, I ask students to write in their journals on the following topic: "What myth or myths have been important to you, your family, or your peer group as you have grown up? From these stories, what can you infer about the values of your family or culture?"

Part of the strength of Kingston's writing lies in the bold use of metaphor. Statements comparing the attacking villagers to "a great saw" (4) and peasant women to "great sea snails" (11) make the stories more vivid. Repetition of traditional metaphors—clichés like "Girls are maggots in the rice" (51)—focuses the young narrator's anger and distress. Finally, Kingston uses metaphor to make connections, to reconcile contradictions. Dreaming of herself as Fa Mu Lan in training, she says, "I learned to make my mind large, as the universe is large, so that there is room for paradoxes" (35). She learns "how working and hoeing are dancing; how peasant clothes are golden" (32). Kingston explores the connections between herself and the woman warrior (62) and, in this play on words, between herself and the wife-slaves: "Even now China wraps double binds around my feet" (57).

Peter Elbow has suggested that such "contraries," and the metaphors that often yoke them, lie at the heart of writing (3). Beginning writers frequently complain that most of the good metaphors have already been written, but I have them practice making connections, with interesting results. In one class activity, students write concrete nouns and abstract nouns on the board. The class pairs the words arbitrarily, two concrete nouns or a concrete with an abstract. I ask students to write a sentence for each of several pairs, using this form: "_____ [first noun] is like _____ [second noun] because _____." Next, after adding a list of adjectives to the board, the class lists pairs (two nouns or adjective and noun) that "fight," or contrast, with one another (as in "wispy anger"). In their journals they write paragraphs featuring one of the pairs. These exercises generally lead to energetic writing and frequent use of analogy to illustrate ideas.

To emphasize the importance of vision, I like to discuss the following quotation from *The Woman Warrior*, which suggests that writers can train themselves to see and think in new ways, often at some cost:

> I had to leave home in order to see the world logically, logic the new way of seeing. I learned to think that mysteries are for explanation. I enjoy the simplicity. . . . Now when I peek in the basement window where the villagers say they see a girl dancing like a bottle imp, I can no longer see a spirit in a skirt made of light, but a voiceless girl dancing when she thought no one was looking. (237–39)

The Woman Warrior suggests that some people can "name" things so aptly and powerfully that they influence the way others see their surroundings. Brave Orchid puts things in their place by naming them; alien, threatening, or unimportant people become "ghosts." The woman who says Kingston has a "pressed-duck voice" is a "giver of American names, a powerful namer"

(223). Novice writers are frequently unaware of the power of language, so it is important to draw their attention to it. In their journals, my students keep track of words and phrases that seem to carry special influence within the context of the book (words like "ghost" and "crazy"). That is, students are to choose words that would have particular meaning for an in-group who had read the book. I also invite them to begin listing key words and expressions from their own writing and speech. Response groups can help with this.

Voice, like names, can be used with power. In Kingston's family, "voice" refers literally to speaking voice, but the writer must carry the concept further, as Kingston points out:

> But even though I draw on talk-story, I'm a writer, and writing is a solitary activity, and reading is a solitary activity. It's a process of an individual mind trying to reach other minds, one at a time. . . . I have to find my individual voice. I have to tell this story in a way that is mine.   ("Maxine Hong Kingston: Exploring" 3)

The class explores what happens to people, like Moon Orchid, who lose or never find their voices. We follow the young narrator's struggle to find, use, and have confidence in her voice. This confidence is hard won, especially as she must face skeptical, critical, or uncomprehending audiences: her family thinks she has a duck voice and a weird point of view, and the Americans don't understand her or her family:

> It is the way Chinese sounds, chingchong ugly, to American ears. . . . We make guttural peasant noise and have Ton Duc Thang names you can't remember. And the Chinese can't hear Americans at all; the language is too soft.   (199)

The cultures find each other mutually unintelligible. In the fifth chapter Kingston, like Moon Orchid in the fourth chapter, feels so alien and alienated that she almost loses her voice. She simply cannot find a way to reach any audience. But by finishing her mother's story at the end of the book, she shows that she has been able to meet one of the challenges of writing—to maintain her own voice and point of view without ignoring the influences of parents, culture, and background.

Early in our class reading of *The Woman Warrior*, we discuss the audience for whom the book is intended—and students often disagree on who the primary audience is. We look at scenes in the book in which writing or some other sort of composition occurs: carving grievances on Fa Mu Lan's back (writing as reporting); Brave Orchid's stories of life in China (preservation and instruction); Kingston's various versions of the drowned aunt's story (writing as exploration); Ts'ai Yen's songs (bridging gaps, creating something new). Students discuss how the audience and purpose affect each kind of writing.

It is useful to examine closely in class a short passage from the book to see how style and voice work together. I encourage students to model a passage of their own from a paragraph of Kingston's; if nothing else, they see how difficult she is to imitate. Near the end of the term, I have students try to reread their journals as if the students were outsiders who had just found the journals; I then invite them to piece together a description of the person who had written the entries. In journals or on exams they sometimes write imaginary dialogues between themselves and Kingston or between Kingston and another author we have studied. I find that these impromptu dialogues often capture her voice more authentically and cleverly than the modeling assignments. These dialogic exercises often result in surprises, new insights, and syntheses. When these things occur, students may have an insider's sense of what happens in *The Woman Warrior* when Kingston creates a new version of her life out of the interaction of various voices and points of view.

A good assignment for a formal, revised essay can draw together these ideas about vision and voice. I have adapted a colleague's idea for a "mythical ancestor" paper. Students write about a relative whom they know only (or mainly) through stories, comments, and reports—not firsthand. (If students find it impossible to write about a relative, a member of the community will do. Students who wish to write about a living grandparent they know well should write about that person's youth.) The ancestors are considered "mythical" because they are known mainly through stories and because their deeds are important in some way to the family, community, or culture. Students should write about the ancestor for an audience who does not know their family, culture, or ethnic background. In preparing for this assignment, students can interview family members and others, check libraries and archives, look at old pictures, read diaries and letters. Their task is to "infer the dragon" and convey their inferences in vivid detail to an uninitiated audience. Response groups have been valuable in supplying this audience.

I do not mean to imply that the class uses *The Woman Warrior* only for the help it gives us with writing. Students are also interested in discussing the people, the social problems, the humor, and other aspects of the work. By the same token, a class does not have to be doing narrative or autobiographical writing to benefit from a study of the writing and writing-related issues within *The Woman Warrior*. Finally, to emphasize the ideas of varying versions of stories, distinctive voices, uses of contraries, and writing for different audiences and purposes, I find it useful to compare *The Woman Warrior* with at least one other book, perhaps one of those I mentioned at the beginning of this essay or perhaps a novel like *The Joy Luck Club*, by Amy Tan.

The Woman Warrior
in the History Classroom

Paul W. McBride

Document makers and signers skew history to their liking. They entice the historian to interpret history through their eyes. Often the historian writes as though the fears, hopes, and sympathies of the document signers were representative of his or her own era or as if their friends and enemies were the historian's own. At times, in *Invisible Man*, Ralph Ellison seems to speak directly to historians. He poses these questions: What if historical records and documents serve as blinders that allow the historian to see only a tiny portion of historical reality? What if they camouflage or altogether conceal the accounts of those

> birds of passage who were too obscure for learned classification, too silent for the most sensitive recorders of sound, of natures too ambiguous for the most ambiguous words and too distant from the centers of historical decisions to sign or even to applaud the signers of historical documents? We who write no novels, histories or other books. What about us? (429)

Ellison's unsettling challenge is difficult to dismiss or answer. History has been written largely by elites and about elites. Only after the GI Bill of Rights pluralized academia was there an attempt to study common Americans and the nation's ethnic underpinnings. Scholarship since the 1940s has created a more balanced awareness of the complexity of the American mosaic. The most imaginative historians have dared to sketch the contours of America's ethnic macrocosmology. They include Marcus Lee Hansen, Oscar Handlin, John Higham, Herbert Gutman, Thomas Sowell, Thomas Archdeacon, John Bodnar, and others. These scholars have refined our understanding of the overarching issues in ethnic history. What is ethnicity and how does it work? Which factors contribute to assimilation and which retard it? Has the United States developed into a melting pot or a tossed salad? Has the success of ethnic Americans depended primarily on Turnerian or non-Turnerian principles? That is, have the dominant factors determining the success of various ethnic groups been those of the American (urban) environment or the "human capital" the immigrants brought with them? The sources that have allowed historians to systematically assess these macro issues have been educational records, mobility statistics, the minutes of Americanization groups, political party records, census reports, church records, city directories, and similar materials. Dozens of historians, specialists in particular ethnic groups, have demonstrated how their group does or does not fit one or another macrointerpretation.

Despite the democratization of the history profession and the sophistication of postwar analysis on the larger issues, historians are still stymied by microcosmological questions. They haltingly confront the history of the inarticulate. "Birds of passage" bequeath few documents or eloquent pronouncements. Their pleadings are often in languages historians have not translated. Contemporaries seldom argued the cause of people "too distant," and few historians do so today. Uncovering and writing the history of the muffled masses remains an intricate and important problem of the historians' craft.

What Americanizers intended is amply documented. What the immigrants thought as they attended Americanization classes is far more elusive. How many Italian women married non-Italians or finished high school between 1900 and 1920, for instance, is statistically established. How they reacted to stringent chaperonage or to educational discouragement remains hidden, undocumented.

Thus historians have not penetrated ethnic microcosmology, the everyday life of ethnic Americans—what they thought, feared, laughed at, cried about, and understood. There are precious few sources to help unlock these mysteries. How are historians to comprehend, much less teach, truth hidden beyond or beneath the comfortable crutch of documentation?

Luckily, in the field of ethnic studies, historians have valuable allies in writers emerging from the immigrant experience. The drama of the most monumental human migration in history, fifty million since 1800, has inspired hundreds of novelists and memoirists to record the strivings, failures, and successes of their people and themselves. Their works reveal the inner dimensions, the heart and viscera of their people. The best ethnic writers, unconstrained by the lack of historical documents, uncover the ideals and feelings of people who were unrenowned, silent, and invisible.

Of course, by disclosing the inner dimensions of the ethnic experience, writers explore the intersection where historical forces act on and are perceived by those who endure them. Historians have written volumes about the patriarchal dynamics of culture, for example, but it remains to ethnic novelists and memoirists, such as Maxine Hong Kingston, to invite the reader into the mind of a person who has lived within (and outside of) the bounds of such a culture. Not only does Kingston represent microhistory; she creatively explains the subjective reality of that history.

An intriguing, yet largely undescribed, aspect of United States ethnic history has been the female experience. That is not to say that ethnicians have ignored women, but rather that their writings have left unexamined their microcosmology. Historians have written extensive macrohistories of women but only scattered microhistories.

Moreover, male novelists have not been much more successful than historians in dealing with the female side of the ethnic experience. To be sure, some of the finest male writers hint at their own lack of understanding. In his famous battle royal chapter, for instance, Ellison allows his protagonist to observe the stripper purchased to entertain the crowd of rowdy good old boys. He saw "terror and disgust in her eyes, almost like my own terror and that which I saw in some of the other boys" (20). Ellison implies that women, like blacks, are invisible to their oppressors. However, since he develops female characters only superficially, the depth of his comparison is left to conjecture.

Like Ellison, most male ethnic writers allow women only bit parts, but some have made them central characters. Mario Puzo's novel about Italian American family life, *The Fortunate Pilgrim*, for example, revolves around the inextinguishable Lucia Santa Angeluzzi Corbo, mother extraordinaire, who protects and defends her family against all the corrosive effects of satanic America. Her daughter, Octavia, harboring American ambitions, announces plans to quit her job to seek a professional career. She defends her request by citing the insidious promise of the Declaration of Independence—the right to the pursuit of happiness. Her mother replies with utter contempt, "You want to be happy. . . . Thank God you are alive" (15). By the end of the novel, because of Lucia Santa's unyielding will, Octavia remains quintessentially Italian.

The image of woman as mother-defender of ethnic culture is echoed in O. E. Rolvaag's *Giants in the Earth*, in which the central character is Beret, wife of Per Hansa, for whom America represents endless accomplishment and challenge. But for Beret there is little joy in her husband's success. She sees her values eroded by the savagery of the American wilderness and the allure of American acquisitiveness. Her native land had given her parental love, stability, and cultural certainty, all of which she had forsaken to follow the love of her life, Per Hansa. While he pursues his American dream, she remains tormented by her memories of Norway. Despite the opportunity of the New World, Beret longs for the comfort and assurance of the Old. At novel's end, Per Hansa perishes in a vicious snowstorm while Beret remains the cultural anchor of her family.

Both Puzo and Rolvaag depict the ethnic woman as mother, protector of established traditions, and fountain of cultural permanence. This interpretation of the relationship between women and culture reveals more about how men view women than about how women view themselves or how they really are. It imparts to women characteristics that men most admire and expect; these mothers and wives accept and even savor their traditional images and roles. Male writers thus tend to ascribe to women a voluntary preoccupation with the dimensions and demands of their culture.

Many female ethnic writers have directly challenged the male view of the relationship between women and their traditional cultures. These writers portray a more complex and ambiguous, even hostile, association. They survey the world of the unattached woman and the unfulfilled wife and mother. Their female characters brim with inner aspirations and defiant self-definitions.

Few writers have voiced female aspirations more forcefully than Maxine Hong Kingston. In *The Woman Warrior* she deftly displays the magnitude of Chinese culture as well as her own unmistakable ambivalence toward it. She chronicles her sometimes painful flight from her patriarchal culture, her reluctant but inexorable reconciliation with much of her past, and the course of her inner journey of self-discovery.

Kingston excavates the invisible and allows a glimpse of the personal and microhistorical truth about which documents say so little. She begins with the story of No Name Woman, her father's only sister, whose name was never mentioned because of the disgrace she had brought on the family in China. The men of the family headed west, where they could "fumble without detection" ancient Chinese traditions. No Name Woman, however, remained to "keep the traditional ways . . . to maintain the past against the flood, safe for returning" (9). Thus her aunt was given in marriage to a villager whom she had met only on her wedding day and with whom she had sexual relations only once before he departed for the Gold Mountain. Like other brides in "hurry-up weddings," she would provide her husband a reason to return, and she would shield Chinese traditions from the forces of the future (1).

No Name Woman betrayed her trust. To make herself enticing, different from other married women, she "often worked at herself in the mirror" and "combed individuality into her bob" (10). Years after the departure of her day-long husband, she became pregnant, and her husband's family exiled her in disgrace to her family's home. The villagers raided her home, destroying the family's belongings to chastise her for "acting as if she could have a private life, secret and apart from them" (14). The morning after giving birth to her child in the pigsty, she walked to the well and drowned herself and her child, "probably a girl; there is some hope of forgiveness for boys" (18).

Narrating the story of the rebellious No Name Woman was itself an act of rebellion. Kingston had been forbidden to tell anyone. By her silence, she had joined in her aunt's punishment—denial that she had ever lived. Yet the author is fully aware of the daring of her opening chapter. She writes, "My aunt haunts me—her ghost drawn to me because now, after fifty years of neglect, I alone devote pages of paper to her, though not origamied into houses and clothes" (19). Indeed, Kingston's memoir is a tribute to all women without identities who have challenged the restraints of their cultures, women who have asserted their own personhood. It puts historians and others on notice that the world of Chinese women is peopled with more than mother figures and culture nurturers.

Kingston also announces that her inner yearnings have contrasted sharply with her traditions. She has not easily accepted the dictates of Chinese society. How could she feel comfortable as part of a culture that holds women worthless? It was her mother, Brave Orchid, an imposing storyteller, who told Kingston the story of No Name Woman and commanded her complicity in keeping it secret. As a midwife in China, Brave Orchid later explained to her daughter, she would prepare a dish of ashes for all birthings in case the newborn was a girl. She had said, "The midwife or a relative would take the back of a girl baby's head in her hand and turn her face into the ashes. . . . It was very easy" (101).

In adulthood, Kingston became an American success, a teacher, and an award-winning writer. Yet she recalls vividly the power of her mother's stories and the assault they made upon her sense of self:

> From afar I can believe my family loves me fundamentally. They only say, "When fishing for treasures in the flood, be careful not to pull in girls," because that is what one says about daughters. But I watched such words come out of my own mother's and father's mouths; I looked at their ink drawing of poor people snagging their neighbor's flotage with long flood hooks and pushing the girl babies on down the river. And I had to get out of hating range. (62)

Such bitter sentiments break the constraints of historical texts and dramatically call into question the traditional image of women as complacent couriers of culture.

In her childhood, the stories and sayings translated themselves into everyday indignities that did not escape Kingston's notice. When Great Uncle visited, he invited the children to accompany him on the weekend grocery trip. The children eagerly answered his invitation. However, Kingston reports, "When he heard girls' voices, he turned on us and roared, 'No girls!' and left my sisters and me hanging our coats back up, not looking at one another" (55). The narrator was acutely aware that, to her parents, she and her sisters were less precious, less an occasion of joy, than her brothers. The neighbors in Chinatown met her and her sister with sidelong glances, whispering their pity for parents who had two daughters and no sons. Only after her brothers were born did that particular indignity stop. But there were new ones, equally galling:

> "Did you roll an egg on *my* face like that when I was born?" "Did you have a full-month party for *me*?" "Did you turn on all the lights?" "Did you send *my* picture to Grandmother?" "Why not? Because I'm a girl? Is that why not?" (55)

The resentment at being "one more girl who couldn't be sold" (62), at being constantly reminded of her worthlessness, propels the narrator to issue her own American Declaration of Self-Worth and Independence. Her parents, she thought, were trying to marry her to a particularly undesirable and unattractive Chinese prospect. "I want you to tell that hulk, that gorilla-ape, to go away and never bother us again," she screamed at both her startled parents. After criticizing her parents for their insensitivity, she continued her remarkable outburst of self-assertion: "I can make a living and take care of myself. So you don't have to find me a keeper who's too dumb to know a bad bargain. . . . I am not going to be a slave or a wife. . . . So get that ape out of here" (234–35).

Despite her declaration, her American successes wrapped around her "like a private shawl" (62), her lifelong quest for her own identity, Kingston never escapes the sway, even the love of her ancient culture, her parents, and her ancestors. During a visit home long after she has become a noted author, her mother pleads with her not to leave again. "[H]ow can I bear to have you leave me again?" she cries (118; see also 126). In the end, Kingston concedes that her culture, her ancestral footprint, is inescapable, inexorable, timeless. She admits poignantly, "Before we can leave our parents, they stuff our heads like the suitcases which they jam-pack with homemade underwear" (102). Unable to escape her culture, her past, she does the best she can—she translates it into barbarian, ghost language. Her concluding sentence is, "It translated well" (243).

What are we historians to make of the wizardry of *The Woman Warrior*? Kingston ushers us into the otherwise inaccessible domain where micro- and macrohistory meet, where the individual understands and reacts to the relentless forces of history. She is acutely aware of her ability to intensify historical sensitivity. "Long ago in China," she teases,

> knot-makers tied string into buttons and frogs, and rope into bell pulls. There was one knot so complicated that it blinded the knot-maker. Finally, an emperor outlawed this cruel knot. . . . If I had lived in China, I would have been an outlaw knot-maker.   (190)

Kingston had just finished her dazzling chapter "At the Western Palace." In fifty-five magic pages, she tells the story of Brave Orchid's reunion with her sister, Moon Orchid, just arrived from China after a separation of thirty years. Subsequently, Moon Orchid is unable to endure the transplantation to the United States. Her mental health deteriorates until she spends her final months confined to an institution. The distance from one world to another, from one age to another, from one culture to another is too foreboding for her nonmigratory soul. The chapter is a funny, tragic tour de force of the unsuspected and unbridgeable immensities between East and West. It also reveals the magnetism of culture, both to those unconsciously caught in its force, like Moon Orchid, and to those, like Kingston, who are attempting to break free of it.

The author admits that she created her intricate account of Moon Orchid's tragedy from a spare remark that her brother had made to her sister. She writes, "His version of the story may be better than mine because of its bareness, not twisted into designs. The hearer can carry it tucked away without it taking up much room" (189–90). But Kingston's tangled tale explores the enormity of Chinese culture and the two old sisters caught in its vortex. Her book is the forbidden knot that both informs and challenges the historian.

The author powerfully portrays the enigmatic and labyrinthine relation between women and culture. Mothers are more than nurturers: they are also rebels and warriors. They sustain the very culture that they renounce. Yet paradoxically, no matter how far the quest for self propels them, they return, like swallows, to their past, their ancestral ways.

In my courses Ethnic America and Learning History through Immigrant and Ethnic Literature, I have been captivated by the common themes running through the literature of female ethnic writers, particularly the assertion of personal independence accompanied by eventual cultural conciliation. In the writings of many female writers there appears a Declaration of Independence scene. For instance, in *Bread Givers*, Anzia Yezierska's novel of Lower East Side Jewish life, the protagonist, Sara, announces to her tyrant father, Reb Smolinsky, that she intends to leave home and his despotism. She shouts, "I'm smart enough to look out for myself. It's a new life now. In America, women don't need men to boss them" (137–38). Like Kingston, however, Sara discovers that escape from history, from culture, is impossible. She leaves home, completes high school while working full time, graduates from college, and becomes an honored teacher—in the old neighborhood, where she plans to marry her Jewish principal, who convinces her to allow her father to live with them. At novel's end, father, unrepentant, chants prayers while, resigned to reconcile with her past, Sara concedes, "It wasn't just my father, but the generations who made my father whose weight is still upon me" (297).

Women ethnic writers like Kingston and Yezierska (one might also consult Zora Neale Hurston's poetic *Their Eyes Were Watching God*) capture both macro- and microhistorical truths about the female experience. They provide insight into their culture and into their ambiguous relationship with the roles and limitations it imposes on them. But one's heritage is not easily transcended, and the attempt often produces guilt and uneasiness. To my knowledge, no historian of women in the United States or of immigration examines these ambiguous topics with nearly the richness and complexity of the novelists and memoirists. The demands of historical documentation deny access to the minds of those who have lived the ethnic experience.

In the cogently argued *Madwoman in the Attic*, the authors conclude that the nineteenth-century female writer found it difficult to assert selfhood

because she first had to define it in the face of "all those patriarchal definitions that intervene between herself and herself" (Gilbert and Gubar 17).
In ethnic writing generally, something of the same dynamic of self-definition
is at work. The environment of the United States boldly invites exploration
and self-discovery by breaking down ethnic customs and by encouraging
confrontation with traditional authority. America's bewitching promise of the
right to personal happiness and its sustained faith in individualism beckon
all immigrants, male and female alike, to discover, even to create, their own
personalities. Consequently, in the world of female ethnic writers, there
has been little room for selfless characters like Lucia Santa or Beret. The
authors of *The Madwoman in the Attic* observed that "to be selfless is not
only to be noble, it is to be dead. A life that has no story . . . is really a life
of death, a death-in-life. . . . [A woman who has] died to her own desires,
her own self, her own life, leads a posthumous existence in her own lifetime"
(25). Such has not been the case of female American ethnic writers or the
women who inhabit their writings.

Teaching *The Woman Warrior* to High School and Community College Students

Marlyn Peterson and Deirdre Lashgari

Despite differences in age and experience, high school and community college students in required general literature courses are often both excited and intimidated by *The Woman Warrior*. They identify with some aspects of the narrator's silencing and her quest to define herself. At the same time, they are often troubled by the way the narrative makes it hard to decide what is and is not "true," and they find its cultural otherness disturbing.

The interplay between these two responses, one of recognition and one of alienation, can deepen students' awareness both as readers and as members of a diverse society. The aspects of the book that initially seem disconcerting, its formal complexity and cultural unfamiliarity, give the students valuable tools for examining their personal and cultural identity. When they find validation for their own experiences, students are better able to enter imaginatively into the unknown territory of others.

In teaching, it is tempting to work outward from familiar ground, to minimize the students' discomfort by presenting as much contextual information as possible before they begin to read. Instead, we propose to let the students encounter the book without that reassuring preparation. As they wrestle with what troubles or confuses them, they can begin dismantling the protective fences they carry in their minds.

In this essay, we suggest ways to work with reader alienation, helping students to move from the unfamiliar to the familiar and back again, to find known ground in what had seemed strange and unsettling, and to learn to see their ethnic traditions with new eyes. We focus on three chapters—"No Name Woman," "White Tigers," and "A Song for a Barbarian Reed Pipe" —defining specific problems in each, suggesting exercises that can turn those problems into advantages, and discussing some results and implications of these approaches. Although our suggestions are drawn from the experiences of several teachers and students, we present them in the context of a hypothetical composite class—taught by "us"—that typifies both high school and community college student responses to the work.

In reading *The Woman Warrior*, students snag on form and content both. We have found it useful to begin with form, focusing on the way two kinds of talk-story, the cautionary tale and the heroic quest, confuse fiction and reality for the reader as they do for the narrator.

The initial assignment asks the students to read the first two chapters. In class, we ask them to list specific passages they find confusing. As they explore these problematic passages, students discover a peculiar shift in the narrator's control over the text. In "No Name Woman" the narrator articulates her frustration as she tries to make "truth" emerge from her mother's sketchy story and leads the reader through her successive attempts to fill in missing details. Here, although it is not clear what is true, the reader shares the narrator's confusion and thus feels, in some sense, on solid ground.

Toward the end of the first chapter, there are progressively fewer signposts, and the second chapter becomes even more complex. Instead of talking about the way fiction blurs into reality, as in "No Name Woman," here the narrator makes the reader experience the confusion directly. Chinese students recognize the Fa Mu Lan legend immediately; according to Jane Young, it is as familiar to them as stories about George Washington are to children in the United States. Even students unfamiliar with the legend realize fairly quickly that the narrator's account of her childhood training as hero cannot be taken literally. What they resent is not that they are being given a fiction but that the narrator does not warn them of the transition. Again, the sense that they are not in control, that the work is moving in directions they are not prepared for, often leads to a feeling of alienation.

We invite the class to use that sense of discomfort to fuel discovery. Asked to examine the first two paragraphs of "White Tigers," students notice how the chapter begins by dancing among talk-story of heroic women (history? legend?), Brave Orchid's chant of Fa Mu Lan, Sunday movies, and the child's dreams. At that point we ask the students, in reading the next few paragraphs, to look closely at the shifts in verb form between the mother's statement that her daughter "would grow up a wife and a slave" (24) and the words "[t]he door opened" (25) on the next page. They realize then that the narrator has employed a deft sleight of hand, using various and ambiguous meanings of "would" to slide into what seems a straightforward past tense "history" of the narrator's life.

As we discuss how the talk-story functions in Chinese culture, students see how the narrator has made them share her frustration and confusion in trying to sift out the truth. We ask the students to do freewrites (later expanded) on "stories" in their own families in which literal truth was embellished or altered, or fantasy presented as truth, in ways that were confusing to them as children. As students share these stories with one another, they find the Chinese use of talk-story less strange, and they gain confidence in their ability to weave a pattern that makes sense of the tangled threads of family tradition and individual experience.

After dealing with formal issues through a focus on genre in the first two chapters, we find it useful to ask the students to reread "No Name Woman," this time exploring what the talk-story is saying. Because the students have confronted their initial resistance to the story and can now understand why they had trouble figuring out what was "true," they can approach the second reading with less alienation and a greater sense of control. This reading will be more sophisticated, more alert to the way in which the point of view of speaker and listener makes it hard to define "truth."

Students can now examine the cultural "strangeness" they have encountered so far in the book, both in the aunt's village in China and in contemporary Chinese American experience. It is helpful here to narrow the consideration of "culture" to gender role differences, specifically the constraints a society places on its female members. We begin by asking students to brainstorm as a group (with one person jotting ideas down on the board) in response to the following questions: (1) What attitudes toward the "proper" female role do you find in this chapter? (2) Where exactly in the text are these ideas expressed? Students tend first to focus on the attitudes implied in the actions of the aunt's neighbors and family. Looking further, they realize that there are attitudes toward the female role implicit in the mother's telling of this cautionary tale in the first place, in the child's response to the tale, in the adult narrator's various responses, and, finally, in the author's shaping of the text.

After reading aloud parts of "No Name Woman" as an example of a cautionary tale for females, students (European American and Chinese American alike) express outrage at the villagers' reaction to the aunt's pregnancy. Their alienation in this case is an illusory superiority: "How *could* they . . . !" "That could never happen *here*!" By pointing out the narrator's remark that "[a]dultery, perhaps only a mistake during good times, became a crime when the village needed food" (15), we help them see that the villagers' actions are rooted in a specific social, economic, and historic context (Kotite-Young).

Male students often sit back, feeling that the book's emphasis on women does not especially concern them. One way of dealing with their distancing is to read aloud the short chapter "On Discovery" from *China Men* as a cautionary tale for males. Suddenly the issues in *The Woman Warrior* hit home. The male students have a hard time listening to the tale of a man who is taken prisoner by a court of women, who has his feet bound and his eyebrows plucked, and who is treated as both decoration and servant. Their discomfort energizes the ensuing discussion of male and female roles in both books, as well as in contemporary United States society (Kotite-Young).

An effective exercise is for students to brainstorm about cautionary injunctions in their own families and society, using the formula "If you do *x*, then *y* will happen." When they are asked to make up their own cautionary tales, they often demonstrate with powerful immediacy their understanding of this mode of social constraint (Kotite-Young).

An important aspect of the cautionary tale, as of the talk-story generally, is its silences—what is left unsaid. During class discussion, students realize that as reader-participants they play a role akin to that of the narrator, as they uneasily juggle what they think they know and what they try to guess.

Returning to the broader discussion of content, we write on the board: "Define the role of women in Chinese culture." After the students have jotted down answers for a few minutes, we ask, "What do you need to know in order to answer this question accurately?" Further questions—What is culture? What does it encompass? *Which* Chinese culture? Where? (in main-land China? Taiwan? San Francisco?) When? What class? Urban or rural? —jolt them into realizing the unexamined assumptions underlying their responses to the initial question.

At this point, a few students can do some quick research and report on what they've found to the class, with each perhaps responsible for a different time period or place. The "three obediences" and "four virtues" of women under Confucian doctrine serve as a useful statement of ideology against which actual practices in specific cultures can be compared:

> The three obediences were "obedience to the father when yet un-married, obedience to the husband when married, and obedience to the sons when widowed." . . . The four virtues were: 1) "woman's ethics," meaning a woman must know her place and act in every way in compliance with the old ethical code; 2) "woman's speech," meaning a woman must not talk too much, taking care not to bore people; 3) "woman's appearance," meaning a woman must pay attention to adorn-ing herself with a view to pleasing the opposite sex; and 4) "woman's chore," meaning a woman must willingly do all the chores in the house.   (Tsai 157–58)

The information the students bring back helps them appreciate the differ-ences between the values a society preaches and those it practices, as well as the obvious dissimilarities from one cultural context to another.

It is useful to bring the discussion closer to home with an exercise that gives students an opportunity to experience the gender role assumptions shaping their own lives (Devlin). Men and women in the class are divided into separate groups to discuss, and then list on paper, the ways their lives would be different if they had been born a member of the opposite sex. Each group contains one observer-recorder of the opposite sex, whose task is to take notes, including surreptitious impressions of group dynamics. According to Pamela Devlin:

> The boys get really silly about it. They think it's frivolous to be a female, and they'll say, "I'll have to spend five hours every morning putting on my makeup." The girls get into critical issues for them: "I would be able to walk around at night and not be afraid." "I would be able to go to the bathroom wherever I wanted and not have to hassle with it." That may seem frivolous, but it's a comment about freedom. This [exercise] lets the students see that they do have clearly defined male and female roles.

In different ways, the discussion on form and the exploration of sex roles helps lessen the distance the students tend to feel initially between self and "other"—male/female; European American/Chinese American. A brief free-writing exercise such as the following can reinforce this shift in point of view:

> Describe some part of your daily routine from the perspective of some-one who has never seen behavior like it before, such as an anthro-pologist from a planet in the Andromeda Galaxy who has just been transported back in a time machine to the late twentieth-century United States.   (Horace Miner's anthropological parody "Body Ritual among the Nacirema" can provide an effective model.)

As students come to see what is "strange" in their own cultural experience, they can better recognize what is in fact familiar in the experiences portrayed in the text.

The theme of silencing in *The Woman Warrior* evokes considerable recognition. Still, students have trouble with the scene in which the narrator, as a child, torments the "silent girl" to try to force her to speak. Although they identify to some extent with the narrator's experience, their initial reaction is that her behavior is extreme, violent, and inexplicable.

Here again, a solution to the problem is to bridge the gulf between the alien and the known, allowing students to acknowledge their own experience of the pain of being silenced and to hear the diverse experiences of fellow students. Two exercises in particular have proved valuable:

1. guided visualization, followed by freewriting, in which each student returns to a real or imagined "grandmother's house" and asks the grand-mother what it was like for her growing up female (adapted from Folsom);
2. freewriting, in which the assignment is to "recall or imagine a specific incident in your life in which you felt silenced (that is, were prevented from expressing yourself by forces outside or within yourself)."

Sharing the freewritings in dyads or small groups, so that students can hear how other classmates have been silenced, enables them to see that the dynamics of silencing are individual as well as macrocultural.

These exercises can form the basis for a discussion of "A Song for a Bar-barian Reed Pipe," focusing on the confrontation with the "silent girl" and the reasons why it was so desperately important to the narrator that her class-mate speak. The issue is the constraining effect not only of gender but also of the tension between two cultures. It can be valuable here to bring in other voices of Asian American writers as they question what it means to be "American"—poetry by Diana Chang and Mitsuye Yamada; sociological accounts like Judy Yung's *Chinese Women of America* (88); Kingston's own af-firmation of herself as "American" in an essay she published when she was fifteen (Yu 95), and her insistence, in a talk, on the uniquely individual as well as cultural threads that weave themselves into her identity ("Tripmaster").

This approach to the issue of silencing establishes familiar ground by drawing from personal experience, both cultural and individual. It also clarifies differences instead of glossing over them by recognizing the unique cultural configuration of each instance of silencing. In addition, it is important to acknowledge that many people live comfortably within their culture's norms without feeling silenced. As one Chinese American student has pointed out, "A person shaped by Chinese culture doesn't see herself as having been silenced until she has looked at the culture from the outside" (Young). The difficult paradox Young expresses here is crucial to the immigrant experience. She acknowledges the confusion of identity that results when a person belongs to two or more contradictory cultures. At the same time, she insists that each of us, including herself, make an effort to see Chinese values from inside, through the eyes of a woman who wears them as a comfortable and unquestioned skin.

As two young Iranian women expressed it, the task is to "appreciate both ways, without judging," even while one accepts individual responsibility for making hard choices, weaving a unique sense of self from a variety of threads (Amanpour and Molanazadeh). This challenge is particularly apparent for the immigrant. But each of us faces a similar challenge at times of great change. Perhaps the high school or young community college student on the verge of adulthood, as well as the returning student risking major transitions in midlife, is especially ready to explore such a frightening and freeing dual vision. Our responsibility as teachers is to help each of our students develop this empowering perspective: the ability to see one's own cultural "givens" with the eyes of a stranger and also to understand how natural these values appear to a person who has known nothing else.

One effective way to bring closure to the study of *The Woman Warrior* is through visual presentations embodying insights the students have gained. Students who prefer to work on their own might prepare an individual "gathering": a graphic collage, perhaps including words, that reflects aspects of gender socialization in their own culture; images defining the cultural threads from which they weave their sense of self; or a "map" of their lives—actual and projected—as heroic journeys (Kotite-Young).

Students can also create a collective articulation of what the text has meant to them. In one group project, students first write down their favorite quotes from each chapter, ones they feel best represent what *The Woman Warrior* is about. The class divides then into groups, where members decide which of the quotes they want to use. Next they devise a graphic way of representing their experience of the book, combining the quotes with symbol, color, and form to give body to their ideas. When the activity is finished, each group has a chance to display its project and explain it, describing what the symbols mean to their group and how the quotes fit. Students not adept at written interpretation are often remarkably skilled at expressing their understanding of the book visually and orally (Devlin).

Especially for young and returning students, who may be uncomfortable with the idea of "literature," our experiential approach to the book has several advantages: it gives students a chance to use discomfort and confusion as a mode of discovery; it sharpens their understanding of narrative point of view and the way talk-story, in any society, requires active participation to discern what is "true"; and it helps students develop a multicultural consciousness, as they look at their own and others' cultures from new perspectives. In particular, as students work from alienation to recognition, they discover a powerful catalyst for personal awareness, and an openness to what had seemed strange and threatening in literature and life.

CRITICAL CONTEXTS: GENRE, THEMES, FORM

The Woman Warrior as Postmodern Autobiography

Marilyn Yalom

Any label affixed to Maxine Hong Kingston will invariably fail to encompass the multifaceted nature of her work. When asked if she was a "feminist," Kingston once replied that she had always been a feminist, but that "feminism is just one modern political stance, like being an ethnic writer. One has to have an even larger vision" (Islas 16). Thus it is with caution that I refer to her autobiography as "postmodern," for to privilege that catchword is to deny others, equally applicable.

Yet it is useful to consider *The Woman Warrior* (as well as *China Men* and *Tripmaster Monkey*) in terms of postmodernism, since that particular word denotes a complex aesthetics that tends to be overlooked in critiques of Kingston's writing. Moreover, it places Kingston where she should be placed—at the vortex of the most vital and innovative literary currents of the late twentieth century.

Postmodernism has, in the words of Ihab Hassan, "become a current trope of tendencies in theater, dance, music, art, and architecture; in literature and criticism; in philosophy, psychoanalysis, and historiography; in cybernetic technologies; and even in the sciences, which are making 'new alliances' with humanistic thought" (304). Those tendencies, when embodied in literature, form a cluster of what Hassan calls "indeterminacies"—that is, expressions of openness, pluralism, marginality, difference, discontinuity,

incoherence, fragmentation, absence, skepticism, irony, playfulness, ambiguity, chance, popular culture, heterogeneity, circularity, and "polymorphous" diffusion, in contrast to their opposites (closed systems, single authority,
centeredness, sameness, continuity, coherence, wholeness, presence, certainty, sincerity, seriousness, design, high culture, hierarchy, and "phallic"
linearity). This dichotomy, by no means exhaustive or universal, helps to
differentiate the likes of Maxine Hong Kingston, John Barth, John Fowles,
E. L. Doctorow, and Thomas Pynchon from their modernist predecessors
(for example, Katherine Anne Porter and Ernest Hemingway) as well as from
their contemporaries more solidly anchored in the canon stretching from
modernism back to Romanticism (for example, John Updike, Robertson Davies,
and Anne Tyler).

Another way to approach postmodern works in general, and *The Woman
Warrior* in particular, is to ask questions about the nature of representation:
How does the author present herself and her world? Is the process mimetic
and "realistic," a direct rendering of the writing subject's consciousness and
a mirroring of the empirical world she inhabits? Or is representation mediated by a literary consciousness whose referential status is uncertain, or
by a framing device (tale within a tale, play within a play) that obtrudes
between the writer and the reader? Does the work offer a seemingly "natural"
sequence of events suggesting an ordered, apprehensible, teleological world,
or does its nonlinear, piecemeal, or circular form suggest the arbitrary rule
of happenstance? Postmodern works are, according to Silvio Gaggi, char-
acterized by "complex, contradictory, sometimes whimsical styles that fly
in the face of the high seriousness and passion of orthodox modernism" (2).
Does the work conclusively resolve its internal conflicts, or does it proble-
matize the issues it raises and open outward toward alternative endings?
In each instance, *The Woman Warrior* corresponds to the second half
of the question: it is marked by a decentering of the author as protagonist
and by the mediating effects of framing narratives, it is informed by an
aesthetics of artifice and ambiguity, and, ultimately, it presents an exemplum
of possibility.

Consider Kingston's use of tales, ballads, legends, and maternal talk-story
as framing mechanisms for the author's personal narrative. Kingston tells
her story through the stories of others—mother, aunts, mythical women
from Chinese poetry and legend. These stories bear a relationship to the
writer as girl and as young woman in that they incarnate various negative
and positive possibilities leading either to mental illness and/or suicide, or
to more felicitous forms of self-expression. (For a fuller study of the negative
possibilities, see Yalom.)

The first, a cautionary tale told by her mother when Kingston began to
menstruate, concerns No Name Woman, an aunt in China who killed herself
and her illegitimate baby following humiliation at the hands of the villagers.

The story of the nameless aunt gives voice to the author's most deep-rooted fears: cruelty and injustice inflicted on women; terror in the face of pregnancy and childbirth, especially out of wedlock; the intermingling of birth, death, and potential madness. The aunt whose name cannot even be pronounced because of the shame she has brought to the family becomes a negative role model in her niece's sense of identity. Yet she cannot simply be abandoned; Kingston assumes responsibility for restoring her aunt's memory, for giving her symbolically the descent line she will never have.

The story of the woman warrior Fa Mu Lan, a legendary character in Chinese literature, provides an alternative image for self-definition. In the original ballad, Fa Mu Lan goes off to fight for the emperor as a replacement for her father; then she returns home to take up the domestic life of a pious daughter. Kingston turns this daughterly figure into a modern, militant heroine—a strong and dangerous swordswoman, a visionary sensitive to ecological concerns, an athlete unaffected by her menstrual days, a feminist wife and mother, a female avenger, the fierce enemy of sexism, racism, and all other forms of injustice. Though Kingston's heroine shares with her literary ancestor the act of replacing her father as conscript during ten years of battle, she is essentially the creation of a twentieth-century Chinese American woman's imagination, a wish-fulfillment fantasy designed to counter the image of the victimized aunt. The chant of Fa Mu Lan that the narrator had sung with her mother, the book pictures and movie images of dangerous Chinese swordswomen she had seen as a child, fuse into a personal scenario, with herself in the leading role. Narrative begetting narrative, lived experience subsuming myth and subsequently becoming myth in its own right, folktales transformed into the personal fictions of childhood, refashioned in adulthood and subsequently subject to the judgment of an authorial "I"— these techniques lead to the confusion felt by many of Kingston's readers. How are we to understand the juxtaposition of different time frames, linguistic modes, and story lines? Do the stories interpenetrate and affect one another? Traditional autobiography does not pose such problems. Typically, it offers a one-plane, chronological account of the author's life history, commencing with birth and ending in middle or old age; the story line follows the evolution of the author-narrator-protagonist as the central character in search of him- or herself.

The reader looking for Kingston in her memoirs will encounter her at first only indirectly, through the framing mechanism of the tale within the tale, each bearing a psychological relationship to the narrator that becomes apparent only in the context of the entire work. The initial chapters produce a sense of disquieting distance, because the author has "decentered" herself and substituted in her place contradictory alter egos. Moreover, their stories are further removed by the overarching presence of Kingston's mother, who relayed them to her daughter in the first place. Various intermediary levels are thus established between the authorial self and her textual incarnations, unlike traditional autobiography, in which the author *of* the text is squarely the protagonist *in* the text (Jay). Kingston has to be found obliquely, in the interstices, *in relation* to the female figures that people her work. (For a discussion of this issue as characteristic of women's autobiographies, see Lidoff, in this volume.)

Most central and most pervasive is the figure of the author's mother, clearly the source of the daughter's contradictory self-images. Mother is the link between Chinese and American culture, the transmitter of myth, the storyteller, the shuttle between dream and reality. "Night after night my mother would talk-story until we fell asleep. I couldn't tell where the stories left off and the dreams began" (24). From her tales of a prewar China, Mother assumes in her daughter's mind the larger-than-life dimensions of a shrewd and dignified doctor whose patients all get well. But how is the daughter to merge that vision with the reality of her mother as laundry worker in Stockton, California? And how can she combine her mother's stories and proverbs conveying female worthlessness ("Better to raise geese than girls") (54) with the legends of female courage and the "great power" she perceives in her "mother talking-story" (24)?

Following the pivotal third chapter, devoted to her mother, Brave Orchid, Kingston turns to the story of her maternal aunt Moon Orchid, the delicate sister who comes to visit from Hong Kong. Unlike Brave Orchid, the tough and fearless, Moon Orchid is a complete misfit in America, ineffectual even in her attempts to communicate with her nieces and nephews or to fold towels in the family laundry. She is pushed over the border into madness by her sister's insistence that she try to recoup the wayward husband, now in Los Angeles, who had abandoned her decades earlier.

Moon Orchid's story, one of the funniest and most pathetic in the book, is also the most overtly realistic. We leave behind a mythical China and encounter a contemporary California processed through the author's eyes and imagination. Although the story is still that of another—Moon Orchid —the narrator seems closer to us because she is no longer distanced by time, space, and a frame tale. The characters in this chapter seem to correspond to Kingston's living kin, flesh-and-blood people we might encounter in the streets of Stockton or Los Angeles. Yet elsewhere the narrator warns us that characters in a text are never the duplicates of living persons: they partake of the freedom to change and be changed that is fundamental to storytelling. Commenting on this matter, Kingston said:

> Students want you to come to class and tell them, . . . "Yes, I have this aunt, Moon Orchid." They want that. But what I want is to see the stories change. Maybe Moon Orchid is like this today, but to-morrow I'm going to tell you something else that she did. I try to keep

> that extra little doubt in the stories. I throw it in. I can't help it, it
> seems to be part of every story.   (Islas 18)

The last chapter, "A Song for a Barbarian Reed Pipe," brings us back to
the ambiguous overlap between art and life. The captive poet Ts'ai Yen,
singing of China to her barbarian captors, offers Kingston a consummate
model of self-realization. Like her revered ancestor, she too will translate
an alien culture to the "barbarians" (Americans) and thereby transcend the
obstacles of language, sex, and station. The final narrative strategy is nothing
less than brilliant. "Here is a story my mother told me, not when I was
young, but recently, when I told her I also talk-story. The beginning is hers,
the ending, mine" (240). Kingston collapses the mother's oral tradition, the
poetry of Ts'ai Yen, and her own written craft. Once again the reader is
reminded that this representation of reality is structured by the language
and forms it invokes. As Gaggi puts it, postmodernism is "art that openly
declares its artifice" (17).

An analogy with postmodern architecture comes readily to mind. As in
certain buildings erected in the 1980s that recall the architecture of the
1920s and 1930s and playfully call attention to their component parts, so too
The Woman Warrior plays with time segments, juxtaposing age-old tales
with twentieth-century experiences and producing the scattered effect of
arbitrary diffusion.

Some critics have singled out the diffuse, disjunctive, fragmentary nature
of women's autobiography as its predominate stylistic mode (Jelinek, *Tradition*). I disagree with this position, for in the history of women's autobiography one finds linear, hierarchical, "phallic" writing, as well as diffuse,
discontinuous, "polymorphous" texts, and sometimes both styles in one. The
disjunctive effect of *The Woman Warrior* is, to my mind, less a result of
Kingston's gender than of a postmodern aesthetics that foregrounds its stylistic devices and makes them an integral part of the work's contents. *Forme*
becomes *fond*, the medium the message. Artistic resolution (if there is to
be any) is wrought out of pluralism and heterogeneity—as in a quilt or
collage—pointing to the possibility of indeterminate combinations. Reading
Kingston, we are constantly reminded that storytelling is an art, to be short-
ened, lengthened, rearranged, parodied, and modified according to the mood
and needs of the author and the times. Kingston is fond of telling the following
illustrative story:

> Did you know that in some Asian cities . . . there are storytellers who
> walk into a restaurant and come to your table and tell you a story.
> Then, just before the climax, they will stop telling the story until you
> pay them. And after you pay them, they tell you the ending. The more
> money you pay, the better the ending!   (Islas 18)

Kingston's skepticism regarding the value of fixed endings and final truths, her delight in ironic twists and unforeseen peripeteia, are expressions of a distinctly postmodern sensibility. Born at the margins of the mainstream United States, bred on the popular lore of Chinese culture, initiated into the mysteries of high-brow American literature, she entered into authorship with an irreverent mistrust for establishment truths and conventions. Stories are made to be retold, art is construction and deconstruction, statement and palindrome, a playful adventure harboring a dangerous threat to the constructs we have heretofore accepted as sacrosanct. At the heart of the two cultures Kingston knows best, there are evils to be exposed: Chinese patriarchy and American racism. As a woman and an ethnic outsider, she is doubly removed from the American literary canon that traditionally privileges white males. Like her exemplars, Fa Mu Lan and Ts'ai Yen, she has to be quick-witted and nimble to find her footing on such hostile terrain. To claim America as her own requires the courage and cunning of Brave Orchid, recast as literary iconoclast. There a blow against chronological time and the illusion of causality! There a thrust against the dual pretense of objectivity and universality! There a parry to deflate the lofty seriousness of high culture and its clichéd fabrications! There a lunge against masculine hegemony! Much that disturbs, disorders, and debunks finds its way into Kingston's art.

If, in 1976, Kingston's first book puzzled her readers, at least there was a recognizable autobiographical persona and a cluster of female characters linked to the author-protagonist. In Kingston's next two works—*China Men* and *Tripmaster Monkey*—women no longer dominated the center stage, and the spotlight was cast on the men.

The grandfathers, fathers, uncles, brothers of *China Men* constitute masculine collectivities that confound distinctions between one's individual blood relatives and the patriarchal heritage common to all Chinese Americans. Throughout the nineteenth century, Chinese sugarcane workers in Hawaii (Sandalwood Mountain) and railroad workers on the continent (Gold Mountain) dutifully sent money to their families in the homeland, sometimes returning themselves and sometimes not. Kingston reworks historical facts and popular legends into an ethnic epic in which heroes and crazy people intermingle and the enemy outsider is the white "demon" rather than the "Indian" or the "Chinaman." The very title of the book, by deconstructing the derogatory "Chinamen" epithet into its two parts, restores dignity to the men of China.

The primary representative of the masculine culture is Kingston's own father, familiarly known as BaBa. In what is perhaps a play on the popular notion that paternity is always uncertain, the prologue "On Fathers" relates how children confuse one Chinese father with another. The narrator concedes that the man she and her siblings had mistaken for their father "probably was not" (6). This anecdote points to the indeterminate tenor of the whole book, its iconoclastic openness to unexpected combinations and multiple interpretations. Born in "1891 or 1903 or 1915" (15), BaBa is remembered as a California gambler and laundry worker, a scholar in China, a dapper dancer in New York. His sometimes dubious history, interspersed with that of his ancestors and sons, is drawn into the piecemeal pattern associated with postmodernism; juxtaposition and subtle interrelationships replace more traditional linear modes of narration.

The last long chapter in *China Men*, "The Brother in Vietnam," is a subversive war saga, with Kingston's youngest sibling incarnating the universal brother, an Everyman in the face of institutionalized violence and racism. Instead of battle exploits, his heroics consist of surviving the Vietnam War without killing anyone. For all its playful ambiguity, *China Men* ends with an unequivocal condemnation of war and a sobering vision of what is morally possible for a man in the late twentieth century.

A decade after *China Men*, Kingston returned to the Vietnam period with a book that dazzles and disconcerts. The protagonist of *Tripmaster Monkey*, a twenty-three-year-old Chinese American English major from the University of California, is male and weird, a 1960s hippie tripping out on drugs and enacting the courting ritual of a monkey in an unsuccessful effort to seduce his Berkeley dream girl. Whereas the reader could sympathetically identify with the narrator and many of the characters in Kingston's two (auto)biographical works, a series of distancing devices over and above his peculiar character traits renders identification with Wittman Ah Sing unlikely. For one thing, the narrator of *Tripmaster Monkey* (a woman?) is situated beyond the sphere of action, like an omniscient seer, and treats the protagonist with irony and mistrust. We are not asked to identify with Wittman or even to like him, though he does entertain us, tease us, goad us into nonconventional possibilities. As in other postmodern novels, identification has gone out of style; indeed, in a play on the traditional terms "minor" and "major" writers, Vladimir Nabokov is reputed to have called those who still identify with characters "minor readers" (Fogel 116).

Like *The Woman Warrior* and *China Men*, *Tripmaster Monkey* draws heavily from popular Chinese literature ("petite histoire" as opposed to "grande histoire") as well as from Western sources. Its Whitmanesque hero combines the exuberance of his American namesake (Ah Sing is clearly a pun on the "I Sing" verses of *Leaves of Grass*), the angst of the German poet Rainer Maria Rilke, and the mischief of the Chinese Monkey King, from Wu Ch'eng-en's seventeenth-century *Monkey* (or *Journey to the West*). The play Wittman is writing is a modern version of Kuan-Chung Lo's *Romance of the Three Kingdoms*. Allusions to several other Chinese novels add to the multileveled parodic effect of the entire book. Story behind story, mask behind mask, the reader is continuously jolted into *Entfremdung* (estrangement from characters and plot)—a far cry from the lyrical directness of Walt Whitman a century earlier.

A more detailed comparison of Kingston's three books would demonstrate the full extent to which a postmodern sensibility suffuses her writing. Her innovative autobiography, *The Woman Warrior*, helped to distend and redefine that genre. *China Men* created a model of collective biography drawn from personal experience, historical facts, and the imaginary. With *Tripmaster Monkey*, Kingston has entered the predominately male arena of postmodern fiction and, in just one novel, secured an enviable position among its leading practitioners.

Autobiography in a Different Voice:
The Woman Warrior and the Question of Genre
Joan Lidoff

Gender does affect genre. Using Nancy Chodorow's and Carol Gilligan's psychological theories, which suggest that women develop a more fluidly bounded sense of self because they do not separate from their mothers in the same way men do, I argue that this less definitive sense of boundary is reflected in women's fiction. The relation of mother and daughter influences women's ways of imagining not only the self but also the whole fabric of social relations and the symbolic structures of literature that express and depend on those conceptions. The concept of fluid boundaries becomes a powerful metaphor for understanding female constructions of experience and for explaining what happens when women write and read.

If we think of a literary work as a set of relations (between author and text, text and reader, individual text and the literary tradition, figures within the text, subjects and symbols), then different perceptions of those relations can alter the forms and functions of literature. In particular, writers' perceptions of the self's involvement with others will influence the style of their work. My premise in thinking about a women's poetics is that specific features of literary style replicate the author's conception of the way relations work. A woman's fiction of identity shapes the identity of her fiction.

The perception of self that arises from the mother-daughter relation assumes that identity is fundamentally relational. As we change our concept of self, we also change the structuring features of narrative. We need a model of literary as well as psychological narrative that doesn't presuppose linear development in stages with a single (oedipal) break that leaves the inner and the earlier definitively behind. We also need a model that allows an ongoing interaction between past and present, inner and outer, self and other. Contemporary writers are developing forms that reflect these altered conceptions.

Women find many ways to soften the absoluteness of a singular narrative identity for their protagonists. In much modern women's fiction, writers have changed the basic structure of major and minor characters. As some characters assume more importance in the fundamental definition of the self, other characters become more important in the literary structure of the narrative; a story that highlights a single protagonist in the foreground, with other characters as background, gives way to structures that foreground more than one character at a time. (This process generates fewer narratives with a single dominant and authoritative point of view.) Women writers often use collective protagonists, multiple points of view, multiple stories.

The collective voice—a voice that defines itself by speaking for others or that interweaves its own story with the stories of others—is one narrative strategy that women writers have found enabling. It allows them to speak for themselves and to express their sense of themselves in unconventional narratives. Fictions of female character show this shaping, and so do non-fictions.

Today women's autobiographies are often written as biography. The early 1980s brought the proliferation of what I call the "forgiving genre": daughters writing their stories as a subplot of their parents'. The story of the other is foreground; the story of the self emerges from the interstices and the background. The film *Entre Nous*, Mary Catherine Bateson's *With a Daughter's Eye*, Kim Chernin's *In My Mother's House*, and Maxine Hong Kingston's *Woman Warrior* fall into this category.

This form of female autobiography validates a speaking voice by placing it in the service of another; it does not place itself center stage but understands itself in context by trying to re-create the parent as other—to see the mother in her own terms and not just as mother. This genre is both more compassionate and more self-effacing than the traditional form of autobiography that dramatizes the self as the starring actor, with other family members cast in minor roles. In each form, the daughter's story emerges, but when the narrative focuses on constructing an inner understanding of the parent, anger and blame are mitigated.

These women writers create singular narrative voices with collective responsibilities; to tell their own stories is to tell those of others as well. The tendency to give others' points of view first before moving to one's own seems to oppose the conventional progress from self-centeredness to an understanding of others. Rather than pursue traditional literary or psychological plots of moral development, these writers follow Gilligan's paradigm in which the self, for women, is the last character to be given full credence. Instead of learning to civilize a selfish self, the writer lets the self emerge from its nexus with others to develop a sense of responsibility for the self as well. Literary genres change when new works no longer focus on a single hero or assert an authoritative point of view.

Kingston's *Woman Warrior* exemplifies the telling of the self's story by the telling of others' stories. The work, which defies classification into conventional genres, is at once autobiography and biography, fiction and mythology, lyric and history. Kingston's story is framed at every point by her mother's talking-story. The author tells us her mother's story, and those of her aunts as well, embedding her own life firmly in the female lineage that stretches back to China. Other women's stories are integral to hers. That multiple story, which often describes suppression of self, and especially of the female self, helps her move from silence to speech to articulate her life story.

The "truth" of narrative is for Kingston as multiple as the elements that make up that narrative: her fantasies, different versions of the same memory

(in her mind and the minds of others), Chinese mythology, historical narrative, and anecdotal reporting hold equal ontological ground in her fiction.
The tracings and shapings of another culture, the inner world of fantasy
ghosts, myths, legends, and daily anecdotes are all powerful, important, and
real in her narration.

Kingston embeds her story in its deeply perceived contexts. Her self-
boundaries encompass otherness to a maximum degree. Both the inner and
the other are given full credence: self includes the realities of other selves
(from their points of view), the reality of a well-stocked inner life, and the
distant culture that lies behind that life. Moving inward moves her outward:
the world of China is imaginatively re-created as it populates her fantasies
and family history.

This ability to assimilate context is consonant with a female habit of perception: the desire and custom of perceiving people and events in relational
contexts rather than as discrete individual actions. In literary terms, this
style of self-perception has led Kingston to create a story of self that book-
sellers do not know how to classify: Is it fiction? nonfiction? autobiography?
novel? The old categories don't hold.

By re-creating and revising generic forms, Kingston constructs a fiction
of the self that questions the construction of the self. She tells her story in
wide cultural context, understanding herself by understanding her mother
and the other women of her family and understanding the family through
its national culture. In ever-expanding circles, she perceives the self as part
of a group system in which an individual's inner world is shaped by family
mythology, which is formed by cultural systems of thought. At the outermost
circumference, she creates an imaginative version of Chinese culture and
the culture clash immigrant Chinese families experience in America.

A fundamental question for the women on the margins of these two cultures concerns the value of individualism. The two cultures differ in the
degree to which personal distinctiveness (and sexuality) is suppressed in the
service of a larger whole—the family, the community—and the degree to
which it is prized and encouraged. The act of telling one's story is an assertion
of individualism that generates intense conflicts. A daughter's loyalty is a
fundamental value within Chinese tradition. In that context, both silence
and telling are acts of betrayal. (To keep her No Name Aunt's story unspoken
betrays the dead. To tell that story, or her own, involves betraying family
secrets.) Avenging family wrongs becomes an act of vengeance against the
family.

Telling one's story in a context that both forbids and requires that telling
creates a difficult dilemma. Mothers are the immediate agents of a child's
socialization; mediated through the mother, immigrant socialization is full
of mixed messages from mixed cultures. Because Kingston's mother ties the
knots of contradictory cultural demands and values, Kingston fights the battle

for self-expression most intimately with her mother. Yet she tells the story from her mother's point of view as well as from her own, thereby framing these conflicts with moral complexity.

Kingston describes incidents from her mother's (and her aunts') perspective, introducing humor and compassion where a description of the same events from her own point of view would have generated complaint or blame. This technique of using multiple points of view produces an irony, like Grace Paley's, of compassion rather than judgment. (Instead of measuring every action by its distance from a single moral standard, Kingston recognizes the legitimacy of more than one point of view, more than one set of standards.)

Multiple narration is fundamental to Kingston's style. Just before the moving tale, in the last section of the book, of her profound struggle against silence, she tells the story of her mother cutting her tongue—either to silence her daughter or to keep her from being tongue-tied (190–91). We never know what her mother's intent is or whether the cutting is real or imagined, fact or family legend. In Kingston we don't get a single account of an incident; we are given alternative conjectures about the same "fact." Questions about reality—madness and sanity, fact and fiction—are reframed in a story about the individual and about storytelling. Memory and conjecture bracket all tellings of the past; fantasy is as real as incident, and any event has multiple interpretations. It is not sanity but madness that has only a single story: "Mad people have only one story," says her mother (184).

The stories Kingston's mother relates and Kingston's story of her mother both have more than one rendition. Her mother said her daughter "would grow up a wife and a slave, but she taught [her] the song of the warrior woman" (24). The mother tells her daughter she's ugly and says it means the opposite:

> "I didn't say you were ugly."
> "You say that all the time."
> "That's what we're supposed to say. That's what Chinese say. We like to say the opposite."   (237)

Her mother is the first power who talks-story. Kingston levels the accusation that she can't tell ghosts from real or fact from fancy because of her mother's way of storytelling. She shouts:

> It's your fault I talk weird. . . . And I don't want to listen to any more of your stories; they have no logic. They scramble me up. You lie with stories. You won't tell me a story and then say, "This is a true story," or, "This is just a story." I can't tell the difference. I don't even know what your real names are. I can't tell what's real and what you make up.   (234–35)

But this very confusion becomes the strength of the daughter's writing voice and the source of her originality. Kingston credits the final story to her mother: "The beginning is hers, the ending, mine" (240). Indeed, her eloquent conquering of silence to tell her story both renounces and uses her mother's storytelling and claims both the continuity and the discontinuity of her story with her mother's.

In the course of the book, as in Kingston's imagination, the figure of her mother changes. As the daughter abandons her fantasy that her mother is a godlike perfect listener who will keep her from existential aloneness, the mother modulates from a heroic fighter of ghosts and a doctor in China to a life-size, cranky old woman whom the narrator loves when she's out of hating distance. Giving up this fantasy of her mother lets Kingston acknowledge "[n]o listener but myself" (237). That recognition enables her to speak.

The multiplicity of Kingston's narrative (multiple central characters, points of view, levels of reality) frames her story as a complex, compassionate, intelligent, and innovative autobiography. In her work, the self-voice is both displaced and enlarged through the telling of others' stories (biographical, legendary, mythic). Kingston's story is all the more powerful for its indirectness. She frames her sadness and anger and the complexity of her struggle from silence to eloquent speech with an acknowledgment of beauty, strengths, and success—her own and those of others. The story she tells is finally both highly individual and broadly cultural, personal and general, unique and shared.

The Woman Warrior demonstrates the strengths of multiplicity as a narrative stance. A difficult story of cultural displacement and immigrant socialization, which could easily have been a tale of mother blaming, instead becomes in Kingston's hands a re-creation of Chinese and Chinese American culture, of both the mother's and the daughter's realities, and of the complex expectations and interactions between the two—from both points of view. Kingston lets us know her pain as well as her triumph but not by blaming her mother.

The complexity of experience that emerges from the multiple points of view is one of Kingston's human triumphs. Her literary triumph is the invention of a narrative style that incorporates many truth dimensions and individual points of view. She makes exemplary use of fantasy, giving it credence as an important reality but not confusing reality with fantasy. She represents fantasy as fantasy even as it widens our definition of reality. This distinction is particularly unusual in portraits of mothers, where an almost universal confusion of fantasy with reality pervades.

The Woman Warrior is an example of female redefining of genre at its best. The responsibility of literary theory, then, is to find a way to talk about this kind of literary production. I suggest that the concept of fluid boundaries can help us accomplish that goal. Focusing on different constructions of the self, as well as on different boundaries between individuals and between and within literary forms, will give us a new way of talking about literature.

A Dialogue with(in) Tradition:
Two Perspectives on *The Woman Warrior*

Colleen Kennedy and Deborah Morse

What follows is not a coauthored article in the usual sense: that is, one voice with two names putting forth a coherent argument. Instead, we discuss, argue about, respond to the different ways each of us teaches *The Woman Warrior*. Deborah Morse stresses the importance of establishing and canonizing this tradition to provide women writers a recognizable and recognized forum. Colleen Kennedy, however, suggests that the notion of any tradition or canon, men's or women's, is necessarily exclusionary and so repeats the very move used against women in the past; consequently, the problem for feminist critics lies in determining who's excluded.

Thus, our debate epitomizes a larger one in feminist criticism. Generally speaking, "feminist discourse" remains in potential, rather than realized, opposition to a discourse construed as "masculine"—that is, one that has historically served the interests of men. Feminists endorsing very diverse theoretical approaches point to the same problem: to articulate opposition to the dominant discourse with any hope of being heard, the feminist writer must gain access to and speak in that same discourse. To give up that discourse is to remain silent, politically ineffective; to adopt it may be to repeat its repressions.

One point we agree on—the narrator of *The Woman Warrior* finds herself in an impossible position, knowing she must speak but aware of the consequences of doing so. Deborah argues that the female artist's voice, which has been struggling to articulate itself throughout the book, will emerge at the end; Colleen asserts that the narrator never resolves her dilemma but instead exploits it to expose the dangers of narrative. Nevertheless, both of us acknowledge that the narrator's accomplishment, however viewed, is a critical construction—just as the "women's tradition," the "great tradition," and "narrative convention" in general are. The text has no ontological status but is precisely the result of critical debate. Our intention, rather than to argue ourselves into a unified position, is to make the terms of the debate explicit.

DM: *The Woman Warrior* can be viewed as a text within the tradition of women's writing—a tradition that is created not only to define women's experience as other but to challenge the patriarchal values in male writing. In my teaching of Kingston's text, I concentrate on its similarities to other female autobiographies, and to other genres as well—particularly the novel—in which women tell their stories. In all forms of autobiography—diaries, journals, fictionalized autobiographies, letters—women focus on the constraints they experience under patriarchy and on the act of writing itself as the most profound resistance to male authority: that of inscribing a female-defined self. Finding her own voice is a triumph over those who wish to silence her, and creating her own forms for the expression of her experience is that "writing the body" of which the French feminists speak.

Kingston's mode of telling her history through imagining and narrating other women's histories is a peculiarly feminine form that masks the self's true story and yet identifies it with the community of women's stories: any woman's story is, in one sense, Everywoman's story, the story of patriarchal oppression. This subversion of masculine forms can be seen in works as different in other respects as the British writer Sarah Scott's utopian novel *Millenium Hall* (1762), the Italian writer Sibilla Aleramo's stark feminist tract, *A Woman* (1906), and the Jewish American writer Kate Simon's lively *Bronx Primitive* (1982), which details her between-the-wars childhood in New York. I also relate Kingston's use of dream-myth-parable to contemporary novels such as Jean Rhys's *Wide Sargasso Sea*, Marilynne Robinson's *Housekeeping*, Rachel Ingalls's *Mrs. Caliban*, and Marguerite Duras's *Lover*, in which the writer creates forms for the depiction of women's experience. Finally, the song of the Chinese poet Ts'ai Yen, which ends *The Woman Warrior*, marks the emergence of the female artist's voice that has been struggling to artic-ulate itself throughout the book. As with, for example, Maya Angelou's singing of the "black national anthem" in *I Know Why the Caged Bird Sings*, this voice is an expression at once of rebellion and of reconciled identity, a song that "translated well" (243).

CK: I teach the book against a tradition still dominated by men's literature. I first introduce students to the terms *discourse* and *marginality*. I use a sheet of notebook paper to explain that to be "on the margin" is to be outside the power structure but still inside the society the power structure dominates (still on the page). *Discourse* presents a greater challenge—I define the term for students as language governed by rules of conversation, whether an informal chat between friends or the all-encompassing "conversations" that comprise the metadisciplines of Western thought. Hence, *discourse* refers to the way we use language to create and convey knowledge; smaller-scale discourses are contained, and frequently marginalized, within large-scale ones. Often the best way to explain the term is through the example of *The Woman Warrior*. The narrator finds herself trapped between two different discourses, neither of which she understands or can control. The power of discourse to create knowledge is evident in the ghost stories Brave Orchid tells. Her children believe these (to the point of believing that the American garbage man is a ghost) until they learn to manipulate the Western discourse, which declares ghosts unreal and so considers Brave Orchid an unreliable source of information.

One discourse common to the two worlds in which the narrator dwells is that of narrative—a discourse of mastery. The narrative voice gains control over the chaos of forces besieging it, wrests control from the discourse of the everyday, and in effect denies the power of that everyday discourse to constitute the narrative voice. Like Milton's Satan or Joyce's Stephen, the narrative voice usurps the right of creation for itself in order to overcome the forces working against it (usually forces associated with quotidian existence and held separate from art). All the narratives within *The Woman Warrior*—the talk-stories Brave Orchid tells as well as the implied conventions of American life (e.g., speak softly and the boys will like you)—share this feature: they demonstrate or promise control. However, control is always control *of*, and it is what the narrator gains her limited control of that keeps her from exerting it with impunity.

The narrator's task is complicated from the start. She is marginal in several ways: she is Chinese in an American culture, American in a Chinese family, and a woman in both. To speak against those who marginalize her, she must learn their languages—both in a literal sense and in the sense of acquiring the discourse, of gaining *recognition*. Re-cognition is the sign of a discourse's power, a thinking-again in terms the discourse recognizes. Hence, opposition is qualified from its outset. However, even as she learns these discourses, she becomes painfully aware of the price of speech. Her mastery of any public discourse threatens to place her, in turn, in the role of oppressor. She adopts that role explicitly in "A Song for a Barbarian Reed Pipe" when she tortures her double, the quiet Chinese girl, to make her speak—not so incidentally, in the very chapter in which Deborah and most critics recognize the artist's voice emerging. More important, she implicitly assumes that role when she is forced to make Chinese women speak—notably her drowned aunt and her mother, Brave Orchid.

As Gayatri Spivak notes:

> When we speak for ourselves, we urge with conviction: the personal is also political. For the rest of the world's women, the sense of whose personal micrology is difficult (though not impossible) for us to acquire, we fall back on a colonialist theory of most efficient information retrieval.   (179)

The Woman Warrior's narrator, speaking in the discourse of narrative, by necessity exposes her mother, her aunts, her sisters to a critical Western gaze. The narrator accuses herself, and so narrative, of this degradation, this reduction to image or stereotype.

However, many critics of *The Woman Warrior* cover up, forget, her self-accusation in the interest of celebrating her song, in order to preserve narrative as a safe (because powerful) mode of female expression. I strongly disagree with Deborah on this point—any woman's story is *not* Everywoman's story. If *one* voice emerges at the end of *The Woman Warrior* (and Western constructions of artistry, as well as critical constructions of *The*

Woman Warrior, stress the unity of the narrative voice), it is certainly not Brave Orchid's. In fact, her voice becomes the discourse to be resisted. Ironically, if what is to be excluded in this book is the patriarchy, it is excluded only as it is embodied in other women.

DM: I view *The Woman Warrior* as a link in a tradition of women's writings fundamentally because I discovered, in teaching Kingston's book in conjunction with other women's texts, that there were striking resemblances among books from varying cultures and historical periods. The perception of a web of women's texts can be enabling rather than exclusionary: instead of determining a rigid canon, it can provide a valid basis on which to connect what might—in a more conventional notion of tradition or canon—seem widely disparate texts. Moreover, Virginia Woolf's notion of a "room" for women in literary history presupposes the need to search out a literary tradition, for we "think back through our mothers if we are women" (79).

The legacy of oppression of women throughout history informs women's writings across cultures and across centuries. Women's voices tend to subvert the forms in which male discourse is carried on and thus to break its patterns of repression. One of the best examples is the nonlinear form in which many women's texts—autobiographies as well as novels—are written. Instead of focusing on the development of one life—the author's—as male autobiography traditionally does, the work is a series of stories about other women told either by the narrator or by the women themselves. The result is a sense of identification with other women for both narrator and the female reader. When I state that any woman's story is Everywoman's story, I mean that women's marginalization provides a context in which to recognize women as linked. The title *A Woman*, for instance, suggests that we interpret Aleramo's autobiographical account of her father's betrayal of her mother (who is labeled "mad" when she denounces him), her rape initiation into sexuality, her deadening marriage, and her compelled abandonment of her beloved child as woman's experience—although she realizes that Italy at the turn of the twentieth century is a particularly repressive society. By telling the stories of others, the female narrator enables the inarticulate other to be known, to have a voice that—if mediated by her own—at least implies both that these women are enacting alternative fates dictated by culturally defined gender roles and that these fates are possible for the narrator herself. Thus the narrators of the women's texts I teach relate stories of mothers, wives, and daughters, of rebels, victims, and outcasts, of madwomen and wisewomen, of housekeeping and of wandering, in an attempt to describe women's experience under patriarchy and to recognize kinship with all women in phallocentric culture.

The multiple narrative form tends to focus on the affinity of women's experience. In *Millenium Hall* the stories of the women who live together in this all-female community are narrated by themselves, within an eighteenth-century epistolary framework in which a British gentleman writes of the community to his friend, convincing him—and the conventional reader—through the women's life stories that patriarchal society is corrupt and must be changed. All the women who have been damaged by male cultural values have names that either begin with "M" (Morgan, Mancel), to indicate their middle—Everywoman—representativeness, or that rhyme with an "M" name (Selwyn, Melvyn), to indicate the similarity of women's fate. Two centuries later, Alice Munro's *Künstlerroman, Lives of Girls and Women*, tells the story not only of its heroine, Del Jordan, but of others whose lives have been constructed according to the gender expectations of their culture: the spinster aunts who ask Del to complete their brother's history instead of writing her own; the beautiful Miss Rush, who dies in childbirth; crazy, birth-damaged Mary Agnes, sexually abused as a child by a group of boys; Del's mother, about whom Del wonders, "Had all her stories, after all, to end up with just her, the way she was now, just my mother in Jubilee?" (67).

Similarly, in *The Woman Warrior* Kingston sees that the stories of other women—her aunt, her mother, Ts'ai Yen—are her story, as well as "her-story," a female inscription of history. One of the repeated figures in this history is the madwoman; the stories of the stoned crazy lady and of Moon Orchid, happy in a community of madwomen after rejection by her husband, represent this figure, embodying in her extreme marginalization not only the symbolic fate for women but also a possible fate for the narrator herself, as a woman and as visionary creator of this text—the rebel knot-maker, blinded by the outlaw intricacies of her art (190).

The creation of modes of narrative seeks to encompass female experience and undermine male narratives by eluding their formal constraints. The terms of gaining power are changed. Thus Kingston uses the myth of Fa Mu Lan—suspect because it has been kept alive in patriarchal discourse, as Sidonie Smith points out (158)—and transforms it, through the other women's stories in the book, into a myth in which the woman warrior's painful song communicates the need to convey subversive feminine history. Other women writers also structure their stories as dream and parable that create new myths. Rhys's *Wide Sargasso Sea* rewrites *Jane Eyre* by telling the story of Bertha Mason/Antoinette Cosway and Rochester, juxtaposing the colonizing male's urge for domination and female psychic geography, mystically allied with nature—the West Indian landscape—and with passionate knowledge of the body. In *Mrs. Caliban* Ingalls embodies the outcast state of woman's experience (the story of the other is indicated by her Shakespearean title) in the form of science fiction, novel of manners, and parable, all of which may be interpreted as her dream—or her madness.

CK: I agree that a woman's tradition is—has been—enabling. My concern is what one is enabled to do. Acquiring power from those who hold it means acquiring it on their terms. The question is: Which aesthetic criteria should feminist critics borrow in order to establish this women's tradition? That tradition is becoming a subtradition (one or two "women's literature" courses taught among dozens in the other tradition), precisely because aesthetic criteria do not change much between the two traditions. Deborah, like many critics of *The Woman Warrior*, insists that the female artist's voice must assert itself, rebelling but of "reconciled identity." "Reconciled" is an interesting term—and the one I resist in discussions of Kingston's narrator. She is not reconciled to the demand of narrative discourse that she speak as one voice in control. While she gives in to the demand so that she is allowed to speak, she nevertheless defies it by exposing it to its crimes— her crimes committed *against her mother* in its name.

DM: One of the ways in which women's autobiography connects is through the narrator's focus on the mother as the source of the daughter's identity. To author her own story, the narrator must tell her mother's story and claim both affinity and difference. She must rebel not only against the patriarchy but also against mothers who try to accommodate her to the patriarchy's values or who participate in its continuance. The mothers in many such works—Margaret Oliphant's *Miss Marjoribanks*, Antonia White's *Frost in May*, May Sinclair's *Life and Death of Harriet Frean*—retreat into chronic illness in the face of demoralizing gender role expectations. Some mothers take refuge in madness, like Aleramo's mother, or Antoinette Cosway's mother in Rhys's text; other mothers commit suicide, like Helen in Robinson's *Housekeeping*, who leaves her children to wait quietly and sails off a cliff in her car, thereafter epitomizing the daughter's vision of enigmatic, tragic beauty. Some mothers abandon or betray their daughters in order to make their own way or to accommodate themselves to the father—Angelou's mother in *I Know Why the Caged Bird Sings* sends her daughter away after the rape she has herself unwittingly facilitated; in *Bronx Primitive* Kate Simon's mother allows her daughter to be denied an education as punishment for refusing to provide her father with a glamorous life by becoming a concert pianist; Marguerite Duras's mother in *The Lover* sees her daughter as a whore, while she holds a fierce allegiance to the elder son. Mothers are in some deep sense the audience in women's autobiography, those who are to watch the performance of the daughter-narrator writing her self.

The ambivalent message that Brave Orchid imparts to her daughter can be linked to the betrayals by the mothers in other women's autobiographies. The mother, acculturated in the patriarchy, teaches lessons of submission, in which the daughter is told she is worthless, told she is crazy, told she is other. But at the same time, the daughter is burdened with a covert expectation, the mother's desire that she will subvert the order. Kingston learns, from her mother's talk-stories, that most women are born to be wives and slaves, but that an extraordinary few may be warriors like the mythical Fa Mu Lan—or shamans, as Brave Orchid herself was in China. And yet, after Fa Mu Lan fulfills her role as female avenger, with the words of the father on her back and a newborn son on her breast, she becomes an obedient wife-slave. It is No Name Woman—whose story of adultery, punishment, childbirth, and suicide her mother tells Kingston as a warning at her first menstruation—who is truly subversive, denying her daughter to the patriarchy, poisoning the well with her own body and her daughter's.

CK: Even though the narrator reacts against her mother who tries to "accommodate her to the patriarchy's values," the American (part barbarian) narrator also tries to accommodate her mother to Western values that are definitely patriarchal, if not in the precise way Chinese values are. However, I do not find the narrator unaware of what she does—instead, she tries to force the patriarchy to see its own crimes as they force her complicity in them. To deny her complicity, to see her accomplishment as a victory for women, is to cover up those crimes once more and to wish the patriarchy continued success.

I teach the book as disrupting tradition because the literary tradition, which many feminist critics embrace as liberating, demands that the voice freed from the constraints of "real" existence emerge victorious, the creator of beauty. Such liberation is illusory, makes pain beautiful, and, in more extreme constructions, something to be sought (a kind of fortunate fall). Feminists need to examine, much more carefully than we have to date, how discourse represses. To be recognized, a speaker cannot threaten the discourse, speak in terms antithetical to it. Psychoanalytic critics argue that any male-dominated discourse would find anything denying its unity antithetical, precisely because the subjects speaking constitute their own sense of unity in discourse in the first place.

Deborah mentioned earlier the French feminists' notion of "writing the body." Such an inscription is, like the one on Fa Mu Lan's back, an inscription of pain that must not be forgotten. The very notion of "writing the body" operates against the notion of speaking as one voice in control, because women's bodies are doubled, multiple. And we are "doubled" not only biologically but because men have encoded "femininity" in the first place. Briefly, women are brought up—as the narrator of *The Woman Warrior* is brought up—within a discourse that both encodes and excludes them for their duplicity. It is precisely the notion of a multiple voice that would, for these feminists, constitute a "female discourse," but such discourse is forbidden. Nor has its possibility been explored by many American feminist literary critics, since it emphatically denies the notion of any self, in control, speaking itself to itself (like God the Father's). These artist's voices in the women's tradition do rebel, but the patriarchal values they rebel against have already determined the form of their rebellion—as a self that will exclude anything threatening its autonomy. So when a narrative is constructed in which a "female-defined self" emerges, patriarchal values emerge as well—the defined, unitary self that little boys chase after from the time they discover that illusory wholeness in the mirror. In pursuit of that image, they repress what they perceive (or construct) as divided, fragmented.

The Woman Warrior suggests that we might want to break out of that demand for unity. Ts'ai Yen's song, which I agree functions as a metaphor for *The Woman Warrior* as a whole, is neither univocal nor celebratory: "Her words seemed to be Chinese, but the barbarians understood their sadness and anger. Sometimes they thought they could catch barbarian phrases about forever wandering" (243). In fact, Ts'ai Yen's song remains unrealized—neither we nor the narrator hears it. Ts'ai Yen is an ambiguous figure to begin with: she represents not only the narrator but Brave Orchid, who feels doomed to "forever wander," who feels lost among barbarians, and whose children do not understand her native language (at the beginning of this passage, Brave Orchid remarks that the narrator has a "seventh-grade vocabulary" [240], too limited to understand the Chinese theater in which Ts'ai Yen's songs might have been performed). Thus, Leslie Rabine concludes, Ts'ai Yen "creates both a difference and a relationship between mother and daughter." Rabine acknowledges that this relationship of difference is painful; nevertheless, she typically (in response to demands from the discourse in which she writes) forgets the pain, formalizes it, almost as quickly as she acknowledges it: "The fantasy of the legendary poetess is on a formal level a fantasy of transforming the conflict from pain into beauty and from paralysis into harmonious movement" (486). One simply doesn't end literature—really, literary analysis—with images of separation, of fragmentation, of unresolved conflict, of pain. One ends with images of reconciliation, of conflict formalized into harmony; one ends celebrating literature's power to unify in a work of beauty. Literature is (an)aesthetic. Numbing.

Part of the pain of *The Woman Warrior* is the daughter's betrayal of her mother. Brave Orchid fears, if nothing else, the prying eyes of the barbarians, of Western ghosts; she guards her language as ferociously as she guards her children (and so berates them for teaching the Garbage Ghost Chinese). Her daughter's narrative subjects her to those prying eyes, reveals the secrets of her language and culture to a hostile audience—one that will call her knowledge "primitive," her power over ghosts "superstition." From Brave Orchid's point of view, her daughter—one of the children for whom she sacrificed her powers as Shaman—has become a ghost. By the time the narrator confesses her sins in "A Song for a Barbarian Reed Pipe," she no longer speaks her mother's language but the rudely direct Western discourse of science, which transforms her mother's into lies, nonsense, and perhaps a bit of craziness. Her mother becomes inscrutable, alien.

The narrator emerges whole only if her mother is excluded (and she does attempt to distinguish her voice from her mother's throughout the book—as she says, prefacing this last story, "The beginning is hers, the ending, mine" [240]). To allow that artist's voice to "sing," the mother-other is silenced. Deborah finds one value in the women's tradition is that it "enables the inarticulate other to be known." But what are we articulating—the crimes of the patriarchy against what it constructs as inscrutable, or the illusion the patriarchy fosters that we can somehow overcome those crimes by writing beautiful stories? I'll give you the chief danger of my position: we become silent again, afraid to talk. It's not a matter of silencing but of exposing our own complicity in the process of exclusion. Discourse never wants to study itself too closely.

Writing may be potentially, as Deborah puts it, the "most profound resistance to male authority," although she thinks of that resistance within a culture in which male authority has silenced women. But male authority doesn't silence women in the 1990s—this volume alone is evidence of that, as is Kingston's success and that of feminist criticism these days. However, male authority still oppresses us. We are allowed to speak within certain limits, limits that permit oppression and yet will not acknowledge that they oppress. *The Woman Warrior* examines the mechanisms by which the discourse makes us complicit in our own oppression: what is foreign is scrutinized; what is usable (Brave Orchid's stories) is appropriated, what is not usable (Brave Orchid) is excluded. We need to expose those mechanisms until the discourse can no longer stand the sight of itself.

DM: Kingston's authoring of No Name Woman's story—imagining her experience and in the process making her a subject, as Sidonie Smith argues (153)—is an alliance that ends the complicity Kingston admits she has had in maintaining the silence, in refusing her an identity. As the book's first story, it serves as a warning of what happens if one does not enter the dominant discourse: women's real history under patriarchy is erased. Kingston's decision to speak, despite her mother's injunction not to "tell," indicates that she has decided to enter the discourse (3, 18). Her comment about the aunt who "haunts" her, "I do not think she always means me well," and the fear that her aunt, "the drowned one," may "pull down a substitute" (19) suggest that she knows the price of telling and has chosen to risk the pain of giving birth to her aunt's story as well as to her own. Similarly, I read the "torture" of Kingston's silent, ultrafeminine double—the more Chinese image of Kingston's selfhood—not as a repetition of the dominant discourse but as a demand that Chinese women speak out against the discourse that inflicts on them the same pain that she has felt when she heard her uncle call her a "maggot," or saw pictures of girl babies being pushed down the river in the flood.

But because Kingston's text is constructed in terms of Chinese paradox, the torture of the other is self-torture. Thus both Kingston and the girl she tried to torment into speaking cry, in a mirroring of each other's pain; when the girl is rescued by her protective sister, who allows her silence, Kingston herself is guilt-stricken and becomes seriously ill. The price of speaking— of rebellion and liberation—is intense pain; the imagined cutting of the frenum by her mother symbolizes this. Nevertheless, Kingston chooses to speak, to tell her aunts' stories, her mother's story—with all the ambivalent consequences for herself—and to tell off her racist boss in the art supply house, after which she is fired. Finally, each section of *The Woman Warrior* ends with a commitment to telling; "No Name Woman," for instance, closes with "I alone devote pages of paper to her, though not origamied into houses and clothes" (19). The telling is at once a work of devotion and a work of mastering, an emergence of voice in the American tongue, not in the Chinese language or in the Chinese form of origami—an art form that itself includes the idea of paradox, for it suggests the protection of "houses and clothes" but in fact is an expression of the culture that sees No Name Woman as having transgressed. Therefore, the telling is always both a betrayal—of her mother's injunction not to "tell," of No Name Woman's choice for silence —and an act of homage, an acknowledgment of the legacy of other women, of their history. The "betrayal" of Brave Orchid by the daughter through the telling of her story in Western discourse must be viewed from this double perspective. The story of Ts'ai Yen issues from Brave Orchid's story of her own mother, who had bound feet and loved the theater. Like Ts'ai Yen's children listening to her song in the desert, Kingston interwines her voice with that of her mother.

Speech-Act Theory and the Search for Identity in *The Woman Warrior*

Victoria Myers

I teach *The Woman Warrior* in a course entitled American Autobiography, a lower-division seminar. We focus on what autobiography is, how it differs from history on the one hand and fiction on the other and yet maintains links with both. We consider also how the account of an individual life (or, rather, its literary construction) reveals the life of a community or even delineates the community's vision of itself. Thus we trace a double theme in the course, the writers' depiction of themselves in relation to their culture and their use of literary techniques to create this self. The texts in the course reflect this double interest, for they raise the question of what defines an "exemplary" American, and each one falls somewhere along a continuum from intended fact to avowed fiction: Franklin's *Autobiography*, Thoreau's *Walden*, Douglass's *Narrative of the Life of Frederick Douglass, an American Slave*, Twain's *Life on the Mississippi*, Hemingway's *Nick Adams Stories*, and Kingston's *Woman Warrior*.

In large part, the course is fueled by the theses of Darrell Mansell and Robert F. Sayre ("Autobiography"). As Mansell points out, writers of autobiography may intend their work to be taken as real life, but neither they nor the reader can escape from the essentially constructive nature of language. Although words are a simulacrum, they do not reproduce the whole event. Moreover, authors purposefully select—not only facts but emphases, expressions—and in this way resemble other artists, fiction writers in particular. All imaginative works, however, are derived from personal experience; events, character traits, feelings come from *someone's* life. This, of course, makes the fiction writer resemble the autobiographer. With any given work, readers oscillate between reading referentially and reading aesthetically—reading with the sense that "this is true" and reading with the sense that "this is constructed."

This thesis provides the underpinning for Sayre's more specific thesis concerning the topic of the course—namely, that "American autobiographers have generally connected their own lives to the national life or to national ideas" (149). They have shown their lives as the fulfillment of ideas; for instance, they may present themselves (like Fitzgerald) as the embodiment of a sham individualism, or (like Franklin) as a model of prosperity and usefulness to be emulated, or (like Douglass) as a living refutation of the white American's self-concept. They have structured different ideas of themselves as Americans, ideas that have revised the description of America itself. Essays by George S. Gusdorf, Barrett J. Mandel, and James M. Cox (in Olney, *Autobiography*) and by Sayre and by Alfred Kazin (in Stone, *American Autobiography*), as well as Cox's "Autobiography and America," have also been helpful in formulating the problems for this course.

The course needed a systematic approach to textual analysis that would give students the tools for exploring these theses in individual texts—in short, for relating style to theme. Speech-act theory enables us to articulate our sensitivity to the constructiveness of language; moreover, its premise that the individual is intimately related to the community in the use of language is compatible with the larger questions we ask. The works of J. L. Austin and John R. Searle describe speech acts in the context of everyday discourse; Mary Pratt applies their discoveries to literature. Like rhetoric, speech-act theory assumes that literature (like all speech acts) is an act of communication in which the main components are the character of the speaker, the audience's state of mind, and the nature of the subject. Like (some) linguistics, speech-act theory attends to the grammatical construction of the utterance while assuming the existence of a deep structure of intended meaning. But it also recognizes that the communicative act takes place in a context whose conditions determine the interpretation and effect of the act. This context includes the kind (or, by extension, the genre) of the utterance, as well as physical, psychological, and cultural facts of which the listener must be aware.

Understanding an utterance is a complex act that requires the listener not simply to decode the syntax but to discern the conditions in society relevant to each utterance. One can thus imagine the difficult task children confront in understanding and assimilating their culture. When this task is complicated by a child's belonging to two cultures simultaneously, we have a dilemma like that described in *The Woman Warrior*. Kingston must create her identity, and it is in large part a verbal identity. But as she does not invent her own words, she must assimilate the language of her community—the customs and assumptions of her Chinese and American contexts, although they compete with each other. That language implies attitude—a *way* of understanding as well as a thing understood—is not a difficult concept for students to grasp. Many can point to misunderstandings based on misinterpretation, to misinterpretations based on a dearth of contextual fact. They recall conversations with immigrants who speak English well but do not completely understand the context of their utterances, as well as with native speakers in which ambiguity, equivocation, and the like hinder communication.

From this minimal starting point, we can develop some basic terms of speech-act analysis. In all communication, we rely on the *cooperative principle*: we assume, and must assume, that speakers intend to communicate and will express themselves economically, truthfully, relevantly, and clearly (Pratt 130). If we can assume that the cooperative principle applies, we can then rely on the operation of *implicature*: the use of bridging assumptions (for instance, about psychology, the culture, the physical environment) that fill in the missing parts of a conversation (Pratt 154–55; Searle, *Speech Acts*

117–36). For example, my husband and I are standing before our front door, he with an armful of groceries. He says, "My keys are in my left pocket." I understand, from the context and from the maxim of relevance, that this statement of fact is really a request for me to open the door.

Of course, the violation of these two principles does not always destroy communication. Violation (as in self-contradiction or ambiguity) can be used deliberately to communicate something different from the surface utterance. Novelists, for instance, systematically have characters violate these principles in order to metacommunicate—that is, to insinuate that the violation itself is significant. The violation may point to personality traits of which the characters themselves are unconscious or that they are unable to control. (*Tristram Shandy* is a wonderful example of the systematic violation of the requirement that one speak economically.) Thus we look for an implicature even to interpret the violation.

Speech-act theory, then, helps us understand literature insofar as literature resembles everyday conversation, but the theory enables us to comprehend the complex relation of fact to fiction as well (Pratt 162–75). One context for knowing how to interpret an utterance is its kind: is it novel or is it autobiography? Unless a work is explicitly labeled, one often cannot tell the difference. (Maya Angelou's *I Know Why the Caged Bird Sings* is a case in point.) Both use techniques of verisimilitude to assert their trueness to reality. Readers like to know which genre the work belongs to: are they to consider this work to be true or merely imitating reality? Even if they understand that both are constructions, the answer to the question makes a difference to them. But the generic classification does not usually cause problems. The book is labeled, and once readers have situated themselves in a genre, they *believe*, they know how to take the utterances. Verisimilitude in a novel means something different from verisimilitude in autobiography. But the problem becomes more complex if the writer is inconsistent. When the writer violates verisimilitude, then either the communication is destroyed or the reader looks for implicatures that will explain the violation. The search for such implicatures constitutes the interpretive process in a work like *The Woman Warrior* (see Myers 117–23).

We spend six to eight one-hour class periods discussing the work chapter by chapter and gradually developing an appreciation of Kingston's mixture of fact and fiction. At the same time, we are interested in her revelations about being a Chinese American, and we analyze her special use of language as an appropriate form for capturing the dilemmas of her identity. At no time do I deliver a lecture on speech-act theory as I have explained it above. Rather, I name and explain these concepts when they emerge as we explore the problems in specific passages. I can best illustrate the usefulness of speech-act theory by sketching the course of some of our discussions.

In the opening chapter, "No Name Woman," Kingston tells us that she was given very little information about her aunt who drowned herself in the well. But we discover that what she doesn't know she makes up. We notice that she shifts back and forth between speculation and assertion about her aunt's experiences and feelings: she violates the maxim of clarity. We can locate these shifts by specific syntactic signals. To indicate speculation, she uses the conditional subjunctive: "My aunt could not have been the lone romantic who gave up everything for sex" (7). "She may have been unusually beloved, the precious only daughter" (12). She also uses qualifiers: "Perhaps she had encountered him in the fields" (7). To signal assertion, she uses the indicative: "Even as her hair lured her imminent lover, many other men looked at her" (11). But the shift becomes especially startling when assertion follows hard on the heels of speculation. After a series of sentences qualified by "perhaps," Kingston says, "His demand must have surprised, then terrified her. She obeyed him; she always did as she was told" (7). If these shifts do not simply signal the author's confusion, what could they suggest? To answer this question, the students must seek the implicature that will complete Kingston's communication with them. Kingston gives a clue to the *kind* of implicature that needs to be used to interpret these shifts when she says, "I want her fear to have lasted" (8), and when she calls her aunt her "forerunner" (9). The indicative does not signal what the reader should take as fact but what Kingston, absorbed in her speculations, momentarily lives as fact. We infer that she is deliberately constructing motives and feelings for her aunt as an act of imaginative identification. Her descriptions of her aunt's feelings test her own potential identities: as slave, as romantic dreamer, as outcast. If the indicative fits, she may have to wear it.

In discussing the second chapter, "White Tigers," students readily notice that Fa Mu Lan is a very different character from Kingston's aunt. In this chapter, the woman is not slave but warrior, a dreamer whose dreams are reality—no outcast but the savior of her community. Here again we notice that Kingston shifts from an imagined world to a real one, but the mixture is much more complex. The students at first have no difficulty separating fact from fantasy. Fantasy, of course, is whatever could not happen in everyday life. And, besides, Kingston makes typographical breaks between the frame narrative and the mythical, or "inside," narrative (25, 54). But then we notice that there are fantasy elements in the frame narrative and, conversely, that the mythical narrative seems in some ways very like everyday life. In the mythical narrative, Kingston uses qualifiers: "the rice pot seemed bottomless, but perhaps not" (25–26); "They had probably left images of themselves for me to wave at" (40). Such usage paradoxically increases the verisimilitude of the narrative by introducing doubt: a skeptical, observant mind is at work. Even the details creating the verisimilitude of the mythic world point to the gestures and measures of earth-bound reality: "We reached the tiger place in no time—a mountain peak three feet three from the sky. We had to bend over" (29).

The students notice that, after the typographical break, the myth creeps into Kingston's daily life to compete with another Chinese identity, that of the female as slave. For instance, when Kingston attempts to stand up to her American boss, she thinks, "If I took the sword, which my hate must surely have forged out of the air . . ." (58). Disappointed with her life in America, she says, "I mustn't feel bad that I haven't done as well as the swordswoman did; after all, no bird called me" (58). At first these reflections appear a reconciliation to the world of fact, then a denial of it, for this observation follows: "I've looked for the bird" (59). When we try to account for this use of language, to find the assumptions that give these shifts meaning, we must look to Kingston's "personality" as the context. We first notice that the myth is a fulfillment of Kingston's desire for importance and love: in Fa Mu Lan, she finds a powerful Chinese female identity to dispel the ghost of her aunt. Does her manipulation of language then simply evidence a desire to escape reality? To assent is to imply that the description of woman as slave is more real than the description of woman as warrior. Yet the heroines of both the first and second chapters have been imagined. If Kingston could achieve the identity of Fa Mu Lan (victim-avenger, with words carved on her back), she says, she could return to her Chinese community. We open the possibility, resolved by the end of the book, that using words—writing this book—will be for Kingston her way of achieving a strong identity and of being accepted. In a sense she could become Fa Mu Lan.

In discussing the third chapter, "Shaman," students rediscover the difficulty, for a child growing up in any culture, of distinguishing between what is real and what is made up. Students have said that the chapter draws them on by stirring up questions about who believes what: Did (does) Kingston's mother really believe in ghosts? Did (does) Kingston herself? Did (does) Chinese society? Finding the answer requires locating the implicature that could link statements. For example, Kingston says, "My mother relished these scare orgies. . . . She could validate ghost sightings" (76–77). The assumption that links these two statements is that her mother was an impostor; she could pretend to believe in ghosts for the sake of pleasure and personal influence. The presence of this implicature seems to be affirmed a little later, when her mother questions the existence of ghosts. Kingston comments: "If the other storytellers had been reassuring one another with science, then my mother would have flown stories as factual as bats into the listening night." The implicature: her mother has no real belief in ghosts, but just likes to dominate discussions. Yet the next sentence undermines this implicature: "A practical woman, she could not invent stories and told only true ones" (77). By depriving readers, at times, of consistent assumptions, Kingston forces them to experience the vacillation and ambivalence of children trying to distinguish what is real and to find their place in that reality, when (as Kingston found) the reality itself is not consistent.

I have tried to give a sense of how speech-act theory informs stylistic analysis and guides it toward questions about achieving identity within a community. In the course of our discussions, we repeatedly compare *The Woman Warrior* with the other texts assigned in the course. I chose Kingston's memoirs as the culminating work of the course because of the complexity of its verbal technique and Kingston's self-conscious use of language as theme: language is both the goal and the way in her search for an identity. *The Woman Warrior* (like Wallace Stevens's jar in Tennessee) centers and gives tendency to the earlier works in the course, which in turn illuminate Kingston's work. For instance, when we analyze the language of Franklin's *Autobiography*, we focus on the concept of persona, pinpointing his selection of detail as it builds his persona and distinguishes it from the character of others; we discuss the shift in personae from the first to the second half of the work, relating this shift to Franklin's conception of his role in history. Such exploration is the basis for our ultimate understanding that Franklin depicts himself as an exemplar to posterity. When we arrive at *The Woman Warrior*, we possess the concept of persona and audience, on which we can build more complex rhetorical and linguistic questions. We can see that Kingston's use of language does not so much create her as exemplar as show the problem of identifying and identifying with an exemplar.

We take up Twain's *Life on the Mississippi* halfway through the course. Here is where we first encounter the problem, embodied in Twain's style, of distinguishing reality from illusion. Frauds and tricksters abound in riverboat society, and lying is a pastime. Twain's persona is complicated by the self-reflective ironies of his prose. Is he basically (as he says) an honest man who fails at lying whenever he tries it, or a consummate liar who places flaws in his lies to cover his identity as liar? This complexity of self-consciousness illuminates the superstitions, sentimentality and maudlin romanticism, and illusions of progress that characterize Southern culture. Twain as liar both represents and criticizes his culture. Again, with this discussion we possess a concept of irony when we reach *The Woman Warrior* that readies us for the self-reflexiveness of Kingston's language: the merging of speculation and reality, fantasy and reality. Wish, dream, madness, and reality characterize Kingston's and the universal dilemma of finding one's identity in relation to a community. What I hope results from the discussions, by the end of the term, is a conviction that we all create our identities by means of language, both when we accept and when we alter the language that was given to us. At the same time, we are accepting and altering our culture: we wrest free from it, just long enough to add to its stock of exemplars one that makes the culture a different kind of nourishing mother.[1]

NOTE

[1]My ideas about *The Woman Warrior* and speech-act theory were presented earlier in "The Significant Fictivity of Maxine Hong Kingston's *The Woman Warrior*" (*Biography* 9 [1986]: 112–25), from which part of my discussion of "No Name Woman" is drawn.

The Woman Warrior as a Search for Ghosts

Gayle K. Fujita Sato

The narrator of *The Woman Warrior* admits, in the last chapter, to being an "outlaw knot-maker," twisting common material into singular designs and favoring intricate patterns that would leave the maker blind (190). This admission usually draws unanimous agreement from students, many of whom remain baffled by the narrator's larger designs. They have little trouble appreciating individual talk-stories but falter when trying to relate them conceptually. My solution is to teach *The Woman Warrior* through an examination of "ghost," an approach requiring close reading but aimed at revealing the text's thematic and dramatic patterns. Concentrating on the meanings of "ghost" provides a comprehensive yet efficient overview of *The Woman Warrior* through the material students often find most alien. [1]

To broach the topic, I usually begin with the book's title: How is woman warriorhood related to "girlhood among ghosts"? Doesn't Kingston imply a connection between the unlikely pair "warrior" and "ghost," and how is this connection realized in the text? Furthermore, is it possible that our assumptions about warriorlike assertion and ghostlike absence have something to do with the many paradoxes the narrator attributes to her bicultural childhood? Once its significance is proposed in this manner, discussion naturally turns to what constitutes a "ghost."

One could start from any number of quotations, but the following passage from the chapter "Shaman" is useful because it builds on the familiar image of Casper or Halloween costumes:

> But America has been full of machines and ghosts—Taxi Ghosts, Bus Ghosts, Police Ghosts, Fire Ghosts, Meter Reader Ghosts, Tree Trimming Ghosts, Five-and-Dime Ghosts. Once upon a time the world was so thick with ghosts, I could hardly breathe; I could hardly walk, limping my way around the White Ghosts and their cars. There were Black Ghosts too, but they were open eyed and full of laughter, more distinct than White Ghosts. (113)

Visually, this passage evokes a child's guessing game in which players are draped in sheets with only a key object to identify them—silver badge, red helmet, cash register—but obviously the narrator is playing more seriously with the implications of "ghost." The passage is about point of view. Behind the child's observation that all whites are indistinguishable lurks a too-familiar question: Whose perspective determined that "all Asians look alike"? The narrator further undermines the notion of racial hegemony by observing that "black" is "more distinct" than "white." We can recall that Kingston's blackened kindergarten paintings were misinterpreted by teachers who were blind to the child's fertile imagination. Nor is the narrator replacing one color hierarchy with another, for in the chapter "White Tigers," white also designates, like the black of Kingston's school paintings, the power of imagination. In fact, the scenes of "White Tigers" are flooded with color, like the Cantonese operas the young narrator imagined behind the "black curtains" of her paintings. In short, the passage about ghosts not only constitutes "ghost" specifically as "white people" but builds on color symbolism to introduce inverse concepts of cultural invisibility (color blindness) and multicultural perspectives. The paragraph introduces the fact that "ghost" is a multiple signifier representing both concrete phenomena and abstractions.

Students can then be asked to name other kinds of "ghost"—the "Chinese" types the narrator finds bewilderingly diverse. A basic list would include the "nether creatures" (98) whom Brave Orchid's medical science cannot defeat and who visit Chinese villages as "ghost plagues" (15), and those, like "Sitting Ghost" (81), who can be vanquished in tests of strength and courage. Harmless creatures of "ghost stories" send only "chills" up the back in an overheated laundry (102), while more vicious varieties plague Kingston in recurrent nightmares. There are also the "ghosts of neat little old men" (118), Chinese bachelor laborers who once boarded in the house where the Hongs live, and of course the spirit of No Name Woman, who "haunts" (19) the narrator but is eventually transformed into a kind of ghost-writer. "Ghost" is a term of endearment, indicating "temporary absence," as when Fa Mu Lan, glimpsing pictures of her family in the water gourd, reflects: "We will be so happy when I come back to the valley, healthy and strong and not a ghost" (37). Yet the same term denotes permanent exile in the case of No Name Woman, who must "beg food from other ghosts" (18) because her descendants refuse to honor her memory with ritual offerings. These contradictory meanings (endearment, banishment) are illustrated succinctly when the suicide aunt looks fondly at her sleeping infant soon to be severed from mother and family—"[f]ull of milk, the little ghost slept" (17). Finally, there is "Ho Chi Kuei" (237), a Chinese counterpart to the reduction of all Caucasians into one uniform "white." "Ho Chi Kuei," at the other extreme of opaque complexity, yields thirteen useless translations when the narrator consults a dictionary.

This list by no means exhausts the narrator's references to "ghost," but it is enough to begin analysis, starting with the point that "ghosts" define two antithetical worlds that threaten the narrator's sense of a unified self. How is she to articulate her own location, which is "Chinese America," when history, tradition, and family have formulated "China" and "America" as reciprocally alien territories? "Ho Chi Kuei" and "No Name Woman" in particular embody the narrator's problematic situation. Identified by a phrase whose meaning is inaccessible to her, enraged by the subjugation and denigration of women in Chinese culture, the narrator comes to identify with her nameless, outcast kinswoman. She tries relocating to the "ghost-free" world of white America (127), where she presumably lives as a Writer Ghost among Urban Renewal Ghosts, Garbage Ghosts, Druggist Ghosts, and others who identify with or are identified according to their jobs, but this entails an intolerable loss for the narrator, particularly because she is an artist:

> I had to leave home in order to see the world logically, logic the new way of seeing. I learned to think that mysteries are for explanation. I enjoy the simplicity. Concrete pours out of my mouth to cover the forests with freeways and sidewalks. Give me plastics, periodical tables, TV dinners with vegetables no more complex than peas mixed with diced carrots. Shine floodlights into dark corners: no ghosts.   (237)

The narrator has liberated herself into a sterile world. A central paradox of *The Woman Warrior* is that the very "ghosts" that drive the narrator from home bring her back, for she realizes that banishing them all means banishing all poetry and magic too, including the legend of Fa Mu Lan. We return, then, to the question implied in the book's title: What role has "a girlhood among ghosts" played in the narrator's development as a woman warrior?

From the list of "ghosts" we can reconsider those that are obviously beneficial or benign. For instance, the narrator is refreshed by ghost stories and feels affection for the lingering spirits of Chinese bachelor laborers. Most important, the ghost of No Name Woman has given the narrator "ancestral help" (10) to become a word warrior: "My aunt haunts me—her ghost drawn to me because now, after fifty years of neglect, I alone devote pages of paper to her, though not origamied into houses and clothes" (19; "origami" is actually a Japanese word for the art of folding squares of colored paper into various objects). Here the narrator equates her writing about the suicide aunt, on the surface a subversive, unfilial act, with the traditional filial act of burning paper symbols in memory of the dead. To understand this analogy, we can turn to the conclusion of the episode of Fa Mu Lan, where we are told that the woman warrior's exploits compose "a legend about [her] perfect filiality" (54). Here, "filiality" is redefined by the narrator so that she can claim Chinese American identity while repudiating antifemale teachings and practices rooted in Chinese Confucian tradition and rehearsed in her own house. The narrator is able to incorporate feminism into a new definition of "filiality" by recognizing a link between Fa Mu Lan and Brave Orchid as lessons in paradox.

The narrator interprets the culmination of Fa Mu Lan's training as "learn[ing] to make [her] mind large, as the universe is large, so that there is room for paradoxes" (35). The specific paradox that Fa Mu Lan's disguise as a male warrior encodes is that Chinese women are potentially and actually powerful regardless of what Chinese culture teaches. Of course, the narrator is quick to admit that she cannot storm across America or China like a modern-day incarnation of Fa Mu Lan to recover her parents' stolen property. She must adapt Fa Mu Lan's behavior to her particular situation, and she discovers how to do so through the example of her mother. Student, midwife, healer, wife, mother, laundry worker, farm laborer, and indefatigable immigrant, Brave Orchid is nothing if not a contradiction of her own pronouncements on the unworthiness of females. The eternally compelling paradox embodied by Fa Mu Lan—that a fearless transgressor can also be a daughter, can rebel and repudiate yet return home—is validated by the contrast between what Brave Orchid says about women and what she actually accomplishes.

Brave Orchid's and Fa Mu Lan's contradictory lives enable a crucial adjustment to the "ghost" metaphor, one that connects "ghost" with "woman warrior." Namely, "ghosthood" can be a self-imposed, willingly embraced, rewarding experience of alienation. In this revision, "ghosthood" still means loss of identity through separation from one's primary social unit (e.g., family), but such loss yields a renewed sense of affiliation and identity. Fa Mu Lan, who furnishes the paradigm, becomes a "ghost" when separated from her family to undergo rigorous training. The first phase develops her ability to survive human isolation and concludes with a visionary experience of complete "ghosthood," or loss of human identity (32–33). The second phase, which trains the mind to entertain paradoxes, can also be considered a supreme lesson in "ghosthood" if we interpret paradox broadly as the absence of single, stable meaning. This combined "tiger" and "dragon" training then culminates in feats summarized by the narrator as "perfect filiality." "Filiality" opens the way for the narrator to emulate the woman warrior. The lesson she seems to extract from the tale is that self-imposed exile from normal human association—the deliberate adoption of "ghosthood"—empowers the self to return from exile with a greater capacity for life and knowledge of human connectedness.

Again, Brave Orchid's particular "imitation" of Fa Mu Lan converts this revised version of self-imposed "ghosthood" from theory into practice. Brave Orchid's battle with Sitting Ghost teaches the narrator how to risk being haunted or temporarily isolated. According to the narrator's imaginative re-creation of this episode, Brave Orchid has begun to feel the pressure of aging and long separation from her husband. She fears that the death of their children in China might undermine his commitment to return or send for her. She risks encountering a "ghost" as a means of controlling these fears of failure and abandonment, and, as if to embody her psychological burdens, Sitting Ghost's weapon is suffocating, paralyzing weight. But Brave Orchid wins through sheer determination, expressed through a steady stream of words. She talks Sitting Ghost out of existence, then celebrates her re-connectedness to the world by narrating the event and by letting classmates chant her safely back home.

Following Brave Orchid's example, the narrator confronts her own ghost adversary—the spirit of No Name Woman. The narrator, too, fights through words by "unghosting" or telling about the suicide aunt. But by valorizing the aunt's life of "extravagance" (7) and writing her back into family history, the narrator asserts her own right to extravagance (living the nonpractical life of a writer) and consumption of communal resources: "I *am* worthy of eating the food" (62). Through "pages of paper," therefore, the narrator "unghosts" both herself and the nameless aunt. It is a victory of legendary proportions in two senses. Ancestors claimed and remembered by living descendants can "act like gods, not ghosts" (18), and this filial gesture of remembrance is inspired by Fa Mu Lan's legend of "perfect filiality." Through "pages of paper," in other words, the aunt's "ghost" becomes ancestral "god," and the narrator redeems the status of daughters by tracing their spiritual descent from Fa Mu Lan. Through such acts, the narrator finds the terms of woman warriorhood in "a girlhood among ghosts."

By the end of *The Woman Warrior*, "ghost" has developed into a capacious literary metaphor through a process reminiscent of the narrator's meditations on "invisibility" in *Invisible Man*. In Ralph Ellison's novel, the protagonist is in the process of converting a painful education in "invisibility" into life-generating strategies, beginning with his practical and symbolic act of stealing electricity from "Monopolated Light & Power" (6–7). In a similar way, the narrator of *The Woman Warrior* discovers a regenerative potential in "ghosthood" after experiencing and witnessing its negative forms of denial, death, misrepresentation, and voicelessness. When reinterpreted as self-empowering isolation, "ghosthood" becomes the means of cultivating physical stamina, self-reliance, and mental agility (Fa Mu Lan undergoing training-in-exile), of exorcising debilitating insecurity while renewing self-confidence (Brave Orchid challenging Sitting Ghost), of reconstructing needed ties to family and tradition (the narrator invoking her aunt's ghost), and of forging kinship across cultures (No Name Woman keeping silence, like Hester Prynne, to honor "extravagance"; Ts'ai Yen finding voice in captivity through "barbarian" language; the spirit of Virginia Woolf visiting Brave Orchid and her classmates in "a room of their own" [73]).

I would like to turn now to Henry James's story "The Jolly Corner" and Kingston's second book, *China Men*, which provide historical and cultural contexts for "ghost." The work that eventually became *The Woman Warrior* originally contained stories of male characters, but finding that their presence mitigated the narrator's feminist rebellion, Kingston published them separately as *China Men* (Kim, *Asian American Literature* 207). The historical context missing in *The Woman Warrior* became the main subject of *China*

Men, which reconstructs the daily life and sensibilities of Chinese male immigrants through several generations. At the book's center is a chapter titled "The Laws," which enumerates thirty-two acts of legislation, mostly discriminatory, affecting Chinese immigration from 1868 through 1978. This journalistic summary of Chinese American history is imaginatively fleshed out through stories of individual men, including the narrator's grandfathers, uncles, cousins, father, and brother. Although this narrator is only partially identifiable as the narrator of *The Woman Warrior*, and although the question of narrative continuity is an important feature of *China Men*, the larger issue of Kingston's autobiographical "I" need not be raised here to make the point about different uses of "ghost" in *The Woman Warrior* and *China Men*.

Both works reclaim ancestors from oblivion and misinterpretation, but they use "ghost" differently to represent these unidentified ancestors. An episode from *China Men* called "The Grandfather of the Sierra Nevada Mountains" provides an illustration. Although this grandfather was not financially successful and died in obscurity, the narrator writes: "They [his family] did not understand his accomplishments as an American ancestor, a holding, homing ancestor of this place" (151). Recast as a home builder, this grandfather is "unghosted" like the suicide aunt. He, too, has provided "ancestral help" of the spiritual if not material kind. In one scene, moreover, the grandfather merges with Guan Goong, a Cantonese deity (149), in a manner recalling the suicide aunt's transformation from "ghost" into "god." The grandfather's "unghosting," however, does not involve the same amount of labor, the untwisting and refashioning of "outlaw knots," that reclamation of No Name Woman requires. Although the narrator of *China Men* must reimagine forgotten personalities and lives, and although the narrative of Chinese American history is a "ghost text" for uneducated readers, this narrative can be *recovered* with less effort and emotional stress than the "ghost text" of Chinese American woman warriorhood, which must to a far greater extent be *created*.

The landscape of *China Men* is thus not ghost-ridden, like Kingston's memories of childhood, but crowded instead with kinfolk caught in the acts of living—clearing cane fields, laying railroad ties, blasting tunnels, casting nets, smuggling stowaways, ironing laundry, planting gardens. *China Men* therefore furnishes a relatively stable reference point for navigating shifting ground in White Tigers mountain or other poetic terrain in *The Woman Warrior*. Equally important, the social history narrated in *China Men* implicitly anchors the narrator of *The Woman Warrior* as a Chinese American and accounts for her desire to be creative and self-empowered within her home culture: "The swordswoman and I are not so dissimilar. May my people understand the resemblance soon so that I can return to them" (62). The immigrants portrayed in *China Men*, in fact, become those "ghosts of neat little old men" inhabiting the Hong residence and representing the narrator's positive identification with Chinese American culture.

"The Jolly Corner" combines into one compact drama the metaphoric and sociohistorical constitutions of "ghost" given separate emphasis in *The Woman Warrior* and *China Men*. Both Kingston and Spencer Brydon react against polarized definitions of culture (America and Europe, America and China). They seek wholeness by returning physically and in memory to their childhood homes, where they recover "ghost" identities formerly denied or unrecognized. Brydon repossesses American habits and values he had once denigrated. Kingston's narrator likewise leaves home to "get out of hating range" (62) but returns to discover her life "branching into" (10) and empowered by all her legendary and real-life female kin.

But *China Men* reminds us that Brydon/James had the luxury of rejecting or embracing "American" identity, while Kingston, as a Chinese American, claims America under different economic circumstances and cultural pressures. As Lawrence J. Oliver has noted, James, in *The American Scene*, refers to immigrants as "ghosts," viewing them as insubstantial yet threatening others incapable of becoming "American." Oliver interprets Brydon's confrontation with the ghost in "The Jolly Corner" on a "social or 'ethnic' level" as James's "coming to terms with the 'swarthy' strangers who were forcing old-stock New Yorkers to 'give ground' " (11). The narrator of *The Woman Warrior* may share certain talents or aspects of her artistic predicament with Spencer Brydon, but in *China Men* she is clearly impatient with James's views of immigrant "ghosts."

Returning to *The Woman Warrior* via "The Jolly Corner" and *China Men* illuminates the cultural signification of "ghost." Brydon's flight from America was from the start a self-imposed alienation, and his "Americanness" is never in danger of disintegrating during his long exile. It lies in wait, quite like his bank account, in the corners of his ancestral home, dusty but more or less intact. Kingston's narrator, however, has to invent self-imposed alienation, or "ghosthood," to keep from being doubly exiled from "China" and "America," these places having been already defined for her as mutually exclusive. "Ghost-free" America means an antiseptic world of concrete and diced carrots, but China is equally inhospitable: "I did not want to go where the ghosts took shapes nothing like our own" (116). The articulation of a "Chinese American" reality had to await the verbal skills and perspective of adulthood, but it was and continues to be complicated by sexism and racism. No Name Woman is willed back with greater effort and ambivalence than Brydon's alter ego. She cannot be "pursued" with the leisureliness or sense of inevitability characterizing Brydon's nightly perambulations. And, once materialized, she does not lead the narrator back to a lost home but toward newly articulated home ground.

NOTE

¹This essay builds on ideas first developed in an earlier piece, "Ghosts as Chinese American Construct in Maxine Hong Kingston's *The Woman Warrior*," which will be published by the University of Tennessee Press in an anthology entitled *Haunting the House of Fiction: Feminist Perspectives on Ghost Stories by American Women*, edited by Lynette Carpenter and Wendy K. Kolmar.

Mythopoesis East and West
in *The Woman Warrior*

Cheng Lok Chua

In several comments about her writing, Maxine Hong Kingston has evinced an awareness of using mythic materials and mythologizing techniques in her works. In her use of such materials, Kingston consciously seeks to juxtapose Asian and Western mythoi to arrive at a synthesis that will be meaningful and resonant to her audience. Thus she says in a *New York Times* interview: "I keep the old Chinese myths alive . . . by telling them in a new American way" (Pfaff 26). And speaking with Arturo Islas about Chinese folk material, Kingston says that "myths need to be changed and integrated . . . into the Chinese American's life" (14). As for her techniques of representation, Kingston records that, with certain characters, she "ended up writing about them from a distance, and [they] became mythic. . . . Past generations become mythology. . . . The[ir] form is myth" (Thompson 8). The imaginative skill with which Kingston practices mythopoeic composition in order, on the one hand, to synthesize Asian heritage and American aspiration and, on the other hand, to intensify dramatic impact can be illustrated by examining two facets of *The Woman Warrior*: first, the interweaving of Asian and American myths into one recurrent motif in the narrative, and second, the synthesis of Asian and Western mythoi to create and valorize a major character in the book.

The theme of *The Woman Warrior* concerns the pursuit of identity as woman, as writer, as Asian American (Chua, "Golden Mountain" 46–55). It is in portraying her protagonist's search for self that Kingston uses a recurrent motif—that of the West—which synthesizes, in a unique manner, disparate Asian and American cultural resonances. In American mythic imagination, the West stands for the virgin land of opportunity, the frontier of freedom and adventure where Horace Greeley beckons and where the Jims and Huckleberry Finns of every generation light out for the territory ahead. In the popular Chinese mythic imagination, the Chinese equivalent of the West is a Western Paradise (Hsi T'ien) in the direction of Central Asia and India (see Werner 162). As written down in Wu Ch'eng-en's Ming dynasty classic *Monkey* (or *Journey to the West*), this West, the repository and origin of sacred Buddhist wisdom, is the goal of a quest for completion in enlightenment and fame (hence identity) undertaken by Wu's protagonist Tripitaka and his companion Monkey (78–118). (That Kingston is familiar with this myth is amply borne out by her highly allusive 1989 novel, *Tripmaster Monkey*.)

At the beginning of *The Woman Warrior*, the West that makes its presence felt is the American West, ambiguously portrayed in the book's opening episode, whose subject is Kingston's aunt in China. In their Chinese village, the American West (California) is also perceived as the mythical territory for opportunity. No Name Woman's husband leaves China to seek his fortune on the "Gold Mountain" (3), the Chinese colloquial term for America. But when the China man lights out for the land of opportunity, his family is left behind. In her husband's absence, No Name Woman falls prey to a seducer, bears an illegitimate child, becomes alienated from family, society, and nature, and drowns the infant and herself in the family well in defiant despair. "But the rare urge west had fixed upon our family, and so my aunt crossed boundaries not delineated in space" (9). The westering urge has helped reduce this woman to a nonentity in the family annals.

The West also figures subtly in the book's second episode, "White Tigers," which re-creates the mythic life of the eponymous woman warrior, Fa Mu Lan, the Chinese Joan of Arc figure, who contrasts in identity with the anonymous No Name Woman. The "White Tiger" is one of four mythic beasts symbolizing geomantic power, each one dominating a quadrant of the Chinese compass and representing an element. As with most myths, there are varying accounts of these beasts. One identifies all the beasts as tigers, albeit of different colors—red, black, blue, and white (see, for instance, Cirlot 324–25; Feuchtwang 123). In another account, the beasts are different animals of different colors—namely, the vermilion phoenix, the black turtle, the azure dragon, and the white tiger (Morgan 15–19); a one-sentence allusion to this in *China Men* indicates that Kingston is familiar with the latter version (145). In both versions, the White Tiger, of Kingston's chapter, reigns in the West and over metals—a useful element for warriors, women or men—and is also a likely protector of gold prospectors in the Sierras. It is in this mythic, mountainous region that Fa Mu Lan spends fourteen years, training to assume her role as liberator-warrior and realizing her archetypal identity.

Both Fa Mu Lan and No Name Woman are models of identity constructed by Kingston's protagonist from hearsay and legend, from figures envisioned from a distance. The next two episodes of the book, "Shaman" and "At the Western Palace," contrast two role models from real life, Kingston's strong-willed mother (Brave Orchid) and irresolute aunt (Moon Orchid). On both of them the American West exerts a decisive influence. Both women came to California in search of their husbands, who had been lured Westward by the dream of success and prosperity. These women's search is also a quest for identity as wife and matriarch.

In "Shaman" the strong Brave Orchid gains mythic stature by becoming a figurative shaman, a human with more than ordinary powers of communication with the supernatural and the dead (Potter 207). First she overcomes her sorrow at the death of her two children (71), an experience that, for a woman, is often the initial step in becoming a shaman (Potter 226). Moreover, Brave Orchid exorcises ghosts by smoking them out with burning alcohol and oil (87–88), a customary shamanistic ritual (see Jordan 54–56). Kingston combines these Chinese mythic powers with those Brave Orchid gains by attending a Western-run school of midwifery, which, in turn, confers on her the power to assist at births or infanticides (101). Consistent with these powers, Brave Orchid traverses oceans to claim her neglectful husband in America and succeeds in rebuilding her family, bearing six children after the age of forty-five.

Brave Orchid's weaker sister, Moon Orchid, suffers a different outcome in confronting her husband. He is living a version of the American dream as a wealthy neurosurgeon, bigamously married to a new American wife. The confrontation of Moon Orchid and her husband, in the chapter "At the Western Palace," occurs in Los Angeles, the westernmost American metropolis. In the shadow of the high-rise glass and plastic palace of her husband's clinic, an epitome of Western high tech, Moon Orchid's struggle echoes the legendary yin-yang conflict for influence over the Chinese Emperor (166) that the Empress of the East (here Moon Orchid) must wage against the Empress of the West (the American wife). In this struggle, Moon Orchid is defeated, loses her husband, her family identity, and, eventually, her mind. (It is ironic that a neurosurgeon's wife dies in a lunatic asylum.) In this episode, then, Kingston has synthesized a Chinese folk legend involving the West with the Horace Greeleyesque dream of the American West, and has elevated the drama and irony of an immigrant woman's search for family and identity to an archetypal plane.

The final episode of the book, "A Song for a Barbarian Reed Pipe," focuses on Kingston's growth into assertive, creative Asian American womanhood in California. In doing so, Kingston draws parallels between her life and the legendary experience of one of China's earliest women poets, Ts'ai Yen (242–43). Ts'ai Yen was kidnapped by the Hsiung-nu (or Hun) marauders, regarded as barbarians by the Chinese. She is taken to Hsiung-nu territory west of China, where she is forced to marry and bear children to a Hun chieftain. After many years she is ransomed back to China, perforce leaving her Hun children, in order to start a Chinese family. Her powerful poems tell how she must synthesize the experience of family, love, and parting in the West beyond China to her similar experiences in China. In the same fashion, Kingston must relate the myths and experience of her youth in the American West to those of her family and ancestors in East Asia. By using both the Chinese and the American West as a recurrent motif, Kingston has integrated these elements into a mythic frontier of experience, at once Asian and American, a frontier where new identities must be sought and may be destroyed or remade.

Kingston's mythopoeic quality is perceptible not only in her use of motif but also in the texture of her narrative. To illustrate this, we may return to the chapter "White Tigers."

Here, the narrator imaginatively relives the career of Fa Mu Lan. Kingston opens the chapter by situating us firmly in a prosaic mise-en-scène in a

Chinatown home in Stockton, California, with her mother telling a tale (24–25). As the girl's imagination awakens, we move subtly into a world in which art and imagination fuse into eternal and archetypal reality.

Kingston's protagonist projects herself into the life of a seven-year-old girl of the Six Dynasties Period of China, by a meditative technique like the Christian "Composition of Place" of Saint Ignatius of Loyola (Martz 25–32). She thus walks into an inkwash painting with black-winged birds, a river winding between misty mountains, and rocks of charcoal rubbings. In this world, Kingston is Fa Mu Lan, and the legend becomes her life.

But this Asian legend is interpenetrated by a common Western experience. Fa Mu Lan's education into heroism starts at age seven (about the age at which many Americans enter grade school) and ends at age twenty-two (when many Americans graduate from college). We notice, too, that Fa Mu Lan is educated in a wilderness, reminiscent of the wilderness in which Jesus, a second Adam, engages in his first combat with the devil, thereby establishing his identity and regaining Paradise for humanity. Indeed, through Fa Mu Lan's education, Kingston seems to place her heroine's power in the ability to see humanity as a unity, to experience humanity and nature as a whole, and to attain a mythopoeic imagination enabling her to *feel* ecologically the phenomena of the universe, not merely to measure them.

To begin with, the old couple who oversee Fa Mu Lan's education live in a home that metaphorizes the ecological union of humanity and nature. There, indoors is like outdoors: for a carpet, "[p]ine needles covered the floor in thick patterns." Their dining table is a "rock [which] grew in the middle of the house. . . . The benches were fallen trees"; instead of wallpaper, this earth household has "[f]erns and shade flowers [growing] out of one wall, the mountainside itself" (26). (Indeed, Kingston's imagery reminds us that our word *ecology* derives from the Greek *oikos* 'house.') Fa Mu Lan, whose name means Magnolia Flower, learns to blend into nature, maintaining a Taoist "quiet . . . rooted to the earth" (28). Attaining fourteen and puberty, she takes an initiation test in a "dead land" (30) resembling the medieval Grail Knight's wasteland (Weston ch. 4). She journeys to a wooded region where the tree "branches *cross* out everything" (32; emphasis mine). While watching these crossing branches, she attains a vision of existence as an alchemic cosmic dance—"Chinese lion dancers, African lion dancers . . . Hindu Indian, American Indian" (32). This universal dance, suggesting the destroying and creating dance of the Hindu Siva or the agon of the dying and resurrecting Christ, also recalls the Taoist rhythm of yin-yang, female-male, dark-light: "one of the dancers is always a man and the other a woman"; "working and hoeing are dancing. . . . killing and falling are dancing too" (32–33).

Another eight years complete Fa Mu Lan's education. She learns "dragon ways" by which she metaphorizes the universe, seeing dragons in mountains, "in quarries . . . the dragon's veins and muscles; the minerals, its teeth and bones" (34). This cosmogonic visualizing is a mythopoesis and, no less so than a cognitive science, a way of grasping nature and the universe, enabling Fa Mu Lan to use imagination rather than empirical reason to understand the world in its spiritual dimensions.

This, then, is Kingston's portrayal of the *enfance* of her woman warrior Fa Mu Lan, who joins imaginative identity with Kingston's protagonist and shares psychological kinship with Kingston the woman writer. It is a portrayal uniquely Asian *and* Western; it compounds Asian and Western archetypes that fuse mythopoetically into a union of the varieties of human experience, and it leads to a view of humanity and nature as whole.

We see, then, that a distinctive feature of Kingston's method of composition in *The Woman Warrior* is a mythopoeic synthesis of Asian and American cultures, producing a unique identity and imagination that throws an Asian slant of light on American realities. It is precisely through such juxtapositions of materials and through such experimental techniques that Kingston, like many other Asian American writers and, indeed, many other ethnic American writers, is staking an important claim to the territory of American experience and its expression in American letters.

Talking Stories/Telling Lies
in *The Woman Warrior*

Timothy Dow Adams

In their initial encounter with *The Woman Warrior*, undergraduate students frequently have trouble adjusting to Kingston's improvisations, in a way that parallels the passage toward the end of the book in which the narrator says to her mother, "You lie with stories. You won't tell me a story and then say, 'This is a true story,' or, 'This is just a story,' " (235). To resolve this problem, I devote the initial class time to a discussion of genre, encouraging students to see that their position as readers of *The Woman Warrior*—including their struggles to sort out truth and lie, storytelling and telling stories, fiction and nonfiction—is the same as Kingston's situation as autobiographer. Autobiography is a particularly apt literary form for Kingston's complicated task of balancing the "double bind" of her Chinese American identity. Like Kingston's ethnic identity, which is impossible to divide cleanly into Chinese or American parts, autobiography is also, in what Amy Ling has called "the hyphenated condition," neither fiction nor history nor exactly a combination of the two but a genre of its own, a complex equation designed to tell the story of one's life with whatever degree of invention is needed to reconcile one's self to that life.

I teach *The Woman Warrior* in an undergraduate class, open to all majors, a course described in the university catalog as including both biography and autobiography. Because my students have usually had little experience with theoretical distinctions between autobiography and biography—and have certainly not tackled the complications when memoir is added—I find *The Woman Warrior* a good text with which to begin the class. The work is partly autobiography, partly biography, and partly memoir. While some students assume that all three forms of personal narrative are nonfiction, and that consequently any deviation from the most factual detail is dishonest, others see little difference between the story of Kingston's childhood and the fiction they may have read in other classes.

That *The Woman Warrior* is subtitled "Memoirs of a Girlhood among Ghosts" introduces more than a mere problem in classification, if A. O. J. Cockshut's distinction between reading autobiography and reading memoir is valid. According to Cockshut, we either read autobiography as art, paying slight attention to interior false notes and citing external mistakes in footnotes, or we read it as a historian would read a record, using all available sources for verification. "It would seem, on the whole," Cockshut concludes, "that autobiography lends itself naturally to the first kind of reading, and memoir to the second" (6).

Because the usual distinction between memoir and autobiography holds that the former focuses outwardly on events and people as observed by the narrator while the latter concentrates inwardly on the author's life story, students have trouble initially in understanding who is talking in *The Woman Warrior* and whose story is being related. The traditional autobiographical beginning doesn't occur until halfway through the book with the words "I was born in the middle of World War II" (113), and there are places where the speaker is described in the third person in a manner similar to Gertrude Stein's complicated narrative strategy in *The Autobiography of Alice B. Toklas*. For instance, when Moon Orchid tries to match her nieces with their description in letters, she says of Kingston: "There was indeed an oldest girl who was absent-minded and messy. She had an American name that sounded like 'Ink' in Chinese. 'Ink!' Moon Orchid called out; sure enough, a girl smeared with ink said, 'Yes?' " (152).

Students seem to have little problem with the truth value of "No Name Woman"; they immediately catch on to the story's improvisational quality, which reminds some of them of the conversation between Quentin and his roommate Shreve toward the end of Faulkner's *Absalom, Absalom!* When the narrator says of her unnameable aunt, "I am telling on her" (19), the deliberate ambiguity of Kingston's words—which could be taken as "I am revealing her secrets," or "I am playing off her story," or "I am counting on her"—still seems to produce few doubts about the veracity of the narrator. Reading "White Tigers," which begins with the words "When we Chinese girls listened to the adults talk-story" (23), some students think at first that the narrator is talking rather than her mother, but by the second paragraph it's clear who is speaking and that talking-story allows for a wider degree of factuality than usually found in memoir. That "White Tigers" partakes of myth and legend and feels like a fairy tale allows students to incorporate the story of Fa Mu Lan into the ongoing story of Kingston's childhood, especially since the story ends with a modern narrator playing on the difference between her actual life and that of the woman warrior.

However, with "Shaman" serious questions about the truthfulness of the whole book often emerge. Because the first paragraph of this chapter presents documentation, actual diplomas and photographs, apparently in support of a biography of the narrator's mother, the sudden appearance of spirits within the mother's story turns a documentary into a ghost story and may sound to students like those tales of Hawthorne and Poe that begin with scientific documents designed to add verisimilitude to an obviously fantastic story. But since most of the students have by this point realized that the ghosts of the title are not ectoplasms from a Chinese American *Ghostbusters* but non-Chinese (and non-Japanese) Americans, the introduction of *Chinese* spirits is unsettling. When, toward the end of the chapter, distinctions between dreaming and talking start to blur, followed by the revelation (or nonrevelation) that the mother's papers are probably "wrong" and that her name and age, as well as the number and order of her children, are not necessarily accurate, the complications in sorting out narrative truth become evident.

While "At the Western Palace" seems straightforward enough, when students reach the last chapter, "A Song for a Barbarian Reed Pipe" and discover not only that Kingston was not actually present during the events described in the previous chapter but that she only heard them secondhand, they often express doubts about her truthfulness, especially since she admits that she has "twisted" the story into "designs" worthy of an "outlaw knot-maker" (189–90). Knotty as the truth of the story has become, the better students will recall that in the preceding chapter Brave Orchid has declared that the difference between sanity and madness lies in the ability to invest talk-story with variety (184). That the most straightforward of the chapters turns out to be largely invented, while the most inventive chapters are based on actuality, begins to make students question the nature of autobiographical truth.

At this point I try to bring the discussion back to questions of genre. That ghost stories are not meant to be taken literally and that all autobiographers are unreliable narrators are not difficult concepts for most students to accept. But for some students *The Woman Warrior* is inauthentic because it is a memoir, which by definition calls for clearer warnings about the degree of fiction and of fact. According to Marcus Bilson, however, all memoirs are subjective:

> The modern historian constantly wages a battle against such subjectivity and the possibility of error, however unsuccessfully: such a battle is a mandatory part of the methodology of his discipline. On the other hand, the memorialist accepts quite freely the subjectivity of his own perception as the *sine qua non* of his work; without it, his work would have little interest or meaning; it would not be memoir.   (264)

The author of a memoir, according to Bilson, writes as an eyewitness, a participant or an *histor* "to evoke the historicity of his past and to argue for the truth of his vision of history" (271). By *histor* Bilson means the theoretical mode, defined by Robert Scholes and Robert Kellogg, in which the writer describes "events he has not seen with his own eyes . . . what he has overheard, read about, or accumulated by research through historical records" (qtd. in Bilson 278). By these standards the search for absolute truth is not appropriate, especially in a book like *The Woman Warrior*, since it is not only memoir but remembrances of a childhood as well.

Just when students seem satisfied that the narrator should be trusted, their worries about authenticity safely suppressed, they come to the awful story about the narrator and the silent child. Suddenly all of their standards are upset again. Was the narrator's tongue really cut? And if so, is it cut to make her talk freely or to keep her silent? Did her mother tell her to keep silent about No Name Woman so that she would protect the family's history, or did the command really mean the opposite? When the timid, silent narrator becomes a bully, teetering on the edge of insanity, suddenly the whole legend of the woman warrior begins to evoke doubts again. Like Fa Mu Lan, who says that her enemies might flay her so that "the light would shine through my skin like lace" (41), a description paralleled by Moon Orchid's gifts of lacy paper warriors and poets "all intricacies and light" (139), the young Kingston worries about confessing to having skinned her even more silent acquaintance (211).

For some students the confusion becomes overwhelming; nothing seems completely true. The narrator has explained that she is Chinese American, not Chinese, and yet she mentions that her parents always advise others, "Lie to Americans" (214), as though she and her siblings were not Americans. She informs us early on that her mother's words are not to be taken at face value: "She said I would grow up a wife and a slave, but she taught me the song of the warrior woman" (24), and yet she seems surprised, toward the end of the book, when she reports Brave Orchid's remark: "That's what Chinese say. We like to say the opposite" (237). While declaring to her mother that she cannot understand "what's real and what you make up" (235), the narrator has of course adopted this very style throughout the book, even joining her mother, toward the end, in a talk-story built on a talk-story, although the narrator has earlier mentioned that she is "mad at the Chinese for lying so much" (25).

As a way out of these confusions, I have discovered that a discussion of the distinctions between lying and fiction making is very helpful. Sissela Bok begins her classic book on lying by distinguishing between "the *moral* domain of intended truthfulness and deception, and the much vaster domain of truth and falsity in general." For Bok "the moral question of whether you are lying or not is not *settled* by establishing the truth or falsity of what you say. In order to settle that question, we must know whether you *intend your statement to mislead*" (6). But for the autobiographer, part of the game includes trying to keep the reader off balance, trying to disturb what Philippe Lejeune calls "the autobiographical pact" (1). Where Lejeune sees the combination of names, title page, preface, and library classification as working together to signal a generic pact, many autobiographers, not entirely certain themselves, remain deliberately ambiguous about genre. That *The Woman Warrior*'s cover carries a label declaring it "the best book of nonfiction published in 1976" as awarded by the National Book Critics Circle, coupled with the fact that the author has named William Carlos Williams's *In The American Grain* as a prime source, makes clear that even Kingston is not willing to be definite about the book's genre.

Although Bok is certainly right to judge lying in a frame outside the general world of true versus false, her claim that lying is determined by the intention to mislead must be modified when applied to autobiography. Bok stresses that in situations where the rules permit mutual deception, lying is acceptable and should no longer be considered lying. But within the complicated, shifting rules for autobiography, the exact degree of deception intended or allowed is open to debate.

As the class completes its consideration of *The Woman Warrior*, a discussion of Kingston's references to photographs is useful in showing the sort of truth that prevails in the text. That the book evokes, as its subtitle suggests, a "girlhood among ghosts" is particularly interesting when we consider the following statement by Françoise Meltzer: "One of the complexities of photography is that, whereas the referent in a painting, a portrait, is the real, living person depicted, the referent for a photograph is once removed from life . . . its ghost, or shadow, or double" (116). Despite the fact that it often talks about photographs, *The Woman Warrior* does not reproduce any pictures. Throughout the book (and in *China Men* as well) photographs are described, often as official documents, the few tangible physical records of Kingston's past. But in describing her ancestor's photographs, the author often comes to express her own doubts about their authenticity. As a result, the photographs described in the text often become less documentary and more the occasions for Kingston to exercise her imagination and memory.

For example, at the beginning of the "Shaman" chapter she describes a photograph of her mother, at the age of thirty-seven, which has a medical school seal superimposed on it:

> The diploma gives her age as twenty-seven. . . . She has spacy eyes, as all people recently from Asia have. Her eyes do not focus on the camera. My mother is not smiling; Chinese do not smile for photographs. Their faces command relatives in foreign lands—"Send money"—and posterity forever—"Put food in front of this picture." My mother does not understand Chinese-American snapshots. "What are you laughing at?" she asks.   (68–69)

The photograph fails as documentation, her mother's age being ten years off, the face emerging from behind the official seal, like one of Lillian Hellman's pentimenti. To the Chinese American daughter, the picture of her mother is a Chinese document, evidence not of what her mother was like as a person of the same age as the author as she is writing this book, but a further confusion of the differences between Chinese and Chinese Americans. Her mother has what Kingston sees as a characteristic faraway focus of the newly arrived emigrant; however, the picture is of her mother in China before she came to this country, and the last chapter of *China Men* suggests that the whole distinction between Asian and non-Asian vision is false.

"There are no snapshots of my mother," writes Kingston in *The Woman Warrior*, though "in two small portraits . . . there is a black thumbprint on her forehead, as if someone had inked in bangs, as if someone had marked her" (71). Her mother's Chinese face is always presented as a sort of photographic palimpsest, showing forth from underneath an official surface, including another version of the same photograph as on the diploma, this time with "Department of Health, Canton" imprinted in English on her mother's face, a literal example of Paul de Man's well-known essay "Autobiography as De-facement." In contrast to these official pictures, Kingston describes the sort of photographs sent from her father to her mother during their separation:

> He and his friends took pictures of one another in bathing suits at Coney Island beach. . . . He's the one in the middle with his arms about the necks of his buddies. They pose in the cockpit of a biplane, on a motorcycle, and on a lawn beside the "Keep Off the Grass" sign. They are always laughing.   (70)

Photographs are valuable for the author, not as documentation but as proof that improvisation, imagination, and memory, the Americanization and feminization of the past, are equally powerful ways to present an authentic portrait. The issue of looking into the camera is part of Kingston's argument in her evocation of these photographs. "Most emigrants learn the barbarians' directness—how to gather themselves and stare rudely into talking faces as if trying to catch lies" (70), she notes, which is exactly what she is doing in examining her parents' portraits.

Because of the exclusion laws applied only to the Chinese, it is not surprising that, for Chinese Americans, stories about entering America frequently include deliberate ambiguities as to the authenticity of names, ages, dates. To Chinese Americans false papers and forged documents seem as accurate as anything else, the truth of photographs residing in what stories they suggest, not in their literal accuracy or in the photogenic qualities of their subjects. Kingston turns to photographs not just in the search for the truth of her family's past but as sources for inventions in the present.

Far from sentimentalizing the past, Kingston seeks to authenticate her present. Because she had not been to China when she wrote her autobiographical books, she had to rely, literally, on a photographic memory to make sense of the contradictory stories her mother told her and the contradictory way in which she told them. Kingston's description of herself while writing the novel *Tripmaster Monkey* suggests how she was working on her first book: "If there is such a thing as reverse memory, maybe that's what I am getting into; because it seems to me, I'm writing the memory of the future rather than a memory of the past" (Rabinowitz 187).

Even if there were pictures of her father in China or if her brother in Vietnam had taken photographs of the Hong family house when he visited

China, the pictures would never be as authentic as the portraits and self-portraits taken by Kingston. Nor would more actual photographs solve her dilemma as an autobiographer. As Michael Ignatieff explains, neither photographs nor mirrors are helpful in producing a consistent self-story: "More often than not photographs subvert the continuity that memory weaves out of experience. . . . The photograph acts towards the self like a harshly lit mirror, like the pitiless historian confronted with the wish fulfillments of nationalistic fable or political lie" (28).

Whatever else a fruitful classroom discussion of these issues of truth and lie may bring out, it should be clear by the end of the discussion that Kingston is best judged by Marcel Eck's standard as expressed in his *Lies and Truth*: "We will be judged not on whether we possess or do not possess the truth but on whether or not we sought and loved it" (160). The precise generic classification of *The Woman Warrior* is less important than the standards of truth brought to the text by the class and its teacher.

CONTRIBUTORS AND SURVEY PARTICIPANTS

The following scholars responded to the questionnaire on teaching *The Woman Warrior*; many of them also submitted essay proposals for part 2. Much of the information in the "Materials" section of this volume was gathered from their generous contributions. Except when new information has been offered, the list indicates colleges where the participants taught when they submitted their survey responses.

Timothy Dow Adams, West Virginia University; James R. Aubrey, Metropolitan State College, Denver; Edith Blicksilver, Georgia Institute of Technology; Kathleen A. Boardman, University of Nevada, Reno; Carol Burr, California State University, Chico; King-Kok Cheung, University of California, Los Angeles; Cheng Lok Chua, California State University, Fresno; Greta Cohan, Westchester Community College; Margaret Dunn, University of Central Florida; Tucker Pamella Farley, Brooklyn College, City University of New York; Ann W. Fisher-Wirth, University of Mississippi; Andrea D. Gim, Charlottesville, VA; Vicente F. Gotera, Humboldt State University, Arcata; Vicky Graham, University of California, Berkeley; Helen Jaskoski, California State University, Fullerton; Suzanne Jones, University of Richmond; Carey H. Kaplan, Georgetown University; Colleen Kennedy, College of William and Mary; Elaine H. Kim, University of California, Berkeley; Deirdre Lashgari, California State Polytechnic University, Pomona; Robert G. Lee, Brown University; David Leiwei Li, University of Texas, Austin; Joan Lidoff (deceased), University of Texas, Austin; Paulino Lim, California State University, Long Beach; Patricia Lin, California State Polytechnic University, Pomona; Amy Ling, University of Wisconsin, Madison; Lisa Lowe, University of California, San Diego; Paul W. McBride, Ithaca College; Judith M. Melton, Clemson University; Lucien Miller, University of Massachusetts, Amherst; Carol Mitchell, Colorado State University; Ann R. Morris, Stetson University; Patrick D. Morrow, Auburn University; Deborah Morse, College of William and Mary; Victoria Myers, Pepperdine University; E. Imafedia Okhamafe, University of Nebraska, Omaha; Marlyn Peterson, Santa Rosa, CA; Joyce Pettis, North Carolina State University; William Pietz, Georgetown University; Lillian S. Robinson, University of Hawaii, Manoa; Gayle K. Fujita Sato, Keio University, Japan; Ruth O. Saxton, Mills College; Paul Skenazy, University of California, Santa Cruz; George Uba, California State University, Northridge; Kathryn VanSpanckeren, University of Tampa; Susan Ward, Saint Lawrence University; Annette White-Parks, Washington State University, Pullman; Sau-ling Cynthia Wong, University of California, Berkeley; Marilyn Yalom, Stanford University.

WORKS CITED

Books and Articles

Aleramo, Sibilla. *A Woman*. 1906. Berkeley: U of California P, 1983.

Amanpour, Mojgan, and Atoosa Molanazadeh. Interview with Deirdre Lashgari. *Sonoma Women's Voices* June 1989: 1+.

Angelou, Maya. *I Know Why the Caged Bird Sings*. New York: Random, 1970.

Archdeacon, Thomas. *Becoming American: An Ethnic History*. New York: Free, 1983.

Aubrey, James R. " 'Going toward War' in the Writings of Maxine Hong Kingston." *Vietnam Generation* 1.3–4 (1989): 90–101.

Austin, J. L. *How to Do Things with Words*. Ed. J. O. Urmsom and Marina Sbisa. 2nd ed. Cambridge: Harvard UP, 1975.

Ba Jin (Pa Chin) [Li, Fei-Kan]. *The Family (Chia)*. 1931. Trans. Sidney Shapiro. Beijing: Foreign Languages, 1958.

Baker, Houston, and Walter J. Ong, eds. *Three American Literatures*. New York: MLA, 1982.

Bakhtin, M. M. (see also Volosinov, V. N.) *The Dialogic Imagination*. Ed. Michael Holquist. Trans. Caryl Emerson and Michael Holquist. Austin: U of Texas P, 1988.

"Ballad of Mulan." Trans. William H. Nienhauser. Liu and Lo 77–80.

Barnwell, William H., and Julie Price, eds. *Reflections: A Thematic Reader*. New York: Houghton, 1985.

Bateson, Mary Catherine. *With a Daughter's Eye*. New York: Morrow, 1984.

Beaty, Jerome, and J. Paul Hunter, eds. *New Worlds of Literature*. New York: Norton, 1989.

Benstock, Shari. *The Private Self: Theory and Practice of Women's Autobiographical Writing*. Chapel Hill: U of North Carolina P, 1988.

Bilson, Marcus. "The Memoir: New Perspectives on a Forgotten Genre." *Genre* 10 (1977): 259–83.

Birch, Cyril, ed. *Anthology of Chinese Literature: From Early Times to the Fourteenth Century*. New York: Grove, 1965.

Blauvelt, W. Satake. "Talking with 'The Woman Warrior.' " *Pacific Reader* 19 July 1989: 1+.

Blinde, Patricia Lin. "The Icicle in the Desert: Perspectives and Form in the Works of Two Chinese American Women Writers." *MELUS* 6 (1979): 51–71.

Bloom, Lynn Z. "Heritages: Dimensions of Mother-Daughter Relationships in Women's Autobiographies." Davidson and Broner 291–303.

Bodnar, John. *The Transplanted*. Bloomington: Indiana UP, 1985.

Boelhower, William. *Through a Glass Darkly: Ethnic Semiosis in American Literature*. New York: Oxford UP, 1987.

Bok, Sissela. *Lying: Moral Choice in Public and Private Life*. New York: Vintage, 1979.

Brombert, Victor. "Mediating the Work: Or, The Legitimate Aims of Criticism." *PMLA* 105 (1990): 391–97.

Brownmiller, Susan. "Susan Brownmiller Talks with Maxine Hong Kingston, Author of *The Woman Warrior*." *Mademoiselle* Mar. 1977: 148+.

Campbell, R. C. *Chinese Coolie Immigration*. London: King, 1923.

Carabi, Angeles. Interview with Maxine Hong Kingston. *Belles Lettres* (Winter 1989): 10–11.

Cavitch, David. *Life Studies: A Thematic Reader*. 3rd ed. New York: St. Martin's, 1989.

Chan, Jeffery Paul. "Jeff Chan, Chairman of SF State Asian American Studies, Attacks Review." *San Francisco Journal* 4 May 1977: 6.

———. Letter. *New York Review of Books* 28 Apr. 1977: 41.

Chan, Jeffery Paul, Frank C. Chin, Lawson Inada, and Shawn Wong. *Aiiieeeee! An Anthology of Asian American Writers*. Washington: Howard UP, 1983.

Chang, Diana. "Saying Yes." *Asian American Heritage: An Anthology of Prose and Poetry*. Ed. David Hsin-fu Wand. New York: Washington Square, 1974. 130.

Chang, Eileen. *The Golden Cangue (Chin Suo Chi)*. 1944. *Modern Chinese Stories and Novellas, 1919–1945*. Ed. Joseph S. M. Lau, C. T. Hsia, and Leo Ou-fan Lee. New York: Columbia UP, 1981. 530–59.

Chen, Jack. *The Chinese of America: From the Beginnings to the Present*. San Francisco: Harper, 1981.

Ch'en, Shou-Yi. *Chinese Literature: A Historical Introduction*. New York: Ronald, 1961.

Chen Ta. *Emigrant Communities in South China*. New York: Inst. for Pacific Relations, 1940.

Cheng, Lucie, and Edna Bonacich, eds. *Labor Immigration under Capitalism: Asian Immigrant Workers in the United States before World War II*. Berkeley: U of California P, 1984.

Chernin, Kim. *In My Mother's House*. New Haven: Tickner, 1983.

Cheung, King-Kok. " 'Don't Tell': Imposed Silences in *The Color Purple* and *The Woman Warrior*." *PMLA* 103 (1988): 162–74.

Cheung, King-Kok, and Stan Yogi. *Asian American Literature: An Annotated Bibliography*. New York: MLA, 1988.

Chin, Frank. "This Is Not an Autobiography." *Genre* 18.2 (1985): 109–30.

Chin, Marilyn. *Dwarf Bamboo*. Greenfield Center: Greenfield, 1987.

———. "Writing the Other: A Conversation with Maxine Hong Kingston." *Poetry Flash* Sept. 1989: 1+.

Chinese Historical Society of Southern California. *Linking Our Lives: Chinese American Women of Los Angeles*. Los Angeles: Chinese Historical Soc. of Southern California, 1984.

Chodorow, Nancy. *The Reproduction of Mothering: Psychoanalysis and the Sociology of Gender*. Berkeley: U of California P, 1978.

Chu, Louis. *Eat a Bowl of Tea*. 1961. Secaucus: Stuart, 1979.

Chua, C. L. "Golden Mountain: Chinese Versions of the American Dream in Lin Yutang, Louis Chu, and Maxine Hong Kingston." *Ethnic Groups* 4.12 (1982): 33–59.

———. "Two Versions of the American Dream: The Golden Mountain in Lin Yutang and Maxine Hong Kingston." *MELUS* 8.4 (1981): 61–70.

Cirlot, J. E. *A Dictionary of Symbols*. Trans. Jack Sage. New York: Philosophical, 1962.

Clifford, James, and George E. Marcus, eds. *Writing Culture: The Poetics and Politics of Ethnography*. Berkeley: U of California P, 1986.

Cockshut, A. O. J. *The Art of Autobiography in Nineteenth and Twentieth Century England*. New Haven: Yale UP, 1984.

Colombo, Gary, et al. *Reading American Culture: Cultural Contexts for Critical Thinking and Writing*. New York: St. Martin's, 1989.

Coolidge, Mary R. *Chinese Immigration*. New York: Holt, 1909.

Costello, Jacqueline, and Amy Tucker. *Forms of Literature: A Writer's Collection*. New York: Random, 1989.

Cox, James M. "Autobiography and America." *Virginia Quarterly Review* 47 (1971): 252–77.

———. "Recovering Literature's Lost Ground through Autobiography." Olney, *Autobiography* 123–45.

Currier, Susan. "Maxine Hong Kingston." *Dictionary of Literary Biography Yearbook 1980*. Ed. Karel L. Rood, Jean W. Ross, and Richard Ziegfield. Detroit: Gale, 1981. 235–40.

Daniels, Jeffrey. Personal interview with James Aubrey. 11 Aug. 1989.

Dasenbrock, Reed Way. "Intelligibility and Meaningfulness in Multicultural Literature in English." *PMLA* 102 (1987): 10–19.

Davidson, Cathy N., and E. M. Broner, eds. *The Lost Tradition: Mothers and Daughters in Literature*. New York: Ungar, 1986.

de Man, Paul. "Autobiography as De-facement." *MLN* 94 (1979): 919–30.

Demetrakopoulos, Stephanie A. "The Metaphysics of Matrilinearism in Women's Autobiography: Studies of Mead's *Blackberry Winter*, Hellman's *Pentimento*, Angelou's *I Know Why the Caged Bird Sings*, and Kingston's *The Woman Warrior*." Jelinek, *Women's Autobiography* 180–205.

Devlin, Pamela. Personal interview with Marlyn Peterson. 30 Oct. 1988.

Di Yanni, Robert. *Literature: Reading Fiction, Poetry, Drama, and the Essay*. 2nd ed. New York: McGraw, 1990.

Duras, Marguerite. *The Lover*. New York: Harper, 1986.

Dworken, Andrea. "Gynocide: Footbinding." *Feminist Frontiers 11*. Ed. Laurel Richardson and Vera Taylor. New York: Random, 1989. 15–24.

Eakin, Paul John. *Fiction in Autobiography: Studies in the Art of Self-Invention*. Princeton: Princeton UP, 1985.

Eck, Marcel. *Lies and Truth*. Trans. Bernard Murchland. New York: Macmillan, 1970.

Elbow, Peter. *Embracing Contraries*. New York: Oxford UP, 1986.

Ellison, Ralph. *Invisible Man*. New York: Vintage, 1972.

Evory, Ann, ed. *Contemporary Authors New Revision Series*. Vol. 13. Detroit: Gale, 1984.

Feuchtwang, Stephen. "Domestic and Communal Worship in Taiwan." A. Wolf 106–29.

Fischer, Michael M. J. "Ethnicity and the Postmodern Arts of Memory." Clifford and Marcus 194–233.

Fish, Stanley. *Is There a Text in This Class?* Cambridge: Harvard UP, 1980.

Fishman, Judith. *Responding to Prose: A Reader for Writers*. New York: Macmillan, 1983.

Fogel, Stanley. *The Postmodern University: Essays on the Deconstruction of the Humanities*. Toronto: ECW, 1988.

Folsom, Marcia. " 'Whence the Lights and Shadows Fall': Teaching and Learning about Differences in English 101." *Wheelock College Centennial Essays*. Boston: Wheelock Coll., 1988. 4–5.

Fong, Katheryn M. "To Maxine Hong Kingston: A Letter." *Bulletin for Concerned Asian Scholars* 9.4 (1977): 67–69.

Gaggi, Silvio. *Modern/Postmodern: A Study in Twentieth-Century Arts and Ideas*. Philadelphia: U of Pennsylvania P, 1989.

Gates, Hill. "The Commoditization of Chinese Women." *Signs: Journal of Women in Culture and Society* 14 (1989): 799–832.

Geertz, Clifford. "Deep Play: Notes on the Balinese Cockfight." *Interpretation* 412–53.

———. *The Interpretation of Cultures: Selected Essays by Clifford Geertz*. New York: Basic, 1973.

———. "Thick Description: Toward an Interpretive Theory of Culture." *Interpretation* 3–30.

Gilbert, Sandra M., and Susan Gubar. *The Madwoman in the Attic*. New Haven: Yale UP, 1971.

———, eds. *The Norton Anthology of Literature by Women: The Tradition in English*. New York: Norton, 1985.

Gilligan, Carol. *In a Different Voice*. Cambridge: Harvard UP, 1982.

Gilman, Charlotte Perkins. *The Yellow Wallpaper*. 1899. New York: Feminist, 1973.

Gunn, Janet Varner. *Autobiography: Toward a Poetics of Experience*. Philadelphia: U of Pennsylvania P, 1982.

Guo, Muro. *Guo Moruo juzuo quanji.* Vol. 3. Beijing: Zhongguo Xiju Chubanshe, 1983.

Gusdorf, George S. "Conditions and Limits of Autobiography." Trans. James Olney. Olney, *Autobiography* 28–48.

Guth, Hans, and Renee Shea, eds. *Essay 2: Reading with the Writer's Eye.* Belmont: Wadsworth, 1987.

Gutman, Herbert. *Work Culture and Society in Industrializing America.* New York: Knopf, 1976.

Hall, Donald, ed. *The Contemporary Essay.* 2nd ed. New York: St. Martin's, 1989.

Handlin, Oscar. *The Uprooted.* Boston: Little, 1951.

Hansen, Marcus Lee. *The Atlantic Migration, 1607–1860.* Cambridge: Harvard UP, 1940.

Hassan, Ihab. "The Culture of Postmodernism." *Modernism: Challenges and Perspectives.* Ed. Monique Chefdor, Ricardo Quinones, and Albert Wachtel. Urbana: U of Illinois P, 1986. 304–23.

Hegel, Robert E. "An Exploration of the Chinese Literary Self." *Expressions of Self in Chinese Literature.* Ed. Robert E. Hegel and Richard C. Hessney. New York: Columbia UP, 1985. 3–30.

Heilbrun, Carolyn G. *Writing a Woman's Life.* New York: Ballantine, 1988.

Higham, John. *Strangers in the Land: Problems of American Nativism, 1850–1925.* New Brunswick: Rutgers UP, 1955.

Hirsch, E. D., Jr. *Cultural Literacy: What Every American Should Know.* Ed. Pat Mulchy. New York: Random, 1988.

Homsher, Deborah. "*The Woman Warrior*, by Maxine Hong Kingston: A Bridging of Autobiography and Fiction." *Iowa Review* 10 (1979): 93–98.

Hsia, C. T. *The Classic Chinese Novel: A Critical Introduction.* 1968. Bloomington: Indiana UP, 1980.

Hsu, Vivian. "Maxine Hong Kingston as Psycho-Autobiographer and Ethnographer." *International Journal of Women's Studies* 6.5 (1983): 429–42.

Hurston, Zora Neale. *Their Eyes Were Watching God.* Urbana: U of Illinois P, 1971.

Ignatieff, Michael. "Family Photo Albums." *Harper's* June 1987: 27–28.

Ingalls, Rachel. *Mrs. Caliban.* Boston: Harvard Common, 1983.

Islas, Arturo. Interview with Maxine Hong Kingston. *Women Writers of the West Coast Speaking of Their Lives and Careers.* Ed. Marilyn Yalom. Santa Barbara: Capra, 1983. 11–19.

James, Henry. "The Jolly Corner." *Eight Tales from the Major Phase: "In the Cage" and Others.* Ed. Morton Dauwen Zabel. New York: Norton, 1969. 314–50.

Jashok, Maria. *Concubines and Bondservants: The Social History of a Chinese Custom.* London: Zed, 1988.

Jay, Paul. *Being in the Text: Self-Presentation from Wordsworth to Barthes.* Ithaca: Cornell UP, 1984.

Jelinek, Estelle C. *The Tradition of Women's Autobiography: From Antiquity to the Present.* Boston: Twayne, 1986.

———, ed. *Women's Autobiography: Essays in Criticism.* Bloomington: Indiana UP, 1980.

Johnson, Kay Ann. *Women, the Family, and Peasant Revolution in China.* Chicago: U of Chicago P, 1988.

Jordan, David K. *Gods, Ghosts, and Ancestors: The Folk Religion of a Taiwanese Village.* Berkeley: U of California P, 1972.

Juhasz, Suzanne. "Maxine Hong Kingston: Narrative Technique and Female Identity." *Contemporary American Women Writers: Narrative Strategies.* Ed. Catherine Rainwater and William J. Scheick. Lexington: U of Kentucky P, 1985. 173–90.

———. "Toward a Theory of Form in Feminist Autobiography: Kate Millett's *Flying* and *Sita*; Maxine Hong Kingston's *The Woman Warrior.*" *International Journal of Women's Studies* 2.1 (1979): 62–75. Jelinek, *Women's Autobiography* 221–370.

Kartini, Raden Adjeng. *Letters of a Javanese Princess.* 1911. Ed. Hildred Geertz. Trans. Agnes Symmers. Hong Kong: Heinemann, 1976.

Kazin, Alfred. "The Self as History: Reflections on Autobiography." Stone, *American* 31–43.

Kim, Elaine H. *Asian American Literature: An Introduction to the Writings and Their Social Context.* Philadelphia: Temple UP, 1982.

———. "Asian American Literature and the Importance of Social Context." *ADE Bulletin* 80 (1985): 34–41.

———. "Visions and Fierce Dreams: A Commentary on the Worlds of Maxine Hong Kingston." *Amerasia Journal* 8.2 (1981): 145–61.

King, Ann, and Sandra Kurtinitis. *Being and Becoming: An Introduction to Literature.* New York: Random, 1987.

Kingston, Maxine Hong. *China Men.* New York: Knopf, 1980.

———. "The Coming Book." *The Writer on Her Work.* Ed. Janet Sternburg. New York: Norton, 1980. 181–85.

———. "Cultural Mis-readings by American Reviewers." *Asian and Western Writers in Dialogue: New Cultural Identities.* Ed. Guy Amirthanayagam. London: Macmillan, 1982. 55–65.

———. "Duck Boy." *New York Times Magazine* 12 June 1977: 55+.

———. *Hawai'i One Summer.* Illus. Deng Ming-Dao. San Francisco: Meadow, 1987.

———. "The Making of More Americans." *New Yorker* 11 Feb. 1980: 34+.

———. "Maxine Hong Kingston: Exploring Old Myths in a Contemporary American Voice." *Humanities Discourse* 2.6 (1988): 3–5.

———. "Postscript on Process." *The Bedford Reader.* 2nd ed. Ed. X. J. Kennedy and Dorothy M. Kennedy. New York: St. Martin's, 1985. 69–70.

———. "Reservations about China." *Ms.* Oct. 1978: 67–68.

———. "San Francisco's Chinatown: A View from the Other Side of Arnold Genthe's Camera." *American Heritage* Dec. 1978: 36+.

———. "Tripmaster Monkey." Reading and talk. Larkspur, CA. 24 May 1989.

———. *Tripmaster Monkey: His Fake Book.* New York: Knopf, 1989.

———. *The Woman Warrior: Memoirs of a Girlhood among Ghosts.* 1976. New York: Vintage-Random, 1989.

———. "A Writer's Notebook from the Far East." *Ms.* Jan. 1983: 85–86.

Kirszner, Laurie O., and Stephen R. Mandell. *Patterns for College Writing: A Rhetorical Reader and Guide.* 4th ed. New York: St. Martin's, 1989.

———. *The Writer's Sourcebook: Strategies for Reading and Writing in the Disciplines.* New York: Holt, 1987.

Kornblum, Lori. "Women Warriors in a Men's World: The Combat Exclusion." *Law and Inequality* 2 (1984): 351–445.

Kotite-Young, Shirley. Personal interview with Marlyn Peterson. 28 Oct. 1988.

Kwong, Peter. *Chinatown, New York: Labor and Politics, 1930–1950.* New York: Monthly Review, 1979.

Lai, Him Mark, Genny Lim, and Judy Yung, eds. and trans. *Island: Poetry and History of Chinese Immigrants on Angel Island: 1910–1940.* San Francisco: HOCHDOI, 1980.

Lan, Dean. "The Chinatown Sweatshops: Oppression and an Alternative." *Amerasia Journal* 1.3 (1971): 40–57.

———. "The Lamentation." Trans. Yi-T'umg Wang. Liu and Lo 36–39.

Latsch, Marie-Luise. *Chinese Traditional Festivals.* Beijing: New World, 1984.

Lauter, Paul, et al., eds. *The Heath Anthology of American Literature.* New York: Health, 1989.

Law-Yone, Wendy. *The Coffin Tree.* Beacon: Boston, 1983.

Lee, Robert G. "The Origins of Chinese Immigration to the United States, 1848–1882." *The Life, Influence, and Role of the Chinese in the United States, 1776–1960.* San Francisco: Chinese Historical Soc. of America, 1976. 183–93.

Lee, Rose Hum. *The Chinese in the United States of America.* Hong Kong: Hong Kong UP, 1960.

Lejeune, Philippe. *Le pacte autobiographique.* Paris: Seuil, 1975.

Li, David Leiwei. "The Naming of a Chinese American 'I': Cross-Cultural Sign/ ifications in *The Woman Warrior.*" *Criticism* 30 (1988): 497–515.

Lim, Shirley Geok-lin. "Twelve Asian American Writers in Search of Self-Definition." *MELUS* 13.1–2 (1986): 57–78.

Lin, Alice P. *Grandmother Had No Name.* San Francisco: China, 1988.

Ling, Amy. "Asian American Literature: A Brief Introduction and Selected Bibliography." *ADE Bulletin* 80 (1985): 29–33.

———. *Between Worlds: Women Writers of Chinese Ancestry.* New York: Pergamon, 1990.

———. "Thematic Threads in Maxine Hong Kingston's *The Woman Warrior.*" *Tamkang Review* 14.1–4 (1983–84): 55–64.

———. "Writer in the Hyphenated Condition: Diana Chang." *MELUS* 7 (1980): 69–83.

Liu, James J. Y. *The Chinese Knight-Errant.* London: Routledge, 1967.

Liu, Wu-chi, and Irving Lo, eds. *Sunflower Splendor: Three Thousand Years of Chinese Poetry.* Bloomington: Indiana UP, 1975.

Lo Kuan-chung [Luo Guanzhong in pinyin]. *San Kuo: Or, Romance of the Three Kingdoms.* Trans. C. H. Brewitt-Taylor. 2 vols. Shanghai: Kelly, 1925.

———. *Three Kingdoms.* Abridged. Ed. and trans. Moss Roberts. New York: Pantheon, 1976.

Lu Guanying. "China's Earliest Anthology of Poetry." *Selections* 97–112.

Luo Guanzhong. *Outlaws of the Marsh.* Trans. Sidney Shapiro. 2 vols. Bloomington: Indiana UP, 1981.

———. *Outlaws of the Marsh.* Abridged. Trans. Sidney Shapiro. Hong Kong: Commercial, 1986.

Lyman, Stanford M. *Chinese Americans.* New York: Random, 1974.

Mandel, Barrett J. "Full of Life Now." Olney, *Autobiography* 49–72.

Mansell, Darrell. "Unsettling the Colonel's Hash: 'Fact' in Autobiography." Stone, *American Autobiography* 61–79.

Mark, Diane Mei Lin, and Ginger Chih. *A Place Called Chinese America.* San Francisco: Org. of Chinese Americans, 1982.

Martz, Louis. *The Poetry of Meditation.* New Haven: Yale UP, 1954.

McCunn, Ruthanne Lum. *Chinese American Portraits: Personal Histories, 1828–1929.* San Francisco: Chronicle, 1988.

McQuade, Donald, and Robert Atwan, eds. *Thinking in Writing.* 3rd ed. New York: Knopf, 1988.

Meltzer, Françoise. *Salome and the Dance of Writing: Portraits of Mimesis in Literature.* Chicago: U of Chicago P, 1987.

Miller, Gilbert, et al. *The Short Prose Reader.* 5th ed. New York: McGraw, 1989.

Miller, Margaret. "Threads of Identity in Maxine Hong Kingston's *Woman Warrior.*" *Biography* 6.1 (1983): 13–33.

Miller, Susan, ed. *The Written World: Reading and Writing in Social Contexts.* New York: Harper, 1988.

Miner, Horace. "Body Ritual among the Nacirema." *American Anthropologist* 58 (June 1965): 503–07.

Mitchell, Carol. " 'Talking-Story' in *The Woman Warrior*: An Analysis of the Use of Folklore." *Kentucky Folklore Record* 27.1–2 (1981): 5–12.

Morgan, Harry T. *Chinese Symbols and Superstitions.* 1942. Detroit: Gale, 1972.

Munro, Alice. *Lives of Girls and Women.* New York: NAL, 1983.

Murasaki Shikibu (Lady Murasaki). *The Tale of Genji.* Trans. Edward G. Seidensticker. New York: Knopf, 1986.

Myers, Victoria. "The Significant Fictivity of Maxine Hong Kingston's *The Woman Warrior.*" *Biography* 9 (1986): 112–25.

Nee, Victor, and Brett Nee. *Longtime Californ': A Documentary Study of an American Chinatown.* 1972. New York: Pantheon, 1982.

Neubauer, Carol E. "Developing Ties to the Past: Photography and Other Sources of Information on Maxine Hong Kingston's *China Men.*" *MELUS* 10.4 (1983): 17–36.

Oliphant, Margaret. *Miss Marjoribanks.* London: Virago, 1988.

Oliver, Lawrence J. "The Re-visioning of New York's Little Italies: From Howells to Puzo." *MELUS* 14.3–4 (1987): 5–22.

Olney, James, ed. *Autobiography: Essays Theoretical and Critical.* Princeton: Princeton UP, 1980.

———, ed. *Studies in Autobiography.* New York: Oxford UP, 1988.

Omi, Michael, and Howard Winant. *Racial Formation in the United States from the 1960's to the 1980's.* New York: Routledge, 1986.

Ong, Paul. "Chinese Labor in Early San Francisco: Racial Segmentation and Industrial Expansion." *Amerasia Journal* 8.1 (1981): 69–92.

Ono, Kazuko. *Chinese Women in a Century of Revolution.* Trans. and ed. Joshua A. Fogel. Stanford: Stanford UP, 1989.

Ordóñez, Elizabeth J. "Narrative Texts by Ethnic Women: Rereading the Past, Reshaping the Future." *MELUS* 9.3 (1982): 19–28.

Pearson, Carol, and Katherine Pope. *The Female Hero in American and British Literature.* New York: Bowker, 1981.

Pfaff, Timothy. "Talk with Mrs. Kingston." *New York Times Book Review* 15 June 1980: 1+.

———. "Whispers of a Literary Explorer." *Horizon* July 1980: 58–63.

Piercy, Marge. *Woman on the Edge of Time.* New York: Knopf, 1976.

Plato. *The Republic.* Trans. Desmond Lee. 2nd ed. New York: Penguin, 1974.

Potter, Jack M. "Cantonese Shamanism." A. Wolf 207–31.

Pratt, Mary Louis. *Toward a Speech Act Theory of Literary Discourse.* Bloomington: Indiana UP, 1977.

Puzo, Mario. *The Fortunate Pilgrim.* New York: Fawcett, 1978.

Rabine, Leslie. "No Lost Paradise: Social Gender and Symbolic Gender in the Writings of Maxine Hong Kingston." *Signs* 12.3 (1987): 471–92.

Rabinowitz, Paula. "Eccentric Memories: A Conversation with Maxine Hong Kingston." *Michigan Quarterly Review* 26 (1987): 177–87.

Rexroth, Kenneth, and Ling Chung, trans. and eds. *Women Poets of China.* New York: New Directions, 1972.

Rhys, Jean. *Wide Sargasso Sea.* New York: Penguin, 1983.

Riffaterre, Michael. *Semiotics of Poetry.* Bloomington: Indiana UP, 1978.

Robinson, Marilynne. *Housekeeping.* New York: Bantam, 1984.

Rogers, Judy R., and Glenn C. Rogers. *Patterns and Themes: A Basic English Reader.* 2nd ed. Belmont: Wadsworth, 1988.

Rolvaag, O. E. *Giants in the Earth.* New York: Harper, 1965.

Rorex, Robert A., and Wen Fong, introd. and trans. *Eighteen Songs of a Nomad Flute: The Story of Lady Wen-Chi.* New York: Metropolitan Museum of Art, 1974. Np.

Rose, Shirley K. "Metaphors and Myths of Cross-Cultural Literacy: Autobiographical Narratives by Maxine Hong Kingston, Richard Rodriguez, and Malcolm X." *MELUS* 14.1 (1987): 3–15.

Rosenberg, Warren, et al., eds. *American Voices: A Thematic-Cultural Reader.* New York: Harper, 1988.

Ross, Jean W. "Interview with Maxine Hong Kingston." *Evory* 291–94.

Rubenstein, Roberta. "Bridging Two Cultures: Maxine Hong Kingston." *Boundaries of the Self: Gender, Culture, Fiction.* Urbana: U of Illinois P, 1987. 164–89.

Said, Edward. *Orientalism.* New York: Vintage-Random, 1979.

Saxton, Alexander. *The Indispensable Enemy: Labor and the Anti-Chinese Movement in California.* Berkeley: U of California P, 1971.

Sayre, Robert F. "Autobiography and the Making of America." Olney, *Autobiography* 146–68.

———. "The Proper Study: Autobiographies in American Studies." Stone, *American* 11–30.

Schenck, Celeste. "All of a Piece: Women's Poetry and Autobiography." *Life Lines: Theorizing Women's Autobiography.* Ed. Bella Brodzki and Celeste Schenck. Ithaca: Cornell UP, 1989. 281–305.

Schorer, Mark, et al., eds. *Harbrace College Reader.* New York: Harcourt, 1984.

Scott, Dorothea Haywood. *Chinese Popular Literature and the Child.* Chicago: American Library Assn., 1980.

Scott, Sarah. *A Description of Millenium Hall and the Country Adjacent.* 1762. New York: Viking Penguin–Virago, 1986.

Searle, John R. *Expression and Meaning.* Cambridge: Cambridge UP, 1970.

———. *Speech Acts.* Cambridge: Cambridge UP, 1979.

Selections from The Book of Songs. Trans. Yang Xianyi, Gladys Yang, and Hu Shiguang. Beijing: China Publications, 1983.

Seventy-Five Readings: An Anthology. 2nd ed. New York: McGraw, 1989.

Shimer, Dorothy Blair, ed. *Rice Bowl Women.* New York: NAL, 1982.

Shishedo, Miles M. *Reflections on the Nature and Style of the Liberal Arts: Woman Warrior, Analysis and Interpretation.* Hiroshima: Keisuisha, 1989.

Showalter, Elaine, ed. *The New Feminist Criticism.* New York: Pantheon, 1985.

Shrodes, Caroline, et al., eds. *The Conscious Reader.* 4th ed. New York: Macmillan, 1988.

Simon, Kate. *Bronx Primitive: Portraits in a Childhood.* New York: Viking, 1982.

Sinclair, May. *Life and Death of Harriet Frean.* New York: Viking Penguin–Virago, 1985.

Siu, Paul C. *The Chinese Laundryman: A Study of Social Isolation.* Ed. John Kuo Wei Tchen. New York: New York UP, 1987.

Skwire, David, ed. *Writing with a Thesis.* New York: Holt, 1990.

Sledge, Linda Ching. "Maxine Hong Kingston's *China Men*: The Family Historian as Epic Poet." *MELUS* 7.4 (1980): 3–22.

——. "Teaching Asian American Literature." *ADE Bulletin* 80 (1985): 42–45.

Smith, Richard J. "China and the West: Some Comparative Possibilities." *Liberal Education* 73.4 (1987): 6–11.

Smith, Sidonie. *A Poetics of Women's Autobiography.* Bloomington: Indiana UP, 1987.

Solberg, Sam. "Between the Lines." *Seattle Weekly Magazine* 10 May 1989: 47.

Sollors, Werner. *Beyond Ethnicity: Consent and Descent in American Culture.* New York: Oxford UP, 1986.

——. "Literature and Ethnicity." *Harvard Encyclopedia of American Ethnic Groups.* Ed. Stephen Thernstrom. Cambridge: Harvard UP, 1980. 647–65.

Sommers, Nancy, and Donald McQuade, eds. *Student Writers at Work: The Bedford Prizes.* Boston: Bedford, 1989.

Sowell, Thomas. *Ethnic America.* New York: Basic, 1981.

Spender, Dale. *Man Made Language.* London: Routledge, 1980.

Spengemann, William C. *The Forms of Autobiography.* New Haven: Yale UP, 1980.

Spivak, Gayatri. *In Other Worlds: Essays in Cultural Politics.* New York: Routledge, 1988.

Stanton, Domna, and Jeanine Plottel, eds. *The Female Autograph.* Chicago: U of Chicago P, 1987.

Steiner, Stan. *Fusang: The Chinese Who Built America.* New York: Harper, 1979.

Stiehm, Judith Hicks. *Bring Me Men and Women: Mandated Change at the U.S. Air Force Academy.* Berkeley: U of California P, 1981.

Stockard, Janice. *Daughters of the Canton Delta: Marriage Patterns and Economic Strategies in South China, 1860–1930.* Stanford: Stanford UP, 1988.

Stone, Albert E., ed. *The American Autobiography.* Englewood Cliffs: Prentice, 1981.

——. *Autobiographical Occasions and Original Acts: Versions of American Identity from Henry Adams to Nate Shaw.* Philadelphia: U of Pennsylvania P, 1982.

Sung, Betty Lee. *Mountain of Gold: The Story of the Chinese in America.* New York: Macmillan, 1967.

Tan, Amy. *The Joy Luck Club.* New York: Ivy-Ballantine, 1989.

Thompson, Phyllis Hage. "This Is the Story I Heard: A Conversation with Maxine Hong Kingston and Earll Kingston." *Biography* 6.1 (1983): 1–12.

Tom, Lily. "Swashbuckling Swordswomen of the Silver Screen." *Ms.* April 1973: 28–29.

Tong, Benjamin R. "Critic of Admirer Sees Dumb Racist." *San Francisco Journal* 11 May 1977: 6.

Trimmer, Joseph F., and Maxine Hairston, eds. *The Riverside Reader.* 2nd ed. Vol. 1. New York: Houghton, 1985.

Tsai, Shih-shan Henry. *The Chinese Experience in America.* Bloomington: Indiana UP, 1986.

Volosinov, V. N. [Bakhtin, M. M.] *Marxism and the Philosophy of Language.* Trans. Ladislav Matejka and I. R. Titunik. Cambridge: Harvard UP, 1973.

Wakeman, Frederic, Jr. Rev. of *China Men,* by Maxine Hong Kingston. *New York Review of Books* 14 Aug. 1980: 42–44.

Wang, Alfred S. "Maxine Hong Kingston's Reclaiming of America: The Birthright of the Chinese American Male." *South Dakota Review* 26.1 (1988): 18–29.

Weber, Max. "Politics as a Vocation." *From Max Weber.* Trans. H. H. Gerth and C. Wright Mills. New York: Oxford UP, 1946. 77–128.

Werner, E. T. C. *Dictionary of Chinese Mythology.* New York: Julian, 1961.

Weston, Jessie L. *From Ritual to Romance.* New York: Anchor-Doubleday, 1957.

White, Antonia. *Frost in May.* New York: Dial, 1980.

Wolf, Arthur P., ed. *Religion and Ritual in Chinese Society.* Stanford: Stanford UP, 1974.

Wolf, Margery. "Women and Suicide in China." Wolf and Witke. 111–42.

Wolf, Margery, and Roxane Witke, eds. *Women in Chinese Society.* Stanford: Stanford UP, 1975.

Women in Chinese Folklore. Beijing: Women of China, 1983.

Wong, Jade Snow. *Fifth Chinese Daughter.* New York: Harper, 1945.

Wong, Sau-ling Cynthia. "Autobiography as Guided Chinatown Tour? Maxine Hong Kingston's *The Woman Warrior* and the Chinese American Autobiographical Debate." *American Lives: Essays in Multicultural American Autobiography.* Ed. James Robert Payne. Knoxville: U of Tennessee P, forthcoming.

———. "Necessity and Extravagance in Maxine Hong Kingston's *The Woman Warrior*: Art and the Ethnic Experience." *MELUS* 15.1 (1988): 3–26.

Woolf, Virginia. *A Room of One's Own.* New York: Harcourt, 1957.

Wu, Qing-yun. "A Chinese Reader's Response to Maxine Hong Kingston's *China Men.*" MLA Convention. Washington, 28 Dec. 1989.

Wu Ch'eng-en. *Monkey.* Trans. Arthur Waley. New York: Grove, 1958.

Wu Ching Chao. "Chinatowns: A Study of Symbiosis and Assimilation." Diss. U of Chicago, 1928.

Xu, Zhongshu. "Mulan ge Zaikao." *Dongfang Zazhi* 22.14 (1925): 72–89.

Yalom, Marilyn. *Maternity, Mortality, and the Literature of Madness.* University Park: Penn State UP, 1985.

Yamada, Mitsuye. "Mirror, Mirror." Beaty and Hunter xiii.

Yao, Darong. "Mulan congjun shidi biaowei." *Dongfang Zazhi* 22.2 (1925): 80–97.

———. "Mulan congjun shidi bushu." *Dongfang Zazhi* 22.23 (1925): 66–75.

Yezierska, Anzia. *Bread Givers.* New York: Persea, 1975.

Young, Jane. Personal interview with Marlyn Peterson and Deirdre Lashgari. 26 Apr. 1989.

Yu, Ning-ping. "Elements of Truth in Maxine Hong Kingston's *The Woman Warrior*." Master's thesis. Sonoma State U, 1985.

Yung, Judy. *Chinese Women of America: A Pictorial History*. Seattle: U of Washington P, 1986.

Zhao, Jingshen. *Minzu wenxue xiaoshi*. N.p.: Shijie Shuju, 1940.

Films, Video Productions, and Recordings

Bonetti, Kay. "An Interview with Maxine Hong Kingston." Audiotape. American Audio Prose Library. 1986.

Carved in Silence. Dir. Felicia Lowe. Felicia Lowe Productions. 1988. 45 min.

Chan Is Missing. Dir. Wayne Wang. New Yorker Films. 1981. 80 min.

Chinese Gold. Dir. Geoffrey Dunn. Gold Mountain Productions. 1987.

Dim Sum: A Little Bit of Heart. Dir. Wayne Wang. New Yorker Films. 1984. 87 min.

Eat a Bowl of Tea. Dir. Wayne Wang. Based on Louis Chu's *Eat a Bowl of Tea*. Columbia. 1989.

Eight-Pound Livelihood. Dir. Yuet-Fung Ho. New York Chinatown History Project. 1984. 20 min.

The Family. Dir. Chen Hsi-ho. China Video Movies–C 7 F Entertainer. Based on Ba Jin's *Family*. 1956. 124 min.

A Great Wall. Dir. Peter Wang. New Yorker Films. 1986.

Inside Chinatown. Dir. Michael Chin. Phoenix Films. 1977. 43 min.

Kingston, Maxine Hong. Interview by Bill Moyers. *World of Ideas*. PBS. 1989.

Lotus. Dir. Arthur Dong. Direct Cinema. 1987. 20 min.

Maxine Hong Kingston: Talking Story. Dir. and ed. Joan Saffa. Prod. Joan Saffa and Stephen Talbot. NAATA. 1990. 60 min.

The Only Language She Knows. Dir. Stephen Okazaki. Mouchette Films. 1983.

Paper Angels. Dir. John Lone and Genny Lim. Screenplay by Genny Lim. *American Playhouse*. PBS. WNET, New York. 1985. 60 min.

Pickles Make Me Cry. Dir. Peter Chow. Peter Chow International. 1987.

Sewing Woman. Dir. Lorraine Dong and Arthur Dong. Third World Newsreel. 1983. 14 min.

Slaying the Dragon. Dir. Deborah Gee. NAATA. 1988. 60 min.

Small Happiness. Dir. Carma Hinton and Richard Gordon. Prod. Long Bow Group. Distr. New Day Films. 1984. 58 min.

Talking History. Dir. Loni Ding and Spenser Nakasako. Asian Women United. 1984. 29 min.

Who Killed Vincent Chin? Dir. Christine Choy. Film News Now Foundation. 1988.

Note: Asian Cine Vision, 32 East Broadway, New York, NY 10002, publishes an annual media reference guide listing extant films on Asian Americans. Information regarding media resources on Asian Americans is also disseminated by NAATA, 346 Ninth Avenue, San Francisco, CA 94103, and Visual Communications, 263 South Los Angeles Street, No. 307, Los Angeles, CA 90012.

INDEX